# Transformational Psychotherapy

## Principles & Practice

### The Edge of Passage Series
### Book Four

## Mathias Karayan

Mathias Karayan

## *The Edge of Passage Series*

To start your journey involves the conviction that *there is more to living than what your world offers.* The desire to step beyond this view is to start your journey home. As you begin to recognize your time as a passing through, being a passerby, you begin to understand the messages of what people and events are really about. This is what *The Edge of Passage Series* is about. Wherever you go you take yourself with you. Are you ready?

The first book in the series; **The Way Home; Stories from the Master** deals with the paradoxical experience of living life on life's terms. To transcend the paradox is an experience in non-dualistic thinking.

The second book in the series, **Symbols of Power in Metaphysics: Life on the Other Side of the Veil,** addresses the experience of brushing up against the veil; life from the other side. Psychic experiences, astral-projection, past life memories, reincarnation and karma are among the topics discussed. Most of us have had these experiences but have dismissed them as a fanciful dream or just strange. This book explores the language of and blocks to experiencing life on the other side of the veil.

**Symbols of Power in Philosophy: What the great minds of our past have to teach us about today's issues,** is the third book in the series. This book deals with the issues of what the great minds of our past dealt with. "Are we evolving or are we spinning our wheels in the mud? There is a common thread among our teachers of days gone by about today's issues.

*Transformational Psychotherapy: Principles and Practice,* is the fourth book in *The Edge of Passage Series.* This book for the 21st century, addresses what Transformational Psychotherapy is, how it is applied to topics of conversation in psychology and how healing occurs.

The fifth book, *Reflections for the Wandering Mind: A Book on Meditation,* is about a unified goal for peace of mind. This book is not about changing your world so you can have peace. Peace is not there! This book is about correction at the level of your mind. It is the experience of your miracle when your mind transcends its conflicted thinking. This book contains lessons that allow your mind to experience the peace that awaits your remembrance.

*Words of Love: A book on Healing Relationships,* is the sixth book in the series which asks, "What is love and how is it to be found?" This book is about your journey to experience love, and the healing of relationships that struggle with a lack of love. It is about the removal of your blocks to love's awareness. *Words of Love* illuminates your journey to love's experience.

The seventh book; *In the Light of Passage: Three Short Stories on Life's Journey,* are stories; of a man lost in the forest, trying to find his way home with the help of some strange new friends. An overworked counselor is sent on an unexpected quest of self-discovery. A climber seeks adventure on an infamously dangerous mountain steeped in supernatural stories. With these characters' journeys, *In the Light of Passage* explores the lessons we learn in life and what it means to live.

Book eight, *Awakening to the Christ Within: What Jesus really taught,* takes a scholarly look at the text of the Bible as a means to experience what Jesus was really about. It is a full circle return to the first book, to the message of the Master, as to how to walk in the world yet not be of the world.

## Also, by Mathias Karayan
*

## Healing the Wound
### The Family's Journey through Chemical Dependency

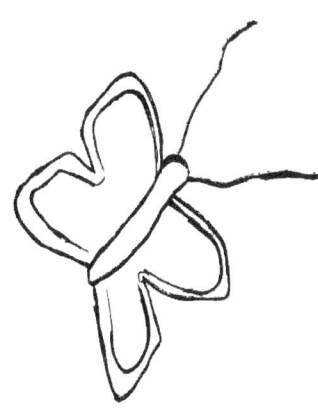

# Contents

# Transformational Psychotherapy
## Principles & Practice

# *Transformational Psychotherapy*
## *Principles & Practice*

This is a book on cause. Your dis-relation with Source is the cause of the world you see. The world and all its problems are a demonstration of complexity. It is a complexity of form (symptoms) that does not imply a complexity of content.

This is an easy text … when you recognize what is cause and what is effect.

## Introduction

> *Those who build castles in the air are neurotic*
> *Those who live in those castles are psychotic*
> *Those who collect the rent are therapists*

I was on a website that involved conversations of issues and therapeutic approaches. One conversation involved dealing with a client's "dark side," trauma and all its differences and complexities. It was asked "How come we as therapists have such a hard time following through with the advice we give?" The responses were as innumerable as the stars … and drawn-out. I decided to get on the ride and stated simply that "The resistance to look within is because of a deep-seated guilt we don't want to look at within ourselves. So, we teach others the indirect lessons we need to learn." The conversation skipped over my suggestion as if nothing was said and droned along in its innumerable complex way. Either the comment was too simple, too definitively inclusive or unintelligible.

## Paralysis by Analysis

*Complexity of form does not imply complexity of content*

The field of psychology is so over intellectually analyzed that a simple approach cannot be seen among the maze of its mental masturbation. In its attempt to be an empirically measurable, relevant science, the field of psychology has become a matter of paralysis by analysis. In my day, it was the DSM-III. What is it now? "Oh" we say "Well, we are better informed to diagnose the finer details of thought and behavior. The finer details will always be legion while missing the point. The point being *complexity of forms seems to imply complexity of content.* The baby with the bath water has been thrown out. Socrates continues to be ignored.

This book is about the recognition that *complexity of form does not imply complexity of content* and that psychology's mental complexity of issues makes it difficult to see all of its nothingness. There is a simple content to all these issues. There really is nothing new under the sun.[1]

*The intangible is the miracle*
*When you are ready the intangible occurs*

*Mathias Karayan*
October 2016

---

[1] *Symbols of Power in Philosophy p5*

# I. The Principles of Transformational Psychotherapy

## A Brief History and Context of the Word "Psychology"

*To know you do not know yourself is not stupidity but the first step to wisdom[2]*

The word psychology is Greek and contains two Greek roots: *Psyche* meaning "mind" and *logos* meaning "study." Traditionally the word psychology referred to dealing with mental phenomena and processes. Along with the Greek word *soma or somatic as* meaning relating to the body, especially as distinct from the mind, today's psychology is defined as "the study of behavior and mental processes." *Unless behaviors are understood as what mind wants them to mean, today's definition of psychology would be misleading.*

### The Ancient Greek Philosophers

The ancient Greek philosophers such as Heraclitus[3] and the Sophists[4] understood the world as being in a constant

---

[2] *The Way Home p100*

[3] Heraclitus (born around 540 BCE and died around 480 BCE), exerted a wide influence on Western philosophy, both ancient and modern, through the works of such authors as Plato, Aristotle, Georg Wilhelm Friedrich Hegel, Friedrich Nietzsche, and Martin Heidegger.

[4] The Sophists were itinerant intellectuals in ancient Greece who provided advanced education in various subjects, shifting philosophical inquiry from the natural world to human affairs and society.

process of ever-changing contradiction … that nothing is for sure. This means that every time a phenomenon arises there is a counter explanation to the phenomenon. Thus, a contradiction in explanation arises which leads to further investigation and further phenomenon and counter phenomenon.[5] The evolution of the world's thinking and its effects demonstrate that this process is endlessly fragmenting. There is always another point of view to your point of view. From this point of view, an absolute point of view is not to be found in the world.

Socrates[6] believed that knowledge and truth reside in the mind and one has to look for and find it there. In other words, *to understand the appearance (phenomena) of an ever-changing external world, one has to look inwards first instead of looking at the outward things (noumena).* In other words, if you don't know who you are, how can you understand what is going on, on the outside?

Epictetus[7] succinctly stated that *"People are not disturbed by things, but by the view they take of them."* He also taught that all external events are beyond our control; that we should accept whatever happens calmly and dispassionately; that individuals are responsible for their own actions, which they can examine and control through rigorous self-discipline.

---

[5] Dualistic thinking, *Symbols of Power in Philosophy p35-49*

[6] Socrates (469 BC-399 BC) is considered to be one of the most important ancient philosopher/psychologist. Laying the foundation of ideas for many philosophers and psychologists to follow.

[7] Epictetus, born around AD 50 and died 135 AD, was a Greek Stoic philosopher influenced by Socrates.

## Psychology's Brief Current History

To many, Søren Kierkegaard[8] is considered the father of modern psychology. In his book *Sickness Unto Death*, Kierkegaard (responding to the Hegelian[9] rage of the day of an impersonal process of moving towards an evolution of greater awareness) talks about the self being in dis-relation with itself as the core cause of mental anguish. To not rest transparently in the power that established you is a tension to wrestle with between the eternal and finite. To Kierkegaard, this spiritual dilemma of dis-relation with your Source of being is an alienation of anxiety, depression, anger, abandonment, fear and despair. It is a sickness unto death. "To be or not to be; that is the question."[10] To decide not to be is the despair of denying your identity in the power that established you. *Everything the world is to you is but the effect of this decision.*

Unlike Socrates and Kierkegaard, rather than looking within for understanding/meaning, many of the existentialists and psychologists that followed focused to look externally at the world of phenomena to explain personal alienation and meaning.

---

[8] Søren Aabye Kierkegaard (1813-1855) was a Danish religious philosopher who focused on individual existence, choice, and commitment. His writings influenced modern psychology, theology and philosophy.

[9] Georg Wilhelm Friedrich Hegel (1770-1831) was a German philosopher who saw all actions and reactions (duality) as the movement of resolution towards pure thought, the absolute principle or God; the dialectic of thesis, antithesis resolving to synthesis.

[10] Spoken by William Shakespeare's Hamlet, Act 3 Scene 1

Friedrich Nietzsche[11] saw the individual as getting lost as a member of herd mentality. It was a "Will to Power" that he emphasized for personal freedom from fear.

Sigmund Freud[12] wrote about stages of development that when blocked by real or imagined childhood traumas result in self-defeating psychological and behavioral compensations.[13] These compensations, in one's later life, manifest primarily through disassociation [14] displacement [15] projection, [16] and from an unconscious source. Freud was correct about an unconscious source to avoid anxiety and punishment. But erroneously, he thought that these dynamics occurred because of childhood traumas.

However, you seem to be born to play out tendencies, compensations, complexities, personalities, *that you*

---

[11] Friedrich Wilhelm Nietzsche (1844-1900) was a German philosopher, poet, and classical philologist who as one of the most provocative thinkers of the 19th century, is still provocative today.

[12] Sigmund Freud (1856-1939) was an Austrian physician, neurologist, and founder of psychoanalysis who through his clinical observations found evidence for the mental mechanisms of repression and resistance. He described repression as a device operating unconsciously to make the memory of painful or threatening events inaccessible to the conscious mind. Resistance is defined as an unconscious defense against awareness of repressed experiences in order to avoid the resulting anxiety or punishment.

[13] To compensate is to make adjustments that justify/defend against your awareness of your disassociation.

[14] To disassociate is to distance yourself from knowing what you substituted (denial).

[15] To displace is to substitute one thing for another.

[16] To project is to put out of your mind that which you do not want to associate with (disassociation).

*brought with you before birth* as projecting an image in space and in time.[17] To displace your projection (denial) is to make a self you are not and then disassociate yourself from knowing what you did to yourself. It is the disassociation from your awareness of an unconscious source.

Take a second look at what your children brought with them. You may be tempted to make sociological and heredity connections of causes as to why your children are the way they are. However, look at all the exceptions to these intellectual connections of why you think they are the way they are. Strip away socialized beliefs of nature and nurture as causal factors so you can see that there is something about them that they brought with them … played out through nature and nurture. How many times do you have to say about your children that "they have a mind of their own" until you get it?

Alfred Adler[18] being influenced by Nietzsche and Hans Vaihinger[19] stressed the need to understand individuals

---

[17] *Symbols of Power in Philosophy p69-89*

[18] Alfred W. Adler (1870–1937) was an Austrian medical doctor, psychotherapist, and founder of the school of individual psychology who emphasized the importance of feelings of inferiority; the inferiority complex as an element which to Adler plays a key role in personality development. Greatly influenced by Vaihinger and Nietzsche, Adler believed that, "at the center of each of our lifestyles, there sits one of these fictions, an important one about who we are and where we are going." In short, we live according to beliefs that have nothing to do with "Being."

[19] Hans Vaihinger (pronounced: häns fihing-r) (1852-1933) was a German philosopher whose system of thought was set forth in 1911 as The Philosophy of "As If." He saw people and society at large making decisions based on and living according to

within their social context. Adler saw an inferiority complex (the duality/compensation of a frustrated "Will to Power") resulting from feelings of inadequacy, or incompleteness arising from physical defects, low social status, pampering or neglect during childhood, or other causes encountered in the course of life. To Adler, education would be the best cure for society's woes. Though Adler put too much emphasis on social context as a *cause* of an "inferiority complex" rather than an *effect* of being born because of an "inferiority complex" (dis-relation), his understanding of "fictions" that one lives by became the foundational steppingstone for later cognitive therapists.

In his book *"The Undiscovered Self,"* Carl Jung[20] argued that many of the problems of modern life are caused by "man's progressive alienation from his instinctual foundation." Jung saw the human psyche as "by nature religious" and made this religiousness the focus of his explorations. To Jung, the psychological process of integrating the opposites, the conscious with the unconscious, while still maintaining their relative autonomy, was the central process of human development and individuation. As introspective as Jung was about a

---

"fictions" that had nothing to do with "what is." Vaihinger argued that human beings can never really know the underlying reality of the world, and that as a result we construct systems of thought and then assume that these match reality: we behave "as if" the world matches our models.

[20] Carl Gustav Jung (1875-1961), a Swiss psychiatrist who founded the analytical school of psychology, broadened Sigmund Freud's psychoanalytical approach, interpreting mental and emotional disturbances as an attempt to find personal and spiritual wholeness.

collective unconscious that we all share (archetypes),[21] he was not able to free himself from a Lockean[22] / Freudian view that said we are products of childhood experiences.

Harry Stack Sullivan (1892–1949), an American Neo-Freudian psychiatrist and psychoanalyst, held that personality lives in, and has its being in, a complex of interpersonal relations. Though Freud, Adler and Jung had touched on the influence of interpersonal relations on personality, Sullivan saw personality development from an interpersonal perspective. Like Locke he saw personality as a product of external influences. David Hume [23] wrote "the mind itself, far from being an independent power, is simply 'a bundle of perceptions' without unity or cohesive quality." Sullivan viewed personality as the "illusion of personal individuality." In Sullivan's psychology there is no room for the innate or

---

[21] Archetypes are images and thoughts which have universal meanings across cultures which may show up in dreams, literature, art or religion. Jung believed that symbols from different cultures are often similar because they have emerged from archetypes shared by the whole human race. For Jung, our primitive past becomes the basis of the human psyche, directing and influencing present behavior.

[22] John Locke (1632–1704), an English philosopher and physician regarded as one of the most influential of Enlightenment thinkers and known as the "Father of Classical Liberalism," greatly affected the development of epistemology and political philosophy. Contrary to Cartesian (Rene Descartes) philosophy based on per-existing concepts, Locke maintained that we are born without an innate self, and that knowledge is instead determined only by experience derived from sense perception of the world.

[23] David Hume (1711-1776) was a Scottish historian, philosopher, economist, diplomat and essayist known today especially for his radical philosophical empiricism and skepticism.

intrapersonal. With his "complex of interpersonal relations," Sullivan is vague as to causality and inconsistent in correlation of effects.

From Emanuel Kant's[24] dividing of the world into two spheres; the *noumena* (what something is "in itself") and the *phenomena* (our sensory experience of "things" in the external world), Edmund Husserl[25] maintained that only that which has meaning is that which you experience directly (phenomena). To Husserl, noumenal existence is irrelevant because it is understood intellectually rather than experienced directly. In other words, the question "if a tree falls in the woods … does it make a noise?" is only relevant if you are there to hear it.[26] The world of past and future tenses is irrelevant to the present mind.[27]

In 1913, John B Watson [28] published the article *"Psychology as the Behaviorist Views It,"* sometimes called "The Behaviorist Manifesto." From the 1920s into the 1950s, Behaviorism, a movement beholding the methodological proposals of Watson was the primary paradigm in psychology. It was a movement in psychology and philosophy that emphasized the outward behavioral aspects of thought, dismissing the inward experiential, and sometimes the inner procedural aspects as well.

Max Wertheimer (1880–1943) was an Austro-Hungarian born psychologist who was one of the three

---

[24] Immanuel Kant (1724-1804) was a German philosopher who is widely considered to be a central figure of modern philosophy.
[25] Edmund Gustav Albrecht Husserl (1859-1938) was a German philosopher who established the school of phenomenology.
[26] *The Way Home p113-114*
[27] *Symbols of Power in Philosophy p27-34*
[28] John Broadus Watson (1878-1958) was an American psychologist who established the psychological school of behaviorism.

founders of Gestalt psychology, along with Kurt Koffka and Wolfgang Köhler. According to Gestalt psychology perception is a whole. To break up, reduce and measure for meaning is to miss meaning altogether. "The whole is *other* than the sum of its parts." [29] Gestalt psychology rebelled against structuralism [30] and behaviorism. Otto Rank, [31] before William Glasser [32] and his book *Reality Therapy*, emphasized short term therapy where the therapist helps the client to exert his own will, to assume responsibility for his own life now. To Glasser, the question of "why you behave the way you behave" is irrelevant to this therapeutic process.

---

[29] The original phrase of Gestalt psychologist Kurt Koffka, "The whole is *other* than the sum of the parts" is often incorrectly translated as "The whole is *greater* than the sum of its parts" and thus used when explaining gestalt theory, and further incorrectly applied to systems theory. Koffka did not like the translation. He firmly corrected students who replaced *other* by *greater*. "This is not a principle of addition" he said. "The whole has an independent existence."

[30] Structuralism as a school of psychology says that everything can be broken down into basic structures or elements.

[31] Otto Rank (1884-1939) was an Austrian psychoanalyst, writer, and teacher. He was one of Sigmund Freud's closest colleagues for 20 years.

[32] William Glasser (1925–2013) was an American psychiatrist who developed Reality Therapy and Choice Theory. Glasser deviated from conventional psychiatrists by warning general public about the potential detriments caused by the profession of psychiatry in its traditional form because of the common goal to diagnose a patient with a mental illness and prescribe medications to treat the particular illness, when in fact, the patient may simply be acting out of unhappiness, not a brain disorder.

Carl Rogers [33] *Client Centered Therapy* emphasized a dialogue of unconditional regard between the therapist and the client that would facilitate awareness to choices for personal freedom. To Rogers, an understanding as to who you are from your past is an irrelevant concept. You make decisions to understand "you" now.

Albert Ellis's [34] *Rational Emotive Therapy* emphasized the cognitive/rational part of being human. Ellis was about challenging his client's "fictions," their magical thinking that caused them to be inauthentic with "the facts of any matter." He is generally considered to be one of the originators of the cognitive revolutionary paradigm shift in psychotherapy and the founder of cognitive-behavioral therapies.

## Full Circle

Coming full circle brings us back to;

1) Heraclitus and the Sophists understanding of a world in the process of ever-changing contradiction … that nothing is for sure.

2) Socrates understood that knowledge and truth reside in the mind, and one has to look for and find it there.

3) Kierkegaard understood that the world of phenomena is not the place to explain personal alienation because it is an effect. The core cause of mental anguish is to be found in a self being in dis-relation with itself. Again, to not rest transparently in the power that established you is a tension to wrestle with between the eternal and finite.

---

[33] Carl Ransom Rogers (1902–1987) was an influential American psychologist and among the founders of the humanistic (client centered) approach to psychology. Rogers' theory of the self is considered to be humanistic, existential, and phenomenological.
[34] Albert Ellis (1913–2007) was an American psychologist who developed Rational Emotive Behavior Therapy (REBT) in 1955.

From the book *Symbols of Power in Philosophy* we found that what the history of humankind teaches us is that you may have temporary relief, but resolution is not to be found in a world of ever-changing form. With the mind as the center for choice, what the world of noumena[35] means is what each mind decides through perception (phenomena). And although the mind has been the center for decision making, the world of dualistic thinking has found no sensible meaning in the world. In fact, the mind has a propensity to hold on to and irrationally defend fictions with resulting irrational feelings as valid experiences. And the bottom-line fiction is in the mind that has decided that your body is to be the center and cause of what you are or are becoming. And no matter how *sacred* you have made a body of dust to defend and protect you as an individual, it is still born to experience one ethical dilemma after another[36] until it dies to the dust from where it came. Your mind's way of dealing with this obvious fiction is an unconscious denial of this absurd contradiction … so the lie, that you think you are evolving, can be believed.

## The Nature of your Mind as Abstract

*Only one deception is possible in the infinite sense*
*Self-deception*
Soren Kierkegaard
Works of Love

---

[35] In Kantian philosophy, noumena means a thing as it is in itself, as distinct from a thing as it is knowable by the senses through phenomenal attributes.
[36] *Symbols of Power in Philosophy p50-68*

By its own nature, the mind is abstract, experiencing the nature of "Being Itself" as One. But part of it is now unnatural. Its dis-relation to Source is a split, experienced as separation. Separation makes the mind a perceiver rather than a creator. This split is the making of a perceiving consciousness which is the domain of an "ego self" that the separated mind identifies with but is not. "Ego self" is other than your experience as the whole. This split allows for fragments of the whole to be perceived as a world outside of your mind. The divided mind now perceives subject and object, inner and outer, temporal and eternal as frames of reference (duality) to try and make the meaningless make sense. Because the ever-changing world is a place where meaning cannot be found, you fearfully attempt to make the meaningless mean something. Through dualistic thinking, your world view[37] is fraught with endless inconsistencies of meaningless connections. This is a consciousness other than the experience of "Being." Transcending this contradiction (non-duality) is what the healing miracle of the mind is all about.

Split from your identity with Source, you become an individual subject, dependent on your identity with your projection of a world of objects untrue to you. This is totally different from knowing you as "Being Itself." Your mind cannot experience duality and non-duality at the same time. Either it is whole, non-dualistic, at peace with itself, or it is sick, split, divided between endless decisions of doubt; an "illusion of personal individuality." There is no in-between because it is a principle of mind that it cannot serve two masters. *Your only decision* is to heal the split and awaken to your identity in the light of Source.

---

[37] Your fiction

Although your dis-relation has not occurred in the abstract, it is experienced from a split mind point of view as a violation. Guilt occurs. Rather than reflect to see what you have done, you project this guilt as specific and concrete; the making of a world of form.

It is the mind that decides what healing is and what the body is for, not the body that dies.[38] In other words, if the body you identify with is an effect of a more fundamental error, to look for resolution for the error in its effects (a world of bodies) is the insanity of looking for resolution in the dust of a world repeating the same thing over and over again. It's like drinking alcohol to alleviate the depression that alcohol causes.

Unknown to you is the truth of the matter; that your identity is still with Source. You don't know this because an "illusion of personal individuality" (pseudo-self) that defines itself through contradiction, is not capable of comprehending the experience of abstract non-duality (resolution). The appearances of form to be examined, compared and explained dualistically is experienced by you as a concrete body of information … meaningful to you only for what it can do for your body. However, *the innumerable distractions of form are appearances of self-deception because they are appearances.*[39] That is why the world of form is not a place to find meaning. Nor are you capable of finding your way out without guidance.

*Confusion looks for its answer in a cloudy pool*
*The unsolvable problem seeks its solution through the mind that imagined it*
*Guilt looks for forgiveness in a world of accusation*

---

[38] *Symbols of Power in Metaphysics p23-32*

[39] This is a non-dualistic statement.

*Wisdom sees Itself*

*Confusion must be shown that its pool reflects itself*
*The unsolvable problem is gone when the mind that imagined it,*
*is changed*
*Guilt is forgiven when truth is allowed to be its guide*

*You are the cause of what you see*
*And this you can change when you choose to see it differently*[40]

## Summary

*Trying to find mental health in a place where it can't be found*
*is self-defeating. Because the means used (the world of bodies)*
*defeats its goal.*

Because of a dis-relation unknown to you, a confusion of unawareness abounds. For the sake of resolution/security, your split-self assumes that you should be a personal identity in process, known to you alone. So, you search in a world of drama, for what you think you can or should be, yet will never find. Because you look for a personal identity in a world that has no meaning, you exacerbate your experience of insecurity and personal confusion,[41] that you brought with you.

From this point of view, it would be easy to look at a *"complex of interpersonal relations"* (society) for meaning through magical fictions of body associations before you

---

[40] *The Way Home p71*
[41] This insecurity of personal confusion is experienced as depression, anxiety, anger, despair, alienation, grief and fear, to name a few. These feelings along with crafty defenses of denial hide the fundamental fact that you are experiencing the insecurity of personal confusion.

die back to nothingness. However, the drama you perceive in your world for meaning is the effect of the drama being played out in your mind … and you brought it with you.

You will never be able to find yourself in the effects of your confusion until you change your mind about yourself. It is for you to interrupt your self-defeating loop of phenomena that you took as meaningfully real. But first you need guidance to recognize how massive your mental loop is.

You may consider this dilemma to be spiritual or existential, but no matter what you call it, the world demonstrates clearly that resolution is not to be found on the level of the world of form. In fact, the world was made so you could not find a way out.

*Because your body dies, putting your body (effect) into proper perspective from the view of your mind (cause), is what is different from most other therapeutic approaches.*

# What Transformational Psychotherapy Is

*The recognition that sickness is of the mind, having nothing to do with the body, is a fundamental shift in perception. This shift will profoundly change how you perceive the world because the world will never again appear to rule your mind.*

Psychology as the study of mental processes makes *psychotherapy* the process towards the healing of your mind. This is first and foremost for a number of reasons.

1) Projection makes perception. What you do not want to see in your mind, you project.

2) Perception is not a fact, it's a mirror. Therefore, what you look on is your state of mind reflected outward.

3) To understand accurately the body of sensation and perception, a clear *mental* perspective is needed.

4) To understand the motives of behavior, a clear *mental* perspective is necessary.

5) To understand the interpretation of what any empirical data collected means for practical application needs a clear *mental* perspective.

6) To understand that all phenomena mean what the perceiver wants it to mean, needs a clear *mental* inclusive perspective to understand its global implication for an accurate world view.

7) To recognize that a shift in perception can temporarily allow relief for the body. However, that the body cannot heal the mind, puts all things into proper perspective.

Since it is only the mind that can be sick, it is only the mind through its own mental process that needs healing. To not recognize this creates confusion and delay. To recognize this allows the body to be free as a means for the mind to heal itself.

*Again, perception is not a fact, it's a mirror. What you look on is your state of mind reflected outward.*

The word *therapy* describes process; a journey you go through with the help of others as you help others. To *transform* is the metamorphosis of the caterpillar into a butterfly. It is the experience you call epiphanies, miracles, that "ah ha" moment, that "I never thought about it that way" release from previous thinking.[42] It is your process of awakening to something other than what the caterpillar thought the world was about.

*Transformational Psychotherapy is the process of helping your client to begin to question their reality.*

## The Need for a Unified Goal

*You are not diligent in guarding your mind against conflicting thoughts. In fact, you are too diligent to protect the ego part of your mind.*

Sickness is separation, a dis-relation from "Source," a Greater Self that your identity is defined by. From this perspective, reality is not yours to select. It is pseudo-self or ego that wants you to think otherwise. Along with ego's alien will comes all issues that dualistic thinking presents, represented as conflicting goals of doubt and projected as a world seemingly outside of your perceiving mind. Your sickness is the giving of your mind over to beliefs that limit your experience to pseudo-self's kingdom of sensation

---

[42] The canceling of a dualistic thought

and perception. Because you are so used to and lost to a condition of separation, differences and judgment, you are unaware of the depths of your denial. It seems impossible to think of the world as one big fiction made out of a conflicted mind. *Transformational Psychotherapy is about the questioning of your reality.*

The basic premise of this book is that separation from your Source of identity is impossible, the body is not you, sickness is an imagined dream and death is not real. It is within the power of your mind to make what is not real and to experience it as true. You are doing it all the time. That is why the changing of your mind is your process towards healing. Miracles seem to be experienced as real, while all that is happening is that your mind is moving towards an *integrated goal* of peace or One Mindedness. Mind over matter is true ... but not to a mind in conflict with itself.

Throughout your day, you can love and hate, judge and be unaware of the hypocrisy of your judgment, be angry and attack yourself at the same time, guilt a self you are not, etc. In the light of a mind in dis-relation with itself and therefore divided and conflicted, your need becomes a unified goal. That unifying goal is peace of mind. The most powerful thing you can do is change your mind. It is the changing of your mind from the duality of fragmentation towards a unified purpose that reframes and thus transcends your contradictions of thought.[43]

---

[43] *Reflections for the Wandering Mind p24-35*

## Forgiveness Properly Understood

*The unhealed healer holds resentment as they teach.*
*The healed healer only knows resolution through forgiveness.*
*You may want to argue that "There is more to therapy than forgiveness!" Not when the only function meaningful in time is forgiveness.*
*Therefore, any kind of healing is always the result of some kind of forgiveness … and to forgive is to change your mind.*

Because perception is not a fact, but your mirror, forgiveness properly understood is the means to cancel dualistic thinking in your mind towards a unified goal. This is the simple process of healing your mind. Your world is a fantasy of fragmented fictions around a body that will fail you. Forgiveness as a means to heal your mind about your body becomes your only function meaningful in time … the way to undo [44] your self-defeating construction of a world of fictional facts.

Your mind is split, has a propensity to misinterpret form (the world) in self-defeating ways. Forgiving your interpretations allows your mind the freedom to choose again.[45] Through forgiveness, your body as an effect, is perceived as a teaching aid to be laid aside at the end of its day. The mind without a body does not make mistakes because it does not use the body as a means to deceive itself. Nor can the mind die or be prey to attack. Beyond your experience of a body, no sacrifice is asked for, nor is pain involved.

---

[44] Speed–up or collapse in time, the undoing of karma. *Symbols of Power in Metaphysics p106-109*
[45] It's called "thinking out of the box."

28

## The Process of Transformational Psychotherapy

*The world is a place of fictional facts, used to defend an imagination of a "you," in a world of fictional facts*

Although the way to healing is simple, it must be taught to those who have lost their way in a maze of intellectual complications of nothingness. Because sickness is an imagined separation witnessed as a separate body self/idea, everyone who comes to a therapist needs help. Their defense against the truth of a world not true manifests itself in forms that seem to threaten the body. For example, all relationship issues involve the body. What issue doesn't involve the body? But these issues are sideshow distractions of delay from where the real issue lies. The resolution of these issues is temporary because the primary problem is a dis-relation with Self. Everything else is symptomatic of this. Thus, your client suffers from a lack of peace while attempting to find resolution in a world of conflicting goals.

For example, you will suffer if you feel abandoned by someone. However, in dis-relation with Source, you have disassociated from the abandonment of yourself first. Because the separation has not occurred but is being experienced "as if" in a dream of relational nothingness, you justify your experience of feeling abandoned as real by projecting it on someone else who may be just as lost as you. Through self-deception, your error of thought is experienced as a someone abandoning you.

Therefore, Transformational Psychotherapy is not about ingratiating an "ego pseudo-self" for raising self-esteem or for the management of an anger that can never be justified or for trying to make right an abandonment that never happened. These approaches to healing are part of your self-deception that an "illusion of personal individuality" needs to stay separated for its healing.

*Transformational Psychotherapy is the process of changing your view of yourself all together.*

An individual "you" is not your solution, it is your existential dilemma, your justification for your issues of abandonment, anger, guilt, alienation and being alone in a world that can never make sense. A unified "You" is healing, the experience of One Mind. The beginning is a process of understanding that you do not journey alone in your confusion. But first you must recognize your confusion.

No matter what you see and how much you feel, your mind is *always* involved in process. If you are in error about "you," all you will see and process in your world of an individual self is your error. And you will attempt to make your confusion born out of error meaningful. That is why your need for guidance is fundamental.

*Transformational Psychotherapy is the process of understanding a "You" not defined by an "illusion of personal individuality."*

Your *willingness* to allow for a new clarification is the start of a process beyond the unconscious limits you have set for what you may think your purpose is. This is a shift beyond religious, political, economic, philosophical, relational and psychological beliefs of how you *think* the world works or "should" work.

These beliefs you think are real are "fictions,"[46] magical beliefs played out as fantasies around the idea of a body image as you.[47] Everything you think, do or say involves the ingratiation of or rejection of a body self-image. Why do you go to the store? Why do you go to work? Why do you take a vacation? Why do you go to sleep? Why do you stand in front of a mirror? Why do you gossip? Why are you angry at someone? Why are you depressed? Why are you anxious? Why do you avoid certain people and situations? Why are you tired of the same-o same-o? Why do you want to commit suicide? Why do you want to kill anyone? Because mind uses a body as a means to justify its beliefs as being a body ... a body that easily feels violation in a world of conflicting contradictions. Your mind's misguided justifications for meaning through a body will always find conflict, pleasure, pain and a shallow happiness, but *never* peace of mind.

If ugliness belongs to the eye of the beholder and you perceive yourself as ugly or falling short of some personal assumption of what your value is, you will exhibit what looks like an inferiority complex. But if you question the reality of your fiction, that to be happy does not involve the achievement of, the accumulation of or the particular appearance of a body image, those beliefs that generated fear, abandonment, loss, anger and guilt disappear. One fiction understood as such and generalized becomes a domino effect to all your other fictions. This is the therapeutic miracle      that demonstrates that all these fictions    are    the    conscious    representations    of    an

---

[46] Hans Vaihinger

[47] Although you are not the product of the duality of nurture vs nature, you do play out your dis-relation (sickness) through the guise of nature and nurture.

unconscious battle going on in your mind. This battle for your mind projected as a world of conflict is where Transformational Psychotherapy begins.

*Transformational psychotherapy is the process of changing your view of yourself in the light of a world of fictional facts used to defend your imagination of a "self" in a world of fictional facts.*

## The Condition of your Mind

*I tried to heal myself of my obsessed and ashamed mind with my obsessive and ashamed mind. You know how well that works.*
Anne Lamott

Since pseudo-self has taken up residency (displacement) in your mind, your mind is habitually analyzing and judging the world it made for a meaningful home of belonging. You do not recognize your displacement because of your disassociation from it; the left hand not knowing what the right hand is doing. Isn't this what the world of perception is all about; tripping over the obvious in an attempt to find it?

Look honestly, you do not recognize that on a massive scale you do not understand what you see. You misperceive daily and don't usually recognize that you do. Because you do not recognize that on a massive scale you do not understand what you see, you do not ask for the guidance you greatly need. Why should you, you have pseudo-self as your guide. So, you look for meaning through an ever-changing whirlwind of little bits of data; things like the newspaper, television, the bell-shaped curve and separate encounters with "special" people, things and events. You find satisfying distraction from the chaos the world seems to present but never release.

It is an open mind that recognizes that it does not know and is thus open to asking for guidance not of itself.[48] There is an underlying theme that brings everything into making sense.

*Your denial is massive, and you do not know that it is massive because your denial won't let you see how massive your denial is*

You have *displaced* or substituted Source's sanity with pseudo-ego's insanity. But because of the integrity of your mind, you cannot live with this split. Through denial you *disassociate* from the awareness of your displacement. The tracks back to where your original error occurred, are covered from your view. Rather than look within, you project. Through disassociation your mind can entertain goals in conflict with each other (the left hand not knowing what the right hand is doing). Now your mind is able to justify the right to be angry and not know that it has to attack its own peace of mind for the right to be angry. You can entertain the idea of a loving God that punishes. You can even kill in the name of truth, justice and God. Simple common sense is denied the viewing of its insane contradiction. A simple example of disassociation is to see hypocrisy against another that you do not see in yourself. You lack the consistency of follow through with what you think and say and do, while you see it in another.[49] That your mind is in conflict (dis-relation) with itself and you are not aware of the depths of this conflict, is what disassociation from your displacement of yourself is all

---

[48] Tao Te Ching #71, Reflections *for the Wandering Mind p24-35*
[49] Cognitive dissonance is a feeling of discomfort that occurs when a person's beliefs or values don't match their actions. It can also occur when someone holds two contradictory beliefs.

about.[50] On a massive scale, through unawareness you disassociate from your inner conflict by projecting it as a world of conflicting forms. This *intrapersonal* conflict manifests symbolically as a world of religious, political, economic and relationship issues. Institutions are made to resolve intrapersonal and interpersonal conflict. These places are not solutions. They are symbols of your conflicted mind. To not recognize this is to look for solutions in places they can't be found; outside of you!

*Trying to find mental health within a sick agenda is self-defeating; because the means used defeats its goal*

To be able to generalize the lesson from being the hypocrite you see in everyone you meet, is to understand that we all teach what we need to learn. This makes no one a hypocrite. To generalize this lesson to everyone would collapse or undo part of the world you thought was real. The word "hypocrite" would no longer be in your vocabulary, and you would be one step closer to integrating your mind towards peace.

*Transformational Psychotherapy is the process of helping your client integrate their mind towards peace.*

To not know "You" is to not recognize your part. To not know your part is to not know "you." How can you find completion through this loop of all the fragmented data the world offers, when you do not know the you "you are" to interpret the data? Because you do not recognize anything you perceive, *instruction in perception is your greatest need*. To help your client question everything they

---

[50] Your inability to be authentic

have learned is your challenge to your client. But every good teacher does not begin there.

A unified goal always lends itself to peace of mind which is foundational for transformational healing to occur.

*It is a principle of Transformational Psychotherapy for you to stop trying to find out who you are through pseudo-self so who "You Are" can tell you.*

## Principles of Transformational Psychotherapy

*The world of people, things and events is your workshop. It is nothing else.*

1) You have conflicts with one another because you have conflicts within yourself first; *always.*

2) Others come along your path as seeming irritants but are actually reminders of your conflict that is *already* within you.

3) Any issue with another is a demonstration that you do not recognize principle #2. That's why you need each other.

4) Joining in a common goal for peace allows for the healing of a split, separated, divided mind.[51]

5) All resistance is pseudo-self's fight for survival; its defense against the healing of your mind as split.

6) Your ability to own your conflict as self-caused without exception is where Transformational Psychotherapy begins. In other words,
*Transformational Psychotherapy allows no justification for blame.*

---

[51] Joining for reasons other than peace is what the alliance of egos is all about.

Your self-deception is hidden from your view[52] or else you would see "the magnitude of your own folly revealed in a blinding flash with all the devices you used for self-deception laid bare."[53] You are the enemy you blame in the form of another that represents your conflicted mind. No wonder the concept of feeling abandoned seems real to you as if it is coming from the outside. You've abandoned yourself first and don't know that you did it!

Beyond your fragmented mind, your completion awaits your recognition. Behind every grievance is the miracle that forgiveness properly understood would show you. Transformational Psychotherapy is the epiphany we say or hear from our client "Oh, I never thought about it that way."

Your conflicts are opportunities telling you to reevaluate what you have decided. Conflict teaches you that you are in self-deception otherwise you would not be in conflict.

*Every conflict is an opportunity.*
*Until you see it that way, it remains as a conflict.*

Defensiveness is a sign of self-deception. Argumentation and blame are self-deception's maneuver. Behavior and feelings are symptomatic of what the mind decides. Those who defend feelings as central to "being yourself," ride an emotional roller coaster. Be honest and look at it. You may think that your thoughts are subject to your feelings, but it is your feelings that are subject to what you choose to

---

[52] What you have disassociated from appears to be out of your mind but is actually in the realm of the unconscious.

[53] JRR Tolkien's *The Lord of The Rings;* part three, *The Return of The King p275;* paraphrased.

think. Therefore, lasting change always occurs at the level of your mind. Self-defeating behaviors and feelings that block your goal towards peace of mind are not judged but are recognized as results of misperception. These same behaviors and feelings are *accepted* as teaching aids that facilitate the changing of one's mind. It is about allowing not judging.

Because Transformational Psychotherapy transcends the limits of nature vs nurture, how you were raised is not a justification for your world view and outcomes. But your world view does determine how you misinterpret nature and nurture as a cause of why you are what you think you are. Because outcomes by and large are not yours to control, you are not responsible for what happens to you in your life. But you are responsible for how you interpret what happens … and that will be your karma. [54] Said another way, because no thought leaves its source,[55] what is, is.[56] How you perceive "what is" (the noumena) will be your experience. Your experience of heaven or hell is the experience you choose through the thoughts you choose to entertain.

*As long as you are lost under your spell*
*It is you that is maker of your personal hell*
*That is why your greatest need is for guidance.*

---

[54] Your interpretation of life events is the script you write. Your script is your destiny, the karma you play out … until you change your interpretation of your life events. *Symbols of Power in Metaphysics p97-109, 254*

[55] *Symbols of Power in Philosophy p252*

[56] If you understand, things are the way they are. If you do not understand, things are the way they are - Zen proverb

## Summary

*You can't distrust the truth. You can distrust your perception of it.*

Socrates said; "Everyone seeks to be happy." Fear is the result of not understanding confusion. What appears to be seen as "evil" in the world is one's attempt to understand confusion. Because confusion cannot be understood, evil seems real, and fear is reinforced as justified. To believe in the concept of "evil" is a fiction to defend that will cost you peace of mind. It is a projection out of your unconscious guilt that punishment is required for reparation. Either it will come from a god outside of you or from the world. They are the same. This fearful fiction will not allow you to look within and thus heal yourself. That is why *your greatest need is for guidance not of your making.*

*Transformational Psychotherapy involves no particular philosophical, psychological or theological approach. It does recognize fear as the primary block to change, and peace of mind through healing the split (forgiveness properly understood) as one's ultimate goal.*

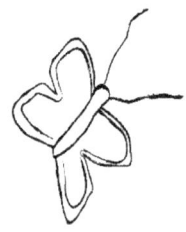

# The Therapist's Role in Transformational Psychotherapy[57]

*You can take your client only as far as you've been*
*Your client can help you take the next step*

1) Every client comes to you for a reason. Though your client may not understand the reason it would be a mistake for you to think you know what to offer everyone who comes to you. This allows you room to be open rather than decided in your approach.

2) Although only fundamental change will last, you start with your client at the level of their presenting problem.

Your client's presenting problem is always symbolic of their dis-relation with Source and therefore with themself. For example, a client may talk to you about issues of abandonment from childhood. Though you recognize this issue as symbolic for their displacement of imagined separation from their Source of Identity, you pace yourself with your client by starting at the level of the presenting problem. You may be steps ahead to help because you recognize their issue as the effect of their dis-relation with Source but be patient.

3) Increasing motivation for change in your client is all that a therapist need do to guarantee change. For change in motivation is a change of mind.

Guilt and blame serve no good purpose as agents of change. They are counterproductive towards achieving a unified goal to peace of mind. Forgiveness *properly*

---

*understood* is the means to undo guilt, anger and fear. This process is simple in approach and application.[58]

4) Strengthening motivation for change in your client is your first and foremost goal. It is also your last and final one.

*Your clients do not represent themselves well. They are tempted to misrepresent the truth. You know this is true because they come to you with a problem.*

Your client is sick because what they think will help hurts them, and what they think helps them are blocks to peace of mind. Progress cannot occur until your client is persuaded to change their way of thinking about the world and themselves. *Therapist, you are not the source of anyone's healing.* [59] You heal yourself by teaching your client how to heal. Through joining, seeing commonality is what healing is about.[60]

5) When the therapist suspends judgment of their client, healing occurs. [61]

Because you take your client only as far as you have gone, lack of judging allows you room to see a new step with your client. Inversely, you become open for the lesson your client has for you.

6) The idea that someone must lose in the therapeutic process is a block to healing towards peace of mind.

Your client comes to you because they believe in loss. Your client's presenting problem is always symbolic of

---

[58] *The Way Home p104-107*

[59] To think you are the source of anyone's healing is what cult attraction to a pseudo-ego charismatic personality is all about. There is only One Teacher, and we join as students.

[60] *Symbols of Power in Metaphysics p170-180*

[61] *Symbols of Power in Metaphysics p30*

their unconscious dis-relation with themselves. The healed therapist can address their client's presenting problem without reinforcing their client's belief in loss. Therapist, somewhere in this process, teach your client that the person they think needs to pay for what your client perceives has been done to them, is the price your client will pay (karma), until they change their mind about it. This makes your client's "enemy" their current best teacher towards peace of mind.[62] It makes your client confront their world view reality, magical thinking, and blocks to a unified goal towards peace.

## A Principled Approach to Transformational Psychotherapy

*I'm not telling you how to do therapy*
*But your world view will be the therapy you do*

1) Without having a personal position, questions are asked, and summations are made to clarify family and relationship issues.

2) Guilt and blame serve no good purpose in this clarification.

3) It is not about needing to be right or wrong. In fact, you don't have to be right about anything. Because there is no position to defend, you can go anywhere you want in the therapeutic relationship without getting caught in counter transference.

4) It is irrelevant as to whether or not you need to trust the client. It is best that you do not ask the client to trust

---

[62] Again, you are not justifying anyone's action against your client, but because no thought leaves its source, in the end it will always come down to your client's experience of how they perceive the action of another.

you. If your client decides to trust you it will have to be on their own volition.

    5) With these principles practiced:

        a. Trust is inevitable in the therapeutic encounter.

        b. Personal issues of counter transference are used as a teaching tool for both the therapist and client.

Remember: It is not about trying to "fix" the client or their problem. It is about creating an environment without blame or guilt that clarifies the family/client reality, so they become motivated to change how they perceive what they perceive.

## Four Things Necessary for Learning to Occur

*The place where you know you know nothing*
*Is your release to everything*

    1) Motivation to want to change has an open mind.

*"Then what's the answer?" asked the testy doubter.*

*"The only answer I have for you is the one you have already decided, for that is the only one you will hear."*

*"Arrgh, but how then do we get beyond our stubborn no-hearingness?"*

*"By admitting that your stubbornness in hearing only what you want to hear, blocks your ability to hear your advocate for freedom."*

*"And who is this advocate for freedom you speak of?" challenged the frustrated doubter.*

*"It is you ... the real you beyond your raging ego," the master replied, quietly and gently. "And when you stop deciding how*

*things should be, you will be free to see … to see your creations unfold … "[63]*

2) When your mind is open to change, guidance will appear. [64]

As I have said, you are not diligent in guarding your mind against conflicting thoughts. In fact, you are too easily taken in to protect the ego part of your mind. Through subtle distractions and sometimes outright defiance to follow guidance not of yourself for a unified goal to peace, you are resistant to learn. Humility is needed here.

*Because he lives beyond the question*
*The master is free to redirect the student to seek the answer*

*Because he lives beyond thought*
*The master is free to respond to the student according to the need of any moment*

*Because he lives beyond the ego*
*The master is free to accompany the student through any conversation, beyond the need to defend*

*Because he lives beyond the desire to possess*
*The master is free to facilitate healing with whatever is provided*

*Because he lives today within the oneness of peace*
*The master knows neither the apprehension of tomorrow nor the guilt of yesterday*

---

[63] *The Way Home p53*
[64] "Communication is not limited to the small range of channels the world recognizes" – A Course in Miracles.

*Therefore, the master is free to extend healing through all that is seen, thought and done[65]*

3) Repetition is your client's best teacher.

You practice meditation. You recognize irrational beliefs. You resolve to focus on changing your thinking. Yet you continue to harbor, wrestle with and placate unreasonable doubt and anxiety. Why?

Since your time began, your mad fictions have gained unconscious hold of great intensity. They have gripped the mind with fright and apprehension so strong that it will not give up its ideas about its own protection. These decisions are made below the conscious level to keep them securely protected from your ability to question their sanity and thus dismiss them. Your continual experience of a gnawing anxiety just under the conscious level cannot be dealt with as long as you believe it is coming from somewhere else. That is why repetition becomes your best teacher.[66]

*A seeker asked, "Master, often you say the same things, just in different ways. Why is that?"*

*The master smiled with an inner delight and responded, "When the only function meaningful in time is forgiveness, there isn't much else to talk about."*

*This time the seeker pressed, "But why the repetition?"*

*"Every one of you has more than one example of a time when you mistook someone the wrong way, reacted to your interpretation of them as if it were true, had a problem with them because you did not recognize you were merely reacting to your own misinterpretation, eventually realized your mistake, and all of a sudden like a miracle ..." the master gestured dramatically,*

---

[65] *The Way Home p189*
[66] *Reflections for the Wandering Mind p36-42*

*"... the 'big' problem was gone. And still you are slow to generalize this lesson to every area of your life. Therefore, repeating the lesson seems to be the necessity ... until you get it."*[67]

4) Generalizing what has been learned to all areas of your life experience is essential.

Your client is a poor learner because of their inability to generalize a lesson learned to other areas of their life.[68] For example: Instead of judging another as a hypocrite, is to see yourself also as inconsistent or a hypocrite.[69] Because you do not do some things very well, you teach it to learn it. This does not make you a hypocrite. And neither is the other person who is teaching what they need to learn.

*It is the body's eyes that sees differences*
*It is the healed mind that does not acknowledge them*

If this lesson is generalized to everyone you see as struggling inconsistently, there is no such thing as a hypocrite as there is someone teaching what they need to learn. Either you are a step closer to peace of mind by undoing a dualistic fiction or you are unknowingly attacking yourself through your judgment of another.

---

[67] *The Way Home p171*

[68] Because complexity of form does not imply complexity of content, when a client generalizes a lesson learned from one seemingly separate issue to other issues, lessons are learned quickly and speed up occurs. This consolidation of learning is a collapse of time or what the shortening of time is all about. *Symbols of Power in Metaphysics p99-109*

[69] The law of karma or "No thought leaves its source" always makes you the hypocrite you see in another.

Either you are the hypocrite you see in another or there is no such thing as a hypocrite. You decide.

Another simple example to generalize is when you see evil; correct your mind by seeing ignorance instead. Generalize that lesson to every event you are tempted to see as evil, and you will undo the illusion of an evil you made real.

The final generalization is when you can see one event of a confusing world as projected from your confused mind. Then you will be able to see what is beyond the meanings you have given movement and noise.

## Forgiveness & Transformational Psychotherapy

*To perceive anyone in a judgmental or negative way is a witness to your own call for healing. Therefore, you have an opportunity to be healed in your mind by forgiving how you perceive that person.*

So easily we tell one another "You need to take responsibility for your life," with little understanding of what that entails. Transformational Psychotherapy says taking responsibility for your life means first and foremost that *how you see what you see is what you will experience.* In other words, you never respond or react to anyone directly; you always respond or react to your own interpretation of them. And because blame is not an option:

*What you see is what you get*
*And what you always get is your own mind set*[70]

---

[70] Your diligence to practice these principal cuts short your propensity to project a world and take it as true.

From this point of view, the role of forgiveness in Transformational Psychotherapy becomes clear. You never forgive someone for what *you thought* they did to you. Because what you thought they did to you is how you perceived it. Therefore, it is for you to forgive[71] you your perceptions of how you made another appear to you through your own interpretations. This you can change.

I am not saying bodies do not do terribly dreadful, shockingly heinous, dreadfully scandalous, criminally wicked, cruelly abhorrent, hatefully disgusting, horribly repulsive and hideously revolting atrocities [72] to other bodies. As the world judges, they do. I am saying that the world is not a place to find reason, sanity, security, justice or peace. Peace will not be found here; maybe relief once in a while, but not peace.

The world is an empirical demonstration that the concept of evolving is a socially conditioned view and that ignorance rules. Rules are not made to keep order but rather to hide that fact that there is no order. Rules are broken because they cannot hold chaos at bay. So, the more rules you have to hold chaos at bay, the more rules that are broken. The more rules that are broken are the more reasons for your client to experience abandonment, betrayal and justified anger. Therapist, from this point of view, you will not be out of a job.

Your client may be vulnerable to tempt themselves to think you are trying to "justify" another's behavior by you asking them to see the madness behind another's behavior. Your client took the other's appearance of madness personally at the level of form and missed the point. To reinforce the process therapeutically, you tell your client

---

[71] Or change your mind about
[72] The descriptions are endlessly endless

that you are not justifying another's behavior but rather clarifying motive so your client can forgive the mistake of interpreting behaviors and attitudes in ways that make themself feel angry, guilty and fearful, etc.

*All appearances are deceiving because they are all appearances.*

That is what the world of the ever-changing is all about, appearances. Allow for no exception.

## Principles of Forgiveness / Healing

*The unforgiven mind is full of fear, believing punishment is warranted.*

*The unforgiven mind is sad, allowing no room for love to be itself.*

*The unforgiven mind is divided, split in allegiance and therefore distracted from focus.*

*The unforgiven mind lacks resolution, lives in doubt and is unaware of its confusion about itself and all it sees.*

*The unforgiven mind anxiously fears a future out of an unforgiven past.*

*The unforgiven mind judges, so it can justify its failure to forgive.*

*The unforgiven mind justifies its reason to engage in rage and attack.*

*All healing is a result of some kind of forgiveness.*

*All forgiveness is a change in perception that leads to self-healing.*

*Forgiveness is the only way to be free and the way out is to see both of you as guiltless.*

*Sooner or later, it will always come down to forgiveness and how willing you are to do it.*

*Only true forgiveness can remove unconscious guilt from the mind.*

*You know who the unforgiven are. They are those who have no mercy to bestow upon another.*

*Because Creation does not condemn you, it is for you to take responsibility for forgiving yourself.*

*The only unforgivable sin is the one you refuse to forgive[73] ... and this you can change.*

Forgiveness *properly understood* is not forgiving someone for what you thought they did to you. It is forgiving yourself for how you erroneously perceived that person or situation. All forgiveness *properly understood* is not about justifying anybody's behavior as OK. It is about the changing of your mind about how you perceive anybody; including yourself. That will be your way through. The result on how you feel will follow.

---

[73] *The Way Home p124*

## The Use of Time

*Because guilt made time, the only function meaningful in time is forgiveness*

True forgiveness is the miracle that sees guilt as an error of thought. The miracle becomes the forgiving of an error that never needed to be forgiven. The last illusion is the recognition that "nothing" needed to be forgiven.

Time made out of guilt becomes your friend, as the time you need to forgive the guilt that made time. You will come to the end of time when you come to the end of an ancient guilt that never needed to be forgiven. In this place the last illusion is dispelled; the understanding that "nothing" needed to be forgiven.

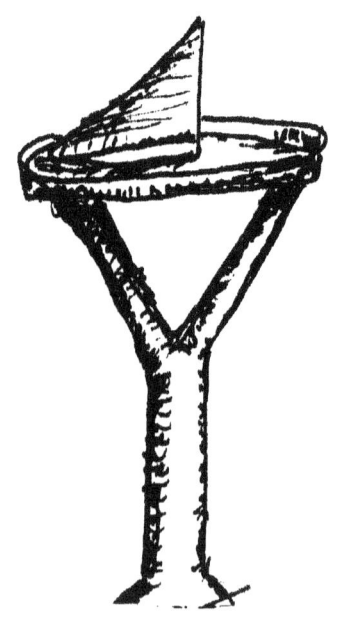

To say it in other ways; your awakening is when giving and receiving are perceived as the same. Your awakening is in the full realization that no thought leaves its source. Your awakening is the undoing of all karma. Your awakening is the place where time ceases to exist because time is no longer necessary to provide the lessons that bring cause and effect together. This is also why;

*Your need is to see you in everyone you meet*
*To awaken you to the "You" You already are*

*Namaste*[74]

---

[74] Namas+te, as believed to be defined by Mahatma Gandhi: In India when people meet and part they often say, Namaste' which means: "I honor the place within you where the entire Universe resides; I honor the place within you of love, of light, of truth, of peace; I honor the place within you, where, when you are in that place in you, and I am in that place in me, there is only one of us."

# II. The Practice of Transformational Psychotherapy

## Transformational Psychotherapy's Approach to Client Issues

Because you do not know what you are, the key principle of Transformational Psychotherapy is "Having is Being." In other words, "You are everything you need." Any thought to the contrary is a conflict in focus, a distraction to look outside for meaning, the acceptance of pain and death as real and a needless delay of your joy.

### Introduction

*Trying to find mental health in a place where it cannot be found is self-defeating, because the means used defeats its goal*

This is a simple curriculum. It may appear to be complicated and confusing, only because you are asked to simplify, make a fundamental shift in how you think about everything. In psychotherapy, the complicating of information for results does make it difficult to see its nothingness The time you take to practice this curriculum is the time you use to heal your split/divided mind.

### Foundation

To the Transformational Psychotherapist the world is not a place to find stability.[75] Because it is ever-changing,

---

[75] Heraclitus (540? BC-480? BC) was a Greek philosopher who maintained that all things are in a state of continuous flux, that stability is an illusion. *Symbols of Power in Philosophy p62-63*

the idea of finding meaning or security in the world is distraction and delay. The world is a place where meaning cannot be found. The world of problems on a global as well as personal scale demonstrates this point.

Your client comes to you with problems related to the same fact that they are trying to make the world of the ever-changing meaningfully real. Yet, it is a fiction they are reacting to.[76] That is why the process of changing their mind about their reality is a step towards transcending their numerous fictions. In the end, all their fictions end up as only one; the world is not a place to find meaning. To generalize this lesson to everything takes the process of patience and vigilance.

The therapist understands that their client can easily tempt themselves to feel like their reality is being attacked by the therapist questioning aspect of their world view, as if it is illusion. Initially, and together they start out by discussing the presenting fiction and go from there. Because complexity of form does not imply complexity of content, the therapist will be content to understand that their client may have to start by undoing one fiction at a time. Eventually, in your client's way and time, they will be able to generalize one lesson learned to all of their fictitious symbols of power. Remember,

*Transformational Psychotherapy is about helping your client question their reality.*

Therapist, to touch upon a larger picture of what you are and the part you play in this picture, we will not focus on external measures of failure and success. They are but

---

[76] This is the definition of a frustrated learner. *Symbols of Power in Metaphysics p110-118*

temptations of delay, misused as a means for self-definition, validation, put downs, and defense. They are irrelevant to the Eternal You. The focus here is directed inward … as far as you are willing to let yourself go. You can take your client only as far as you have gone in questioning your reality. Your client can help you take your next step.[77] Join with them.[78]

*Every conflict is an opportunity to look within. Until you see it that way, it will remain as a conflict. To change your mind about this is to look where the miracle is found.*

---

[77] *Symbols of Power in Metaphysics p30-32*
[78] *Symbols of Power in Metaphysics p177-180*

# Self Esteem: What you are not[79]

*An esteem that can be raised up as well as brought down by words and behaviors, is nothing but a whim*

Being, self-esteem and meaning in a universe of stars has been the topic of conversation since the beginning of conversation. [80] As previously stated, sickness is separation, separation from "Self," a Greater Self that your identity is defined by. From this separation, pseudo-self or ego[81] is made to occupy the throne, to try and convince you that you are something you are not. The world is its proof. This battle between the eternal and the temporal is a battle in your mind projected as a world not true ... yet believed by you.

From a body image point of view, attack is inevitable. Under the conscious level of awareness is a nagging anxious buzz; the effect of your dis-relation with Source. Your need to fix this dis-relation is witnessed by the fact that at times you are aware of how unrealistically hard on yourself you can be. Or how hard you try to make yourself be something you are not. Your dis-relation is also witnessed by the fact that a word from another can devastate you.

---

[79] David Hume wrote "the mind itself, far from being an independent power, is simply 'a bundle of perceptions' without unity or cohesive quality." Harry Stack Sullivan viewed personality as the "illusion of personal individuality."

[80] *Symbols of Power in Philosophy* addresses this issue.

[81] The ego is an aggrandized collection of fictions; magical thinking; a self-contradicting thought system needing the vigilance of constant defense against the truth.

## An Inside Job

*Only one deception is possible in the infinite sense, self-deception*
**Søren** Kierkegaard
Works of Love

An inside job for an outsider is to masquerade as an insider and make it look like the attack on the establishment was done by an outsider. When done right, this so-called insider does not get caught for its betrayal while some unsuspecting outsider is blamed. That is why it is so easy to be hurt by a word from the outside, as it seems. In other words, the threat you feel as coming from outside of you is your ego from within.

Because of your dis-relation with Source into a confusion you deny, you made an ego-self to be your guide through all the uncertainties of perception. Because this ego guide is a substitution (displacement) out of your dis-relation, it was made to protect you from seeing what you did (disassociation). The ego is always threatened because it is not real and therefore has no ground to stand on. Your ego mind projects threat as coming from the outside of you so you do not look inside to see your conflict of threat as a split within. However, what you are is beyond the world, not decided by you and therefore cannot be threatened.

Fighting for its survival, your ego does not want you to look inside as to what is really going on. Think about it; when you react to a nothingness of words, your ego has been exclaiming loudly that you have been hurt, violated, justified in anger, guilty of punishment, abandoned, etc. Why does your ego want you to look to it for help?

Because the value you give it is the measure of its life and death. You are the maker of its survival.

All your boundaries you use to protect you from the threat you perceive as coming from the outside, are not for you. They're for the ego. And, out of fear of violation your vigilance to protect your ego self is a vigilance you need to keep … although, you feel violation anyway. Regarding relationships, how does love fit into this? Only as conditional, which is not love. Now your vigilance has become a prison because it keeps love out. The threat you perceive as coming from the outside is a sidetrack from the fact that your threat, your sabotage to peace of mind is an *inside job* coming from an ego esteem you made to protect you from finding "You."

The "You" you are can never feel threatened. That you can be threatened is an indication that you have identified with an ego identity for survival through a body image. That you don't always feel the threat is your ego at work directing you to look outside at other things to occupy your mind.

*Why are you unhappy?*
*Because 99.9% of everything you think,*
*And everything you do,*
*Is for yourself,*
*And there isn't one.*
Wei Wu Wei

What an absurd contradiction you have put yourself in. What you think and feel as a threat to your peace of mind as coming from the outside, is an inside job, coming from you alone. This you can change. You can fire the insider!

## How Others View You

*What you identify with is what you want to be*
*What you want to be is not what you are*
*Because you already are*

Self-esteem does not come from how others view you. It comes from how you think others view you. And how you think others view you comes from how you view yourself. If you ask how you should view yourself, your ego quickly says, "Look to me, I will tell you how you should view yourself." From this foundation is the birthing of your world view.

*I am afraid because I do not know who I am*
*Because I am afraid I will hang on to the safety I think I can find*
*in my search for who I am not*
*This is all done in self-deception*

In dis-relation, your client's persistence to remain sick is their attempt to validate what they are not. It is a battle of the mind for the mind; and the ego needs your undivided attention to win the battle.

*When you think your something other than what you are, you experience the world: and all its trappings.*

Because you are not what you think you are, trying to find out what you are from the view of what you are not is a fruitless journey to nowhere. The source of your client's frustration has been in their attempt to learn an impossible lesson. How do you help them out of this dilemma?

## Dialogue (for the religious)

*Some may experience a loving God*
*Some may see the concept of a loving God as a useful fiction*
*Some might see a loving God as a contradiction of religious inconsistencies*
*And others might see a loving God as outright deception*

When you ask a client "Who or what are you?" Other than giving you their name, gender and occupation, they can't tell you. If you ask your client "How do you come to a value of yourself?" Other than accomplishments, they can't tell you.

If you ask your client "Are you the one who decides your value?"

Most people will say "Yes I am."

If you ask your client "Is there something bigger than you that decides your value?"

Most people say, "You mean like God?"[82]

If you ask your client "Who created you?" If your client is religious in their thinking they will say "God created me" yet be clueless as to what that means.

"And what is the nature of this God of yours?" you ask.

Your client will usually answer "What do you mean?"

With a little redirection you talk about a God of love and that God creates only out of what He / She is and nothing else. "And if God only creates out of Self as love, what does this make you?"

"Well, love" your client rethinks.

---

[82] For the atheist you can ask your client if there is a power greater than themselves that they participate in. The world of change is greater than the body that participates in it. Also, science can be a useful fiction.

"If you are love's creation, stop trying to find out who you are so who you already are can tell you."

This is a non-dualistic way to tell your client to "Get out of the way!" The implication here is that *reality is not theirs to select.*

Principles of meditative thinking, or assignments for your client would be non-dualistic thoughts like:

1) "It is not for you to decide who you are. In what ways do you try to do that?"

2) Or "Stop deciding who you are so who you are can tell you. In what ways do you try to do that?"

3) Or "Reality is not yours to select." (Control Issues)

4) Or "You think too much. In what ways can you be open to redirection?"

These statements all have one thing in common. They are statements of non-duality that diffuse the intellectually dualistic, ruminating battle going on in their mind. Give your client only one thought at a time to take home with them, to use as a reframe of their inner world.

These are simple truisms for a cluttered mind. Though it is simple, often your client will say "This is not easy." Clarify with them that:

1) "You think it is hard because the lessons you have been trying to learn are impossible.

2) This is a different lesson because it is coming only from within "You" to you. From this point of view, you will change the way you view your world, and your world will seem to change."

## Body Gender Identity and Integration[83]

*He who defines himself can't know who he really is[84]*

Regarding the issue of gender/transgender identity, the language may be complicatedly confusing, but the content is not.

1) Accepting your client where they are at is to allow them time and space to facilitate clarification. They will have anger, guilt, shame and fear to deal with because of their *perception* of how society at large has fearfully perceived the "seemingly unnatural" as not normal. This is the work of helping your client *identify* with the fact that all ego alliances *identify* themselves as gender bodies. *This is the human condition.*

2) When they are ready, remind your client that the world does not make sense. Fear is the primary motivator that attempts to make sense out of the senseless. "Appropriate" roles of conduct and behavior prescribed as "norms" are ever-changing. What does not fit neatly into roles of how things should be is a threat to the paradigm of male, female and is fearfully rejected as deviant and fixed. The eccentric are also misunderstood. *This is the human condition.*

3) When your client is ready, remind them that *the world is not a place to find meaning or identification of worth.* When you remind your client that they took the insanity of others personally you will also need to reinforce the fact that you are not justifying what happened to your client from the fearful ignorance of others. Yet, the way through for your client will be to understand that it is ignorance

---

[83] *Symbols of Power in Philosophy p62-64*
[84] #24 Tao Te Ching, Stephen Mitchell translation

that rules the world of everyone's attempt to make meaningful their perception of uncertainty, including your client's. The way through is to *identify with the perception of uncertainty as being a part of "the human condition"* lest you make the same error that was perpetrated on you; the ignorance of selective non-acceptance.

It is one thing to validate your client's anger. It is another thing to reinforce your client's justification of anger out of how they have been perceived and treated. Because complexity of form does not imply complexity of content, whether it is from within or outside of the context of family, culture, minority, relationships, gender identity, religion, etc., we have all felt misunderstood as bodies. The world of selective perception out of uncertainty leaves everything up to be misunderstood. Get there.

## Justified Anger as a Sacred Fiction

4) You would not reinforce guilt or shame as justifiable. Why would you reinforce anger as justifiable? To reinforce anger as justifiable is a delay that attacks your client's ability to be at peace with themself. Justified anger is a sacred fiction to be disputed. In the end it will be for you to forgive your perception of the ignorance of another that you perceived as hurting you, just as the other will need to forgive their perception of you. Their error about you is not about you unless you want to make their error real for you … and this you can forgive. I am not saying that how another acted out of their perception of you is justified. I am saying the "you" taking it personally is about you, not them. To protest "But how could I not take it personally" is an objection, a delay to not look at the work you need to do!

5) Therapist, when you are ready, you will find that all bodies of gender are illusion. You know this to be true because when it comes to selecting a reality to live by all things are *always* up for grabs ... but never definitive. The justice you look for in the world will never be found. No matter how hard you legislate for change, violation will occur.[85] *This is the human condition.*

Whether you are heterosexual, homosexual, bisexual, transgender, male or female is irrelevant to the point. The point being that your mind cannot integrate (be one minded towards a unified goal) and heal as long as it is distracted to believe it is a body image that dies. That's the battle ground of a split/dualistic mind. Just like you, this is everyone's dilemma that comes here. It is to see our common dilemma that heals, not how different we are.

*It is the body's eyes that sees differences*
*It is the healed mind that does not acknowledge them*

6) One could argue that sensitivity to gender/transgender identity is an asset. But this would involve the final step towards an integration of a "YOU" as being One Mind, not a body. To be able to forgive the confusion of ignorance in another is to be able to forgive your confusion of ignorance. It is a demonstration of healing beyond body and words. It is a transcendence that recognizes "YOU" as Spirit united with Source, beyond body identity. From this point of view, it does not matter what your gender identity is.

---

[85] I am not saying "don't be an activist for social justice." I am saying "there will never be an end to it." *The Way Home p115-120; 139-144*

*All this time you have been fighting for gender identity acceptance when the fact of the matter is that you are none of them. Get there.*

7) Mindful thoughts that transcend your belief in a body identity become essential to practice and apply. When you can do this, you can use the body as a means to heal; a means to teach a tolerance you have longed for that transcends body identity.

**Challenge to the Therapist**

*All comparisons are about you perceiving "a self you made" against other selves you made to dance to the tune you make.*

Therapist, stop trying to reinforce or ingratiate an esteem your client is not. Your client suffers low self-esteem because the esteem they have decided on does not work. Why? Because it is not them! Throw all your esteem building tactics away. Work with your client to start anew with an understanding that their worth does not come from them alone. Nor is it for them to decide what it should be. Reality is not yours to select.

*To "think positive" thoughts about your fiction of what you are not, leads you nowhere.*

This issue is one of authority; either in humility you accept your role as love's creation or decide in arrogance that reality is yours to select. Thank God you have been wrong. That you begin to journey to the fact that your value comes from Source, is your journey to heal the separation of dis-relation.

## Summary

*Self-esteem is a ruse, a fiction, a concept without substance*

Simply stated; you are not what you think you are. You can't comprehend this as long as ego-self is your guide. With ego's guidance, what you think you are is lacking. From this point of view, you can only look upon what you are not, as lacking.[86] You know this is true because you constantly try to be something presentable. You have used a body self-image as a means to remain deceived about what you really are. *This is the human condition.*

The primary tenant of Transformational Psychotherapy is that sickness is a dilemma of separation from your ground of Being. Because your separation is witnessed as an individual self in a sea of individual selves, healing this split is *identifying with* everyone you meet. It is a different way of thinking that eventually lends itself to an experience beyond a way of thinking. Although you do not have to believe in God, eventually it comes down to an authority problem. Your journey to authenticity is to recognize that reality is not yours to select. How's it going boss?

*It is a principle of Transformational Psychotherapy for you to stop trying to find out who you are so who you are can tell you.*

*Namaste!*

---

[86] Your mental loop

# Addiction: Obsession with the Body

*How can you work through anything from the disposition of what you are not?*

## Introduction

*All addictions involve a body that lacks. Your client's primary addiction is the belief they are a body. From this one belief all other addictions of form hinge. Beyond the body is the disposition of no addiction at all.*

In one way or another, most everything you do, think, or say is motivated towards a body as "YOU." You can argue "well of course I am centered on my body because it is me." If this is true, close the book and pitch your tent. Your search for truth, meaning, security and healing is over because the body you think you are will die. You can have temporary relief but never release.

## Distraction & Delay

*Every addiction grieves for its next fix*

All addictions are mental distractions. They are delays your mind uses through objects, people and events of the world to deceive itself to believe it is a body. They are preoccupations your mind uses to look for meaning through the pleasures, securities, pains and fears that a body experiences. In other words, all addictions are effects that symbolize a mistaken identity or dis-relation from "Self" for a self you are not. Your split mind, in an attempt to deceive itself, looks for an individual identity through a body it is not. Maintaining this deception is what preoccupation, obsession, distraction and addiction is all about. The forms this preoccupation takes is legion; chemical dependency, workaholism, shop till you drop, gambling, hoarding, greed, sex, food, etc.

As opportunity, all addictions can also be used as steppingstones for transcending your belief in a fictitious body image. Ego can be described as a cunning, baffling, powerful preoccupation.[87] So is your world of fictional facts used to defend your imagination of a "self" in a world of fictional facts. The term co-dependency is the catch all. It is the belief that a fictitious you can find happiness in something or someone outside of "a you" you are not. According to this definition *we are all co-dependent and addicted to looking outside for meaning and connection and a security that is not there.* That's why your endless search for meaning outside of you is a fruitless search to nowhere. To identify inclusion of mutual dependencies in different forms diffuses your client's frustrated mind of judging, failure and being alone. Now your journey to peace of mind becomes a joined endeavor that you do together through learning detachment with love … or misery loves company. You choose.

## What You Identify With

If I am Spirit and not a body, the only way to describe my dilemma is that I am addicted to the body and in denial that I am. The hallmark of all addictions is that they are protected from detection by denial. That's why you refuse to see that you are addicted to a body you are not.

---

[87] So can "the devil," so can ignorance, so can the world of change, etc. In the book *Alcoholics Anonymous*, alcoholism is described as "cunning, baffling, powerful!" p 58-59

"What you identify with is what you are" is not a true statement. However, your mind does adapt to what it identifies with. The body you identify with tells one story. If you are not the body you identify with then your adaptation to it allows you experiences not real to you. This would make everything you experience an illusion and a block to the experience of what you really are. The mind that transcends the body, does not know addiction.

You may justify your experiences as real because "I feel it." This is body identity, not you. For example, the spouse that wants to save a relationship makes adjustments to an abusive drinking partner. It is a mental dance between bodies. There may be all kinds of abuse in the dance … a very sloppy looking dance. In the end, *your release* from this attraction will be a change in mind, in how you view yourself beyond ego esteem body identity. It has to be beyond ego esteem because it was you listening to ego that got you caught up in something more cunning, baffling and powerful than "the you" you are not. When blame is not an option, and you see beyond the appearances of an insanity you could not see before, you can walk through it. Until then, you will have to struggle with the dictates of the ego.

Your experience of fictions makes them your experience of fictions. Don't validate as real the experience of something that isn't "You." If you are eternal, you are not temporary. If you are temporary, you are not eternal.

*It is the principle of a healed mind that you can't serve two masters.*

To believe your experiences of a body are real, you must lie to yourself.[88] Are you eternal or temporary? You choose; but you cannot choose both … and the choice you make will be the experience you ask for.

## Moderation

There is wisdom in "all things in moderation." However, a mind in dis-relation, split between pseudo- ego's kingdom of the temporary battling for dominance against your Eternal Self which does not know conflict, can have no moderation. Between the eternal and the temporary there is no negotiated peace; only reprieve, for a little while. The world of constant and interpersonal conflict demonstrates this fact.

In Bill's story, he comes to an awareness of what he must do to take his first step. It involves the "experience" of what "an entire psychic change"[89] is about.

*No words can tell of the loneliness and despair I found in that bitter morass of self-pity. Quicksand stretched around me in all directions. I had met my match. I had been overwhelmed. Alcohol was my master.*[90]

It is a principle of mind that you cannot serve two masters and have peace of mind at the same time.[91] To hide this fact, the left hand and right hand must not know what each is doing. Clients say many times "I get it, it is master over me." What your clients do not understand is what "an entire psychic change" means in lifestyle and

---

[88] *Healing the Wound; the Family's Journey Through Chemical Dependency p42-60; Symbols of Power in Metaphysics p162-169*
[89] Alcoholics Anonymous; The Doctor's Opinion xxvii
[90] Alcoholics Anonymous p8
[91] *Symbols of Power in Philosophy p252 #2*

thinking. That is why relapses are pervasive. To them I say "I believe you mean what you understand. But you do not understand what is involved when it comes to making "an entire psychic change." That is why a *unified goal for peace of mind is the only goal in Transformational Psychotherapy.*

## Clarification of Terms

For the addict, whatever their presenting master is, to move them along when they are stuck in their mud hole of guilt and denial, you can provocatively argue with them.

You question: "You don't really think you are an addict?"

"How can you say that" some indignantly reply. "Of course I do."

"I have proof that you don't believe you are an addict," I respond tongue-in-cheek.

Some clients will express a confused "HUH?" or want to angrily justify their point of view that you don't think they are serious about their addiction or that you don't know what you are talking about.

Here's the educational paradox: Addiction from the view of cunning, baffling and powerful preoccupation suggests that if you understood these terms;

1) You would understand *cunning* as "you didn't see it coming," rather than all your "I should haves and should not haves" self-attack. Your self-deception to not see it coming with your first chemical use demonstrates how cunning it is.

2) *Baffling* as "no matter how hard you try to figure it out, it will never make sense." You know it doesn't make sense because of your anger and guilt about it.

3) *Powerful* as "it is more commanding than your ability to fix alone." How many times have you tried to control and/or quit your addiction with the results of failure?

4) *Preoccupation* as an obsessive and hostile takeover of the mind. "Otherwise, you would be able to see your way through, to forgive your perception of your past."

We are not talking about justifying or rationalizing fictional excuses.[92] To think the addict should be punished is your ball and chain. Nor am I saying as the world perceives it that society should not be protected from them (institutions, jail). What I am saying is because of karma, no matter how you think about it or how you think the addict should think about what they did, they will carry the consequences of their addiction with them. Just like you.

For those of you who have a co-dependent relationship (addiction) with a body looking for satisfaction in a world of lack, it is your saving grace to grapple with what cunning, baffling and powerful preoccupation means. Because in your right mind you would not have done the things you did.

---

[92] There are some who believe "pain is gain," that we learn from our consequences and therefore, guilt is a good thing. On one level, it seems to be in the nature of your dream to need consequences to awaken you to the awareness of your fictions. Yet, on another level, if consequences worked to reform we would have no prisons. All are born because of unresolved guilt (karma). No matter what socialization and educational opportunities are available, you live with the consequences of a memory to play again & again with the opportunity to resolve it. That is why the world of educational opportunity is irrelevant to the child who will have to play their life out in their way and time. Guilt does not motivate you away from your obsessive temptation to make a cunning, baffling, powerful preoccupation a fictitious world to defend as real. Rather, guilt justifies your fictitious world as real.

## Zen It

Creation flows through you continuously. All minds that find themselves in the dream of a world not true to your Eternal Self, are obsessed with trying to make their world real. This obsession blocks your experience of Creation's flow. Because complexity of form does not imply complexity of content, your conflict of trying to make a world real that is not true to "You," is the conflict of all conflicts. The battle ground between the eternal and the temporal is endless tension. To Zen the conflict is to see the temporal as it is; a cunning, baffling, powerful, preoccupation. What was once your enemy to judge as lacking is your way through to forgive. In your right mind you would not have done the things you did. This is not a justification, but a way through to forgive. When you Zen it, you use the conflict to express your creative self.[93] It is the Tao of balance until you create to resolve the tension, to transcend it.[94] To forgive one addiction is to be able to forgive them all. You made the world out of tension. Use it to create healing.

## Responsibility or Opportunity?

Some clients, whether it is a parent, sibling or friend, have a distorted idea that in some way they should have helped their loved one through an addiction. To diffuse the guilt of a client feeling responsible for not helping enough to stop another's addiction, you talk about the proof of your client's inability to stop another's addiction. It is not proof of failure. It is proof that "they are not yours to fix."[95] Even more, your client's guilt is proof of their

---

[93] *Symbols of Power in Metaphysics p148-161*
[94] *Symbols of Power in Philosophy p280*
[95] *Healing the Wound p17-24*

own preoccupation with cunning, baffling and powerful. Diffuse the dualistic battle ground. Zen it by asking "What is the addict trying to teach you?" Eventually the conversation turns to "The addict is teaching me detachment with love." The therapeutic situation has taken an entirely different turn.

Some become angry over an addict blaming their addiction on the comment "I can't help it, I am an addict, I have a disease." Be honest, why are you mad at them? You are angry because you did not take care of yourself and are preoccupied out of your own fear. Either way, your anger and fear are about you, not them. Stop blaming them for your inability to not see the fictions you are addicted to.[96] The addict may be deflecting. They may even be blaming you. This is what addiction does. Be assured, they cannot escape the consequences of their denial. Their karma will catch up to them. That is of no concern of yours. Your concern is in your own back yard of making their error real for you. Become aware of the consequence of your denial. The addict is teaching you detachment with love.[97] They have never been yours to save from the journey they must take. Just like no one can save you from the journey you took by misinterpreting and defending your fiction about them. That is your fiction. You can't see your fiction while you are looking outside to fix theirs. They are for you to love so you can experience love. This is their gift to you. Receive it.

---

[96] *Healing the Wound p 46-50*
[97] Al-anon material

## For Spouses

*It's not that your relationship did not work*
*It's that you gave it the wrong goals*

Spouses will ask, "What can I do, how do I support the chemically dependent loved one?" You help your client to see that "your attempts to help have been an enabling of their addiction. It actually helps them do it easier."[98]

Present the dilemma to your client by stating, "You can do years of therapy or take a short cut." Ask your client, "What is your passion in life?" If they don't know it is because they have adjusted their life around living with their chemically dependent loved one, putting their life on hold. There would be anger in this. Explore this with your client.

If they do know what their passion in life is encourage them to pursue it. This may involve a dilemma between perceived abandonment and anger. To your client you say "It is OK for you to walk your passion. If you are tempted to reach back and help your chemically dependent loved one *again* in their struggle, that's OK."[99] There is no guilt or blame in this because that is what your client still needs to work through. "Just don't blame them for your choice if it does not work out," is a therapeutic opportunity. "And don't think yourself as 'stupid' for *again* wanting to believe them when they promised you the earth, moon and stars saying they would change," is another therapeutic opportunity. "There is no need to judge anyone in this journey. But it is your lesson to learn as much as it is theirs.

---

[98] *Healing The Wound p27-39*
[99] This is what a choice between to competing illusions is all about.

Without anger and guilt, you can learn your lesson through real forgiveness. If you are inclined to walk your passion, the chemically dependent loved one will either step-up and walk with you, or not. Should they work through their issues to step up, you have a partner. If not, walk your passion with love, not anger, because it will be either anger or love you bring with you to the next relationship."

**Summary**

Each and every addiction is master over you. Your mind is addicted to a body as you. This is fundamental to Transformational Psychotherapy. To see this fiction is the only way out of a loop that has no resolution in all the forms your addictions in denial seem to be.

Why is addiction an opportunity? It pushes us out of our comfort zones to look at our fictions as to how we think the world "should" work. It makes us more honest with ourselves as to what it means to live life on life's terms. Working through your addiction makes you more aware of your journey through. It is your road to awakening. Life will never be the way it was.

*To live life on life's terms*
*Is to live without "fiction"*

Again, *Transformational Psychotherapy is the process of changing your view of yourself in the light of a world of fictional facts used to defend your imagination of a "self" in a world of fictional facts.*

*Namaste!*

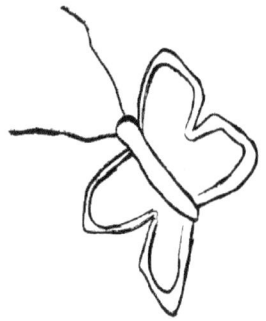

# Anxiety: The Dizziness of Choices

*Anxiety is another form of fear … just more subtle*

## Introduction

The basis of all your conflicts lay in the fact that you are in dis-relation with Source. If this is not the case, we as human animals are irrational beings, lost to the fate of our fictions, magical thoughts and desires, doomed to worry about nothingness. This is not skepticism but a fact of history.[100]

## Under the Conscious Level

*Anxiety is the dizziness of choices in a world where choice is irrelevant*

To be in dis-relation with Source is to not know your "Self." To not know "Self" engenders fear. Now you must find a self, a home to ward off the fear of the unknown. Out of fear, you bury your dis-relation in the unconscious, away from your awareness, away from your ability to deal with it. That is why you are often anxious but are not always sure why.

Just under the conscious level is a buzz, a gnawing unresolved doubt. If you allow for a moment of mental clarity, you can experience the awareness of an ancient buzz … grinding on just under the conscious level. This ancient buzz has been since the beginning. In fact, it is the making of a beginning that never was, yet persists today.

---

[100] The book Symbols of Power in Philosophy attests to this fact.

You cannot resolve your existential dilemma because you have buried it under the conscious level, out of reach. Your dis-relation in secret breeds insane beliefs (fictions) about yourself and others that have gained unconscious hold of great intensity. They grip your mind with a terror so strong that it will not give up the idea of its own protection from its insane irrational fictions. Your decisions to defend these insane beliefs are protected from awareness, not to be disturbed from question, reason or doubt. That is why you persist in defending, wrestling with and appeasing unreasonable doubt and anxiety.

## Anxiety as a Self-Defeating Process

*When you think you are something other than what you are, you experience the world of fiction, and all its trappings.*

In dis-relation, you look outside for meaning because you do not know who you are. When you look outside for meaning you experience anxiety. Why? Because meaning cannot be found outside of "You." And the more you try to understand the un-understandable outside to appease your anxiety, the more anxious you become.[101] That is why *the gathering of information for meaning is a complexity that makes it difficult for you to see its nothingness.*

---

[101] These are the labels Freud called neuroses, a mental condition not caused by organic disease. Neuroses involves symptoms of stress, depression, anxiety, obsessive behavior, hypochondria. Some common examples of neurotic behavior can include obsessing over what others think and exhibiting an anxious temperament. Someone who lives with neuroses may have trouble when they make mistakes at school or work. They may also be overly critical of themselves and others. The need to control one's world and future becomes a paramount stressor.

How can you not feel anxiously disturbed when you are reacting to a world that isn't through a self you are not? There is no empowerment in this; just the need to try and control what you can't control, which breeds your anxiety. This is the dizziness of choices in a world where choice is irrelevant; which only feeds your justification to be anxious. Because of your resistance to see your fictions, magical thinking on the conscious level as what they are, self-defeating, diligence is needed.[102]

*To be free of conflict requires only one thing: A goal that is not itself conflicted. Trying to change anything is a form of battle; wanting something that can only be ours in the future is to block our potential to be happy now. Therefore, set for yourself a goal that can be fulfilled where you stand. Make this instant your door to freedom and you will find that it will crack open a little further each time you return to this moment in peace.*
Teach Only Love
Gerald G. Jampolsky

## Dialogue

A conversation of challenge from a specific anxious dilemma that your client can eventually generalize to each and every anxious thought might go like this:

Have your client identify the object of their anxiety. Simply ask them: "What are you anxious about?" Whatever they tell you, know that the object of their anxiety is always a future possibility, out of the experience of doubt.

---

[102] The book *Reflections for the Wandering Mind*

After your client tells you about their future anxiety that isn't, ask "Has it happened yet?"

When they want to answer "Well, no, but ..." you interrupt their thinking.

Ask again "Has it happened yet?" and interrupt them until they stop saying "Well, no, but ..."

Ask "Is what hasn't happened real?"

When they want to answer "Well, no, but ..." you interrupt their thinking.

Ask again "Is what hasn't happened real?

Finally, when they say only "No" without a "Ya but," you ask, "If it isn't real, what are you anxious about?"

When they say "Well ... nothing."

You say "Exactly!" and tell them "Say it again."

When they say "Nothing."

You say, "Say it louder!"

"Nothing."

Repeat this with them until they get it.[103]

Anxiety as the symptom of out-of-control thinking needs to be interrupted. Because anxiety is the dizziness of a choice in a world where choice is irrelevant, your encounter with your client is about challenging their fiction without your client feeling threatened that their fiction was challenged.

*A nightmare is a panic attack in your sleep dream*
*Anxiety is self-attack in your awake dream*
*The object of your anxiety is always "Nothing"*
*On its most fundamental level, fear is the result of not knowing*

---

[103] *The Way Home p87-89*

## What is Today?

*Today is the tomorrow you worried about yesterday*

Each and every anxious thought is of the nature of a future tense, the tense of unreality.[104] "But if only I could control, yes, secure tomorrow by today's planning," is the anxious thinker's thought, "then I will be content." This thinking chases after the possibilities of tomorrow for resolution today. However, your happiness that can only be found today is robbed by the thoughts of a tomorrow that never arrives. But why would this be of concern to anybody when the past is gone and the future is never to be? These concerns are to be looked at as defenses against a present change in focus; the only place you can free yourself from anxiety.[105] That is why;

*Every ghost of days gone by will haunt the imagination of days to come until every problem of days gone by finds its answer now.*[106]

## Taking your Mind Back

*You have a battle raging inside of you … as you look outside for a resolution that is not there.*

Acceptance of where you are "now" is demonstrated by taking things as they arrive. Because the world is ever-changing nothingness without teleology, [107] there is

---

[104] *Symbols of Power in Philosophy p27-34*

[105] This was the emphasis of Albert Ellis, William Glasser and Carl Rogers

[106] *Symbols of Power in Metaphysics p107*

[107] Without, aim, purpose, goal; *Symbols of Power in Philosophy*

nowhere else. Your only work to do is to interrupt all the anxious thoughts that seem to find you along your way. Any anxious thought can be used to remind you to say, "I forgive how I see this situation because how I see it hurts me." And because complexity of form does not imply complexity of content, you can use this mindful thought for everything. And because all applications have their experiences, be diligent to do the work. [108] Your opportunity to practice interrupting your anxiety is your opportunity to take your mind back. If nothing seems to happen, that does not mean nothing is happening. Be patient, you are working through your unconscious fictions. Repetition is your best teacher. Do the work!

## Summary

You are caught up in a loop. You are anxious because you have no real choices you can make. And you can't see the one choice you need to make because you are anxious. That is why you have panic attacks, an existential dread that there is "no exit."

You have found many games of distraction to occupy your mind. But now, you are doing something different. Through meditative thoughts of forgiveness, you are using your anxiety to remind you to take your mind back. Breaking the loop puts you back on the path to "Self" discovery.

*Transformational Psychotherapy is the process of helping your client to empower themselves, to take their mind back.*

---

*p172-174*
[108] *Reflections for the Wandering Mind p36-42*

# Fear: Your Reminder of the Truth

*The one who fears suffering*
*Suffers from what he fears*

## Introduction

What I said before: This is a book on cause. Your dis-relation with Source is the cause of the world you see. The world and all its problems are demonstrations of complexity. But it is a complexity of form (symptoms) that does not imply a complexity of content.

This is an easy text … when you recognize what is cause and what is effect. Your dis-relation with Source is the cause of the world you see.

## No Exit

*You make the world you see. And what you make, you defend against. And what you defend against you make real. The only escape from this is the miracle of a changed mind.*

Fear is the reminder that your safety resides on a fiction. Your body is the primary fiction that your safety relies on. In the world, acts of violence occur between bodies … then the body dies. In the final analysis, your body is not your place of safety. But where else do you turn to for safety?

How can you trust the self you made and ingratiate along the way? It has been the primary self-deception that causes all your fear. Your attempt to deny this fact through a busy mind makes you all the more anxious because you do not know where else to turn. So, you project your fear into a place of hopeful possibilities. Yet, that can't save you because the projection of fear into the future of possibilities only gives you the unrest of a future of fearful possibilities that you need to control and plan against.

## Fear's Making

Your identity is in Source. To be in dis-relation with Source is to be in dis-relation with "Self." Eternity does not know of change. When you left Source, there was a change. That change was a fearful upset. That is why change all too often involves fear or possibility.

You don't know "You." And to not know engenders fear. Now you must make a self to protect, ingratiate and be something through a world of complicating effects that hide what you have done. To not know "YOU" is a dis-relation that fears the unknown. Out of fear, the unknown is always the temptation of a future possibility that is not yours to control. Your attempts to secure a future that is not yours to secure results in constant adjustments/compensations that rob you of present peace. You are tired because it takes work to defend and ingratiate a self you are not.

## Ego Alliances

*The body's eyes may see differences, but it is the healed mind that does not acknowledge them*

Ego alliances are for security out of fear of being alone. They are self-destructive because they rely on similarities of being "different" from other groups of people who rely on similarities of being "different." This is the making of nationalisms of false pride. This is a binding of commonality through fear. This is what cults and ideologies are all about. Because fear is exclusive to people and groups of people, these alliances cannot know of the freedom of inclusion. Inclusion is a forgiving of your boundaries made out of fear, a fear of exclusive righteousness. While joining leads to healing, the remembrance of a Mind we all share as One.

One way to deal with fearful projections is to label them as "evil." The concept of evil brings tangible meaning and justification to certain behaviors, to your fearful projections in a world of chaos. Ego alliances gravitate towards the justification of their fears as real.

Prejudice is a projection that attempts to understand through fear, those who are different in appearance. To understand through fear is a *selection of perception* to only see the justifications of why you should fear them. These selections manifest fearfully in forms of others being different in gender identity, color, culture, religion and ideologies, etc. It is the power of your mind to project away what you do not want. Yet because you entertain it, you manifest it in a world of effects, a world of innumerably complex differences of ever-changing inconsistency. How scary can that be?

Ideologies are made out of fear to protect you from fear and thus the truth. Because your fear remains, they do not work. The making of a zealot [109] with an exclusively justifiable cause is what all terrorists are about. Your investment to make meaningful a world made out of fear of the unknown is your block that hides the truth of what you are really about. You are about passage. You are a stranger in a strange land. Be a passerby.

All prejudice is symbolic of your dis-relation from your Authentic Self. In dis-relation you experience the aloneness of separation. Out of fear you try to make sense out of the loneliness of being different. Ego has a plan to

[109] *The Way Home p108-110*

ease this loneliness by finding a superficial commonality with others. However, this superficial commonality justifies your alienation from others. Misunderstanding needs to hide under the collective justification of ego alliances. These alliances fall under the banners of being different in culture, language, color of skin, gender identity, national identity, religious affiliation, economics, ideology and separate causes, to name a few. The perception of uncertainty reigns. How ingenious a plan this is to keep you lost in the loneliness of your fear rather than to journey to experience the peacefulness of inclusion.

*You don't need a sword to cut through flowers.*[110]

To understand is to recognize scary shadows for what they really are. Then you won't misuse them as reasons to justify righteous anger out fear.

## Doubt & Denial

*All of us on this side of the veil are terrified to a degree we are not aware of. You are not alone in your fear.*

Doubt is also the result of not knowing. Denial becomes doubt's protection against finding out that you need not fear the unknown. Denial helps you get involved in the seriousness of the everyday to occupy your time with meaningless tasks that avoid reflection. In that void of meaningless seriousness, your choices of diversion appear in innumerable forms to live out through a body. And each diversion you make to avoid fear is an unconscious cultivation of fear in the form of interpersonal conflict.

---

[110] John Lennon, Whatever Gets You Through the Night

Disappointment, hope, frustration, accomplishment, anger, relief, depression, excitability, pain, pleasure, etc. are examples of dealing with fear. These are forms (effects) ego-self in denial can handle. Even though these expressions (effects) are opportunities to remind you that you have *fictions* of how you think the world should work, you deny yourself these opportunities to see that the complexity of all these forms have the same content in common; a dis-relation with your ground of Being. This is the ego's plan of delay. Looking for solutions in a world of diversion is self-defeating because the world is one big diversion, the feeding of and justification for your fear.

> *The greater your denial, the greater your fear*
> *The greater your fear, the greater your denial*

Here, the cycle of fear is exposed for what it truly is; a meaningless effect without a cause in truth.

## The Boogie Man in the Closet

With an open mind, the only need you have is the need to want to know the truth about "You." Do not allow for any exception. Argumentation and justification are diversions, hills to die on from wanting to know inclusion.

This is not an exercise in the denial of fear. This is an exercise of steps towards opening the door to see what's in your bedroom closet. It's OK to be afraid. Fear is only the result of not knowing "You." All you need is a little willingness, a courage to want to move beyond fear to the truth. The truth about you is beyond comparisons of good and bad, beyond interpretations and evaluations of value, beyond measurements of success and failure. All of these approaches evoke experiences of fear. However, you did not establish truth, nor did you establish who you are. You just denied your remembrance of it. In the light of Source, reality is not yours to select.

Therefore:

1) Be diligent to stop trying to decide who you are so who you are can tell you. Remind yourself daily; "The truth about me will not harm me, but free me from the fear of what I think." Interrupt judgments of comparisons and failures. They serve no good purpose.

2) When you are afraid (panicky), to the best of your ability, *allow it*. Talk to someone, make a phone call. Your connection to someone is an extension out of your room of dread. It will pass; it always does. Don't isolate!! *To allow* the experience of fear and its passing is a big step in recognizing that it really does pass and you really can live through it.

Fear (dread) seems to be debilitating until you are able to look through your denial of what is beyond fear itself. Your reaction out of fear says you are vulnerable. But it also says that you have fictions about how you think the world *should* work when they don't.

I am not saying that acts of violence on a body is justified. I am asking, how long will you hold on to taking another person's confused ignorance personally, as a justification to build your fortress of safety that can never keep your fear out? If you continue to justify your reasons to be afraid, vulnerable and violated, you will set up more boundaries to try to keep you safe from violation. And the more boundaries you have, the more opportunities you will have to feel violated. That is the power your mind has to miss-create, to make the illusion of fear a power to adjust your life around.

3) It is not necessary for you to deny or minimize your fear. That only breed's a conflicting fearful resistance. Be

willing to take a different look at what you fear. Take a step towards your closet door to ask "Is it true that my interpretations of life events give me reasons to fear? It does involve introspective *courage* to take a look at your world view. Where there is fear, there is fiction.

4) Ask yourself "What am I angry, guilty and fearful about?" List them.

Look through each one you are willing to find and ask if that interpretation towards that person, thing or event is helping you to cope or is it making you feel miserably angry, guilty and afraid. To deny confusion and ignorance as a cause is to want to hold dear a fiction as to how you think the world *should* work; of how people should be.

5) Keep a note of those interpretations you do not want to keep anymore.

When you find yourself using one, tell yourself *"I forgive the way I see that person or situation because that way I am choosing to see it hurts me. It makes me feel angry, guilty and afraid."*

6) Ask a friend for help; not a friend who will help justify your fear, but one who is willing to listen to you from a different point of view

In the end it will be you who decides when it will be time to freely rise above your cycle of fear. For in the end, it will be you in your *willingness to know,* to open your door to find the truth about YOU that lies beyond all your vain imaginings. You do not have to open your door alone.

7) When you open your door to see what is not there, you can step back into life. Invite a friend(s) to join with you in your celebration back to the remembrance of your freedom.

Although you have been afraid of what another can do to you, *fear's reminder* is that you have invested in a fiction you are not. You can change your mind about this. With courage, you really can free yourself to see the truth of the matter.

## Thought is a Function of Mind

*I am afraid of my world because I am afraid of the power of my thoughts*

Doubt is the thinking; fear is the feeling. Thought is a function of mind, nothing more and nothing less.
Stop Right Here!

"Did you hear me? I just said that your thoughts have no reality in themselves."

"How can you say that? "You ask.

"The boogie man in your closet told me" I say. "He may seem fearfully real, but it was you that thought him that way. And because you have the power of your mind to make him up, you also have the power of your mind to undo him … actually, you can undo anything."

Thoughts are neither good or bad, right or wrong, positive or negative. They are merely thoughts. Yet, through your thoughts do you choose to assign power to people, things and events. In your choosing, these meanings come back to either help or haunt you. You may think the boogie man in your closet was just childish imagination. But until you find the courage to rethink all that you assume to be true, you will not open your hidden (sacred) closet doors to find that there is nothing there.

You depreciate the power of your mind by thinking what's out there can hurt you. When what is out there you made as the imagination of your sleepy dreams. Someday, you will realize that what you "thought" was so, was but a passing thought; nothing more and nothing less.

## Simplicity & Complexity

Truth is always simple. But it must be taught to those lost in complexity. Because of your attempt to make the complexity of nothingness meaningful, you have scared yourself. You can't see any way out, just more complexity of fearful possibilities. Out of fear you easily feel justified and compelled to control people, things and events ... or you hide out.

*People are crazy and times are strange*
*I'm locked in tight, I'm out of range*
*I used to care, but things have changed*
Bob Dylan
Things Have Changed

Forms of control are numerously subtle. The obvious is perfectionism. A perfectionist is one who reflects a need for order in their external life. It is symbolic of their fearful inner struggle. Order represents control as a means of security. In this way the need for external adaptation beyond reason becomes justified.[111] But security never comes. Your adaptations into the extreme merely represent your internal dilemma of being lost in the complexity of insecure thinking.

Spontaneity and creativity flow out of simplicity. They are unpredictable irritations to those who need to control complexity. Because there are too many variables in complexity that cannot be controlled, feeling violated becomes the norm. In the name of self-protection, you

---

[111] Obsessive compulsions

justify additions to your list of boundaries. However, the more rules you have for safety, the more opportunities you have for your rules to be violated. This complication of "more" makes it difficult for you to see the nothingness of it all.

## Fear's Reminder

*Change is easy for those who let go*
*The first step is willingness, a willingness to flow*
*But I've got a long … a long way to go*
*Think not of perfection, think not of lack*
*Think only of willingness, and you're on your way back*

Peace of mind understands that control is unnecessary. Everything flows within its proper time and place. But this is unimaginable to the mind experiencing a threatening world. Fear screams "control is essential for the survival of myself." Instead, let fear remind you that it was made out of an insecure self. And that an insecure self can never feel safety because it was made out of fear. Your continued failures to find security for an insecure self demonstrates that you are not what you think you are. *This is fear's reminder for your awakening.*

*Fear reminds you* that your boundaries do not work. If they did, you would not be afraid. To not know this is to attempt to control a complexity outside of you that is not yours to control. You are suffocating in the boundaries you made to protect you. Open a window!

Society's conditioning is an effect that says, "it is you as an individual that decides your worth." Yet, societies messages are vaguely ever-changing parameters of appropriateness. And "insanity is doing the same thing over and over again while expecting different results."[112] Don't deny the insane situation you have thought yourself into so you can begin to move beyond the self-defeating loop. It is the thoughts you choose to entertain that scare you or free you of your fetters. Use fear to remind you of your dis-relation from Source. Ask for help.

**Exercise**

> *What if there is no tomorrow?*
> *There wasn't one today!*
> The movie Ground Hog Day

An exercise you can do with your client:

1) Without exception and just for a moment, put all your thoughts of past of fond memories, guilt and resentment[113] aside.

2) Without exception, put aside all discomforts and distractions of your physical body. These are all considered to be *anticipations of the body*.

3) Third, without exception, put all your thoughts of future anticipation, anxiety, possibility, fear of the unknown, fear that the past might repeat itself in the future, aside.

4) With these three set aside, tell me, what problems do you have as you sit here and now in this present moment? Only list the thoughts that have nothing to do with the past, the future, bodily distractions/discomfort and anticipations.[114]

---

[112] Albert Einstein

[113] Resentment is anger held on to.

[114] Sometimes your client will talk about a body ailment, a hunger pain or the need to go to the bathroom. Remind them "that is what the anticipation of the body is all about."

When you have worked through this process of elimination with your client, you can ask "what problems do you have in this present moment?" They will realize the answer to the question to be "None."

5) Then you can ask "When you were in yesterday what tense were you in?" The eventual answer after some guessing is "the present." Then ask "When tomorrow comes, what tense will you be in." After some guessing the answer will be "the present." When are you not in the present? The answer is "Never." They may say they are not in the present when they are thinking in tenses, but the fact of the matter is that whether you realize it or not, no matter what tense you are thinking in, you are always in the present.[115]

Any present moment in which you choose to be beyond thought and body will be your epiphany, your experience of peace. You will not forget this experience in this lifetime. In fact, it will be a memory you will feed on, on your journey through fear. Because there is no agenda of your own that gets in the way, you cultivate a place where you can once again remember your real relationship with Source and one another; relationships that transcend the world of tenses and bodies.

6) You can close with your client by saying: "When you leave this place, you may again take up your worries and cares. But this place of peace will always be with you, waiting for you when you again choose to want it more than anything else. And every time you come back to this

---

[115] Just because you are experiencing the "illusion" of tenses that are not real to truth, does not make the illusion real as much as it denies you your experience of the present. As a matter of fact, experiencing tenses that are not real is what the experience of illusion is all about. And you are doing it almost all the time! *Symbols of Power in Philosophy p27-34*

place, the door will open a little wider, until this place of peace is the only place you want.

## Summary

Often, have you felt guilty or the hurt of an impending criticism. Though you have tried to overcome these fears by employment achievements, relationship belonging and ideological or religious zeal for salvation. Yet, there has been no release. You also use your perceived failures to chastise yourself in an attempt to better yourself. If you must use your failures as a measure, let them *remind you* of all the effort you have put into your attempt to want to know the truth about "You" beyond fear.

Because of dis-relation (cause), you live in a state of fear (effect). Out of fear, for safety's sake, you struggle to make meaningful the effects of a world you make. Again, you make what you defend against. And what you defend against, you make real. You cannot escape this because you made it. No wonder you often feel uncomfortable but bury it in your many distractions of your life in a body of constant change. You are not at home. Fear is your primary reminder that you are a stranger in a strange land. You know this is true because you experience fear (effect). Because you are not what you think you are or should be, you can be comforted in the fact that there is a way through to "You." And this is through the changing of your mind (cause).

*Transformational Psychotherapy is the process of changing your view of yourself in the light of a world of fictional facts used to defend your imagination of a "self" in a world of fictional facts.*

# Feelings: Barometers of Your View of Life

*Feelings betray you when they reflect your fictions*

## Introduction

Because you are not grounded in the Source of your identity, you live a life of made-up roles. Ever shifting are your roles from a frustrated student to a blissful lover, from a proud to embarrassed parent and a defeated mourner. At a moment's notice, you can go from laughter to weeping ... and greet the day with welcome or with tears. You seem to change through the experience of a thousand shifts in mood. Your emotions raise you high ... and then dash you to the ground in hopelessness. What 's going on?

## Who Decides How You Feel?

A barometer is an instrument that reflects or indicates change. Your feelings are a barometer that reflects the interpretation you have chosen for any given situation. Depending upon the view you choose for any given situation, that will be the feelings you reflect.

To be responsible for your feelings involves more than recognition, allowing and verbalization. It involves the ownership of feelings being self-caused by the thoughts you entertain. Again, this book is a book on cause. Although we talk much about effect, they are used to bring you back to the cause. If you want to make changes that are fundamental to your well-being your changes will be about looking at the fictions you entertain that cause you mental pain.

When your client says, "so and so makes me mad," they believe a certain person or event caused them to feel a certain way. Whether it is anger, grief, guilt, fear or happiness and all the rest, as different in form as they are, they all have the same cause. The thoughts you entertain is the cause of your discomfort. In other words, you decide upon a view of each and every situation and feel accordingly to the decision you make. Because of the fictions you hold dear to protect your understanding of the world you see, you do not always understand why you feel the way you feel

## You are Deciding Continuously How to Feel

Just below the conscious mind you are making decisions continuously. That is why you have so many mood changes and are not aware of why. This also witnesses to the unawareness of an undisciplined mind. Who would choose to harbor interpretations of any situation that are self-hurting (guilt, anger, fear) unless you did not realize you choose it for yourself? Your fickle nature to express a wide range of emotions in a short amount of time, is not "human nature." It is "the human condition" of an undisciplined mind in dis-relation with itself.

It is temptingly easy for an undisciplined mind in unawareness of your fictions, to feel hurt. And because, to the ego attack is salvation, you respond with justified verbal and/or physical aggression. These attacks are based on thoughts of how justice *should* prevail. And though you may have a satisfaction with the results, these thoughts you harbor still lack resolution. That, *"no thought leaves its source,* is a principle of karma that you will have to pay.[116] There is no escape from this.

---

[116] *Symbols of Power in Metaphysics 99-118*

In other words;

1) Whether it is directed at you or from you, attack thoughts are always thoughts of personal conflict entertained in your mind. There is no escape from this.

2) Because it is a principle of your mind that "no thought leaves its source," [117] your justification for attack leaves you no room for peace. You always experience the attack thoughts you wish upon another That is how you always attack yourself first. There is no escape from this.

3) Whether you take responsibility for your feelings as self-caused or not, is irreverent to the point that it is you who lives with the experience of your thinking. There is no escape from this.

## Circular Reasoning

The feelings you experience from your interpretation of any situation is the justification you use to defend your view as correct. You think your view is right because of how you feel about it ... not realizing that how you first viewed it caused you to feel a certain way. With cause and effect turned around, circular reasoning can only find its power in unawareness.

To feel a certain way about something does not make your view right when your view (fiction) makes you feel a certain way in the first place. Those who defend feeling therapies as opposed to analytical therapies are those who are in a constant state of defending feeling therapies through analysis. It's self-defeating circular reasoning. Recognize your projections for what they are. They are yours!

---

[117] *Symbols Of Power In Philosophy p252-259*

## Principles

1) Feelings are not good or bad or right or wrong. They are the experience of "how" you view "what" you view.

2) Feelings don't lie as much as they "expose" mistaken thinking. That all of us can "feel differently" about the same thing we see or hear, witnesses to mind's propensity to selectively perceive uncertainty. You are not objective! On the contrary, you have a strong tendency towards bias. Your ever changeable feelings are but a witness to this bias.

3) All feelings are self-caused. If you do not believe this, you depreciate the power your mind has to change your feelings through changing the thoughts you choose to entertain. In the end it is each of us who decides how to interpret anything. This interpretation decides how you will feel about what you see or hear. It's that simple.

4) Developmentally speaking, when beliefs stabilize, perceptions stabilize. When perceptions stabilize, moods are more predictable, less impulsive.

## An Issue of Therapy

*Feelings are the expressions of what you are thinking*

Focusing on your client's view of any issue rather than the events of how they were "unjustly" treated can be disagreeable to your client. Often, they come to you for validation of what happened to them to be unjust.

"This is what happened to me!" they will say, wanting to make it an issue of justice.

So, talk about what happened, processing back away from "How do you feel about that?" to "I wonder what makes you feel that way?" Now we are at the place of talking about what makes your client feel a certain way.

We are moving towards your client's fictions. Be empathetic yet resist the temptation to align with their ego.

I am not saying feelings are not important. Nor am I saying they are important. I am saying that no matter who you are, talking about feelings is always an intellectual process. The process can be about accepting feeling how you are right now. Which is fine. So then, just sit there and look at each other and just feel. Don't think! But you can't do that because your feelings are the expressions of what you are thinking.

Feeler, when you justify any view through how you feel about it, you are intellectualizing! Rather than spending time expressing the justification of how you feel, use your feelings to identify the fictions you are defending behind the feelings. This is not about justifying anybody's behavior. It's about owning your feelings as self-caused. This, you can change.

When feelings are involved so are thoughts. In fact, your thoughts help you understand the nature of your feelings because they are the cause of them. To not understand cause and effect is to emote over and over again without the resolve a changed mind brings.

*Be aware of what gets you to where you are*

**Orientation Exercise**

*To allow is to feel without judging*

Feelings can be useful tools. If you allow them to, feelings can be aids to reflect the awareness of what's going on with your thinking. Talk to your client: "Whenever you have a feeling you do not like, what are you thinking?"

1) Allow yourself to feel it.

a. There is no reason to judge or analyze the rightness or wrongness of a feeling. They are not good or bad. They are there as a witness to the way you decide to view your life events. Your feelings make the events of movement and noise seem "personally" real to you.

b. To place a value on your feelings exhibits an attitude of either non-acceptance (that I should not feel that way), or justification (you wronged me). Either way is self-attack because you leave no room for peace of mind.

c. Fighting your feelings will not change your perception. It only feeds the fire. It makes them true to you. Your only other option here is to recognize your non-acceptance and allow yourself to own them as where you are, as where you need to be, because that's where you are … and "there's nowhere you can be where you're not meant to be."[118] This is a statement of non-dualistic non-judgment as to you being always where you are supposed to be. Because, no matter how you feel, that's where you are. But only for a moment *in* time.

2) Regarding the situation you are talking about, write down all your feelings. Don't evaluate them as right or wrong or good or bad. Just write them down.

3) What are the thoughts you have that lie behind those feelings? Write down your thoughts that correspond to your feelings.

4) Look honestly at your thoughts. Are they realistic as to living life on life's terms or is there fiction in them? Take the courage to reflect with honesty.

---

[118] Lennon & McCartney; All You Need Is Love

5) When you look beyond defending your thoughts, you can finally ask yourself "What am I thinking to make me feel the way I do?" WOW! Now you are getting to the source of every problem, the propensity of your mind to think erroneously.

6) Reflection: Ask yourself "Do these thoughts make me feel good?" Feelings you do not like have attack thoughts attached to them. Recognize that you are attacking yourself by how you are thinking about whomever or whatever you are thinking about. Remember: No thought leaves its source. The feelings you feel are connected to the thoughts you think about anything. You are not diligent in guarding your mind from thoughts that attack your peace of mind.

7) Recognize and own that you blame others for how you feel. To blame another as the cause of your feelings, e.g. "You make me sad!" is not only a block to self-reflection but is also a denial of self-caused feelings. Those who "feel" that others make them feel a certain way will interpret experiences of life events as a victim.

8) Reinforce that you are not asking your client to blame themselves. Nor are you asking them to forgive the other person. This removes the tendency for battle in your client's mind. You are asking them to *practice diligently* this mantra whenever they have feelings they don't like or thoughts that are judgy: *I forgive how I see this situation because how I see it hurts me.*

> *Those who look outside dream*
> *Those who look within awaken*
> Carl Jung

If you are not stuck on being right about your ideology, world view and thoughts, you can change your feelings by changing your mind about these people and events. If you want to stay stuck in your justified anger, that's your choice. And it will be you who pays for your justification.

## Summary

*There are only as many views as there is your mind's ability to change them*

If how you have a view that says someone hurt you, you are in need of love. Love yourself by recognizing what was done to you was not really about you. This does not justify what another did to your body or bruised ego. But you have no justification for taking movement and noise personally. You, like the other person who reacted to their own projection, have made the same mistake. You made the world of bodies real in your thinking. It was just played out in different forms. Complexity of form does not imply complexity of content. To forgive another for what you thought they did is your road to release. To forgive yourself for how you perceive another's ignorance is your release.

If you are judging yourself by something you did or failed to do, remember that what you are in truth, has nothing to do with what you did through a body image. Your body will pass and be forgotten as the dust of the earth … so will what you did. Forgive yourself for making absolute in your mind, that which has no lasting value.

That you have decided upon a particularly serious view wit attached feelings, is a fact. No one view of any given situation is any more or less real in experience than any other view. In a whirlwind of thought, the only value any view has is that which brings your mind healing resolve from the problem at hand. Therefore, allow your feelings to remind you what you are deciding to think so you can freely change your mind about what you are thinking.

*Transformational Psychotherapy is the process of helping your client to begin to question their reality through any means your client allows.*

# Blame: A Maneuver to Protect Pseudo-Self from Detection

*Blame's reason is to hide guilt*

## Blame as a Maneuver to Protect

Simply stated, you feel violation out of a dis-relation from your identity with Source. Because "You Are" as identified by Source, to be in dis-relation is to not know the Self you are. From that cause, your effect is experienced as guilt and the fear of punishment. Blame is your maneuver (defense) to protect the pseudo- ego-self[119] you made out of the void of not knowing "You" in Source. Ego-self, made out of fear to protect you from fear, blocks your ability to heal the split. Your set-up to avoid the experience of fear, exposure, embarrassment and guilt remains ... until you change your mind about yourself.

## Blame as a Block to Healing

*Only you can deprive yourself of anything*

The best way to protect a mistake from exposure is to deny responsibility. Blame is a projection away that enables you to deny ownership of your mistake. Rather than correct the mistake of an intolerable dis-relation, you deflect through blaming to protect this mistake from exposure. However, when you recognize that you are guiltless, that violation never occurred, you have no need

---

[119] A pseudo- ego-self is a defensive facade or a self-created self out of fear of punishment to protect against perceived threats or vulnerabilities, at the expense of authenticity and genuine self-expression.

to blame. In the meantime, the threat you feel projected away as coming back at you from the outside (the world), is coming from within. You can't see this as you spend your energy blaming to avoid the punishment that a vulnerable self deserves. Again, you set yourself up.

The need to strike out and shift responsibility (blame) on another because of misfortune, emotional pain and fear of punishment will seem justifiably necessary to the vulnerable. It also leaves no end of time and energy to what you have to do to protect yourself from detection, embarrassment and a punishment that you think is coming from the outside but is actually coming from within. Again, you set yourself up.

*Failure is an opportunity*
*If you blame someone else, there is no end to the blame*
Lao-tzu[120]


Like any defense, blame is a block to healing because it does not allow you to look within to the only place where your healing can occur. All justified anger has one focus and one focus only, to blame someone or something for your mistaken view. And when you blame, you can't deal with it as an issue from within to resolve because blame looks out. Even when you seemingly look within to feel guilt, it is looking through the need to punish the vulnerable self you are not. But when you own your part, you can forgive it the power it seems to have over you. Then, you can walk through the fear of exposure, embarrassment and a guilt that isn't. This can only happen through the healing of a changed mind.

---

[120] Tao Te Ching #79

## Blame's Karma

All appearances are deceiving because they are appearances. Therefore:

Blame is like a tiny hole in your bucket. Wherever you go, the trail follows ... leading back to the owner of the bucket.

Blame is self-deception; it sees the problem outside away from where it was made. It was made by you.

Blame is blinding; it cuts you off from your Source of healing.

Blame is judgment displaced; it reflects self-condemnation placed somewhere else.

Blame is a whitewash; it attempts to do its own dirty laundry in someone else's backyard.

Blame is nakedness exposed; it reveals to others your worst fears of self-condemnation.

Blame is denial; it can't see what it is really trying to protect.

Blame is defense; it attacks to protect its own self-deception.

Blame is a leech; it sucks all of your strength to defend a weakness you are not.

Blame is self-defeating; it attempts to take back by force what it perceives to have lost ... your innocence.

Blame is a nightmare; its scenario seems fearfully real.

Blame is self-attack; no matter where you point, you always expose your reflection of weakness.

Blame is self-betrayal; to hide behind blame for safety is to expose your vulnerable self to attack.

Blame is a scab wound: it continues to fester from your own picking. Leave it alone and it will disappear.

*Like begets like*
*Power begets power*
*An inadequate self begets the need for defense*
*The need for defense begets blame*
*Blame begets misery*

Blame as a defense is a call for help. Only those who perceive themselves as vulnerable to attack, attack to defend through blame. However, your threat is not coming from out there. No one has deprived you but you. There is no distinction between your outer and inner world. If you fear what is out there it is because you fear looking within at the weakness you've identified with; the weakness you are not. What you see out there is the weakness you do not want to see within. However, there is nothing out there!

## Blame and Relational Healing

*It's not that your relationship did not work*
*It's that you gave it the wrong goals*

In any relationship where there is blame, there is the attempt to hang the failure for that relationship on someone else. This you do in hopes of denying any responsibility for the relationship's failure. Although *you choose the fiction of what you thought the relationship should be for,* through self-deception you have a justifiable anger for the injustices caused to you.

Listen to your clients' statements; "They make me feel …" or "Because of them …" or "They would be easier to deal with if they would …" or "They always …" or "They …" This is your client trying to represent the other person in a way that justifies their view of why the relationship failed. Interrupt the monologue by telling your client to "stop trying to represent the other person."

*It's not that your relationship did not work, it's that you gave it the wrong goals* is a non-dualistic view that tells you that you don't need to blame the other person to protect yourself from the responsibility of failure. You can both walk away blameless. But it is essential for you to give the other person the same courtesy of innocence so you can be both free of judgement and blame. This change of mind is a forgiveness that heals the relationship.

*You were just two ships passing in the night. Let it pass*

**Principles of Ownership**

1) You are responsible for your own happiness and unhappiness.

It matters not who you blame for your lot in life. Blame will not make you happy or save you from living your destiny.

2) You *never* react to another's message. You *always* react to your own interpretation of that message.

It is you and you alone who decide how to interpret another's message.

3) You are responsible for your own decisions in life.

It is not the situation you find yourself in that decides your fate. Rather, it is your interpretation of any situation that decides your journey through the illusion."[121]

4) You did not begin when you were born to a body. You entered into an experience of distortion.

I am not saying that social conditioning does not happen. However, you have been conditioned to try to draw intellectual connections from the past to explain why

---

[121] *Symbols of Power in Metaphysics p133-144*

you are the way you are now. And those connections are fraught with massive contradictions. [122] Through social conditioning we all play out the distortions we brought with us. But the conditioning is assumptions of correlations through selective perception that seem to tell us erroneously that we are a product of our past. Do not forget that there is a very low level of correlation that disputes the past as being the determiner of who we are now. Why are appearances deceiving? Because they are appearances.

*The complication of information for outcomes, makes it difficult to see it's nothingness*

Blame is a self-defeating decision to justify your correlations as to why you are the way you are. It is your maneuver to protect you from seeing your dis-relation within yourself.

## No Escape

*You are the Mind I share with you*
*The mind split is experienced as another point of view*

Because what you give you always give to yourself first, or said another way, no thought leaves its source, there is no escape from the thoughts you think. Your blame to defend a vulnerable self always attacks you first. You know attack is accomplished because when you blame, you always blame as a defense to avoid the fear of punishment. But it is too late because fear is always your immediate punishment.

---

[122] *Symbols of Power in Philosophy p69-89*

## Blames Opportunity

Everything that happens as a distraction can be reinterpreted as opportunity. Courage is needed for you to recognize when you are blaming. If you can catch yourself doing it one time, you can see that you are trying to protect a vulnerable self you are not. Blame as a defense is always your witness to your investment in a vulnerability of incompletion/loss. Your connection with Source could never feel the fear of incompletion. To realize without exception that no one can deprive you but you, you begin to unleash the power of your mind to heal. All things become opportunity.

The temptation may be to withdraw from blaming the world and harbor it on you. However, because there is no distinction between your inner and outer world, you are still doing the same thing … blaming. A reframing that blames no one is a forgiveness that is needed here. The way through to remembering your innocence, is to also see it in the other. Namaste.

## Orientation Exercise

1) How do you *try* to make others responsible for your feelings? Your verbal language reveals this to you when you say things like "*You make me* angry" or "*you make me* sad" or "you should have or should not have done that …" List the verbal responses you use.

Don't get into justifications of looking at another's behavior for why you blame. Your justifications will be an endless denial of blame. They only make you an angry victim! Don't deny that you blame. Then you can deal with resentment honestly.

Instead of focusing on what has been done to you, focus on what you have done to you through blame. One thing you do have the power to do is to get in touch with the fact that you blame. "But they also do it!" you tempt yourself to say. This is another sidetrack from taking responsibility for your life now! "But it's not fair!" you speak to justify.[123] That's one way to look at it. There is another way.

2) What feelings do you occupy with your attempts to blame? List them.

3) Do these feelings make you happy? I did not say do these feelings bring you revengeful satisfaction! Do these feelings make you happy?

Be honest because you cannot have peace of mind and resentment at the same time.

4) Does blaming solve your problems? Or is there a seething resentment that abates over time? "Oh well, I'll get over it" denies the hurt and saves you some karma to have to repeat this over again for another time until you get it right. And by the way, you are doing it now over again for an opportunity to get it right.[124]

I am not saying people do not commit heinous, wicked, evil crimes that they should not be punished for. I am saying your perception of it will be the determiner of how you use it as a block to heal or as an opportunity for your healing through this body life journey. As always, in the end *it is always you who will choose how to perceive what you perceive happened to you.* There is no escape from this. This is your karma.

5) Is there a reoccurring theme of people doing you wrong that you need to take a look at?

This may be hard to look at but if there is a reoccurring theme here, it is about how you set yourself up. If you can see the counterproductive nature of blaming, you open yourself to new and different options for problem solving.

---

[123] *The Way Home p101-102; 115-120*
[124] *Symbols of Power in Metaphysics p133-144*

Your willingness to see and discard blame facilitates the availability of the following options:

1) Ask yourself, where does the problem really lie? Be honest.

Therapist, this is where you heavily reinforce the idea that you are not trying to take the responsibility off of another's behavior, nor are you blaming your client. It is a matter of bringing your client back to the power of their mind for a resolution that will be found nowhere else.

2) Now you can ask; what will solve your problems? Be open. Therapist, because perception leads you into the world of uncertainty, teach the art of reframing. In the end it will be your client's willingness to look at anything and everything from a different point of view. This is the miracle of release, the substance all epiphanies[125] are made of.

3) One more thing. What are you really afraid of? This question goes to the core of what you believe about you.

**For the Therapist**

Therapist, it's very simple. Blame is not an option. The allowance of blame in your therapeutic encounter is a distraction away from your client's ability to look at and heal themself. Simply stated, their choices on how they chose to view any situation, sets themselves up. You can be nice and consoling, pacing with your client's explanations of how they were wronged. But somewhere in your therapy you will need to interrupt the regurgitation. So-called cathartic venting will grind on and on until they have a change of mind. If you don't

---

[125] An epiphany is a sudden intuition or insight into the reality or essential meaning of something; like an "Ah ha ..." moment.

interrupt the grinding, you are wasting your time and their money.

Therapist, be brave to redirect. Don't try to rescue them from looking within at what they did to themself. Educate your client that there is another way to look at anything and everything. They may not at first like hearing it. But a healed healer understands that it is the power your client's mind has to heal them. Help them to free their mind along with yours.

It is understood that not everyone is ready to hear this. But after hearing your client complain on the first half hour of every session, it would be the therapist's responsibility to educate what the power of a changed mind can do. Pain is not gain. But we seem to need to go through self-inflicted pain to get to the other side.

## Summary

*Blame is self-deception; it sees the problem outside away from where it was made. It was made by you.*

No matter what the form is, all errors in thinking have the same cause in common; a dis-relation of vulnerability with Self. Because your thinking is *the cause* of your feelings, you are your own worst enemy. You also are your best friend. Don't blame yourself for your mistaken error of thought. But to change it, you must own it.

*Transformational Psychotherapy is the process of changing your view of yourself in the light of a world of fictional facts used to defend your imagination of a "self" in a world of fictional facts.*

# The Truth about Abandonment

*How could you not feel abandoned when in dis-relation you have abandoned yourself first? Everything the world seems to offer you is out of your fiction that you think your abandonment has been accomplished.*

### Abandonment as a State of Mind

One of the most common assumptions to explain Sociopathic or maladaptive behavior[126] is that it is a result of childhood abandonment. Because the exceptions to this assumption far outweigh any low-level correlation, this assumption is a classic example of selective thinking to reinforce intellectually what you already believe to be true. Do not teach abandonment as real.

In denial your client projects a world untrue to deal with the discomfort of interpersonal dis-relation. You perceive what you project. And if in denial (disassociation from) you project your dis-relation, all you will perceive is the separation that your dis-relation causes you to see. You feel abandoned because you have abandoned yourself first. Do not teach abandonment as real.

The fact of the matter is, no matter what the circumstances are in one's life history, no one who knows themselves feels abandoned. Issues of abandonment are not conditions of circumstance. It is a state of mind. If you are not secure about who you are, you will be tempted to project this discomfort on some unsuspecting life situation as abandonment.

To feel abandoned is proof that you do not know who you are. Only bodies with attachments to other bodies will grieve the loss of an abandonment. Because you are love's

---

[126] Whatever those behaviors look like?

creation, there is a connection through love that could never abandon itself.

Therapist, appearances are deceiving because they are appearances. I know it is tremendously tempting to get sucked into your client's attributing the cause of their issues to be from someone outside of them, especially when they can point the finger at someone who apparently left them. And for how long have they been reinforcing that intellectual tape? You do not want to reinforce the idea of the cause of one's dilemma as coming from the outside and therefore the solution as also coming from the same place; outside. There is no resolution in that place

Carl Jung said it well "Those who look outside dream. Those who look within awaken." Projection is a loop that solves nothing. You might say that you are not talking about projection but rather clarification. All clarifications that tempt you to look outside for your solution are the deceptions of delay. Work it out for yourself; any abandonment issue come first from yourself otherwise you could never experience feeling abandoned.

*No thought leaves its source*
*You are the source of how you see what you see*

## A World for the Self-Abandoned

*Made out of dis-relation is the appearance of people feeling abandoned … exiled as a world for the self-abandoned*

Of course your client feels abandoned. They are in dis-relation with themself before they met who supposedly abandoned them. Everyone who incarnates to this world does so because of a self-dis-relation of being abandoned.

Only the delusion of magical thinking can make you believe there is a way out through a connection with the world, when the world was made by and for the self-abandoned. Connections in the world work when unconditional love is present. That is the one thing that transcends abandonment through death. Otherwise, everything else is transactional.

## Abandonment as a Self-Defeating Fiction

Self-esteem is what you think you are. However, it has nothing to do with "what you are." Self–esteem is the ego's kingdom of self-evaluation. Rules, boundaries, and safety are the measures of protection for what you value. There is just one problem in this bubble of safety; it makes you totally vulnerable to hurt. Do the work; no matter how hard you try to ensure safety you feel anxiety, hurt, pain, violation, etc. Why? Because what you think you are, you are not. You who try the hardest to protect "a self," are the most hurt. Why? Do the work; what you have been "trying" to protect is what you are not. That's why your attempts to protect your self-esteem have been a frustrating impossible task to failure. However, what "you are" cannot be hurt. It needs no protection.

Your identity apart from what you thought you were, is secure. Mind is not vulnerable. It cannot be attacked. However, pseudo-self looks for a home to identify with for security's sake. But when it associates as a body of instinct that is vulnerable to change, you experience fear. All of everything you think you are as a self, becomes a body that will one day fail you and die. What a set-up for the experience of an abandonment that can never be.

Not only is abandonment the experience of a fiction, but so is all grieving over the illusion of what is not yours to control; the possession of other bodies as love

119

connections when they are addictions of dependency. Your reactions of loss as real are the testaments that you believe meaningful love connections are attained through bodies that die and fail you. What an insane fiction.

Do not teach abandonment as real! The fact of the matter is that no one ever feels abandoned when they know who they are. And if you are not secure about who you are, you will feel abandoned because you have abandoned yourself first.

Remember: The recognition that sickness is of the mind, having nothing to do with the body is a fundamental shift in perception. This shift in perception will change how you perceive the world because the world will never again appear to rule your mind. Your abandonment is not out there. It is a projection from your mind of a fundamental fiction; the fiction of dis-relation from Source.

*Transformational Psychotherapy is the process of helping your client to begin to question their reality.*

## What your Client's Presenting Problems Represent

Because complexity of form does not imply complexity of content, your client's presenting problem is always symbolic of a deeper underlying issue; their unconscious dis-relation with Self.

A client may talk to you about issues of abandonment as a child. Though you recognize this issue as symbolic of their fundamental error of imagined separation from their Source of identity, you will pace yourself with your client by starting at the level of the presenting problem. You can listen, be empathetic, help them clarify, but what you do not want to do is reinforce their error as real. To do so is to reinforce a false perception and then have to someway resolve this error of thought through magical thinking.

How can they ever be unabandoned if they believe they were abandoned as a child? How can the truth of being abandoned be undone? I guess you have to live with this lack of resolution for the rest of your life. Or recognize that abandonment never occurred except through an error of perception, and this you can undo.

It is tempting through selective perception to try to understand current issues by looking into a dissatisfying past. This is the fiction of cause-and-effect correlations in a world of change where cause and effect correlations are meaningless … through the eyes of real forgiveness.

There are all kinds of mantras of "positive thinking," that ingratiate the ego, cuddle the monster, as being wonderful, lovable and worthwhile. But nothing changes. All you do is ingratiate the ego.

*Reality is not yours to select*

Ego identity for worth is a meaningless concept. Do the work, every issue you have has to do with a self-esteem you are not.

*Your ego feels abandoned because it is incapable of love*
*Stop trying to make your ego lovable by ingratiating it*
*What you are as Love's creation could never abandon itself*

*You experience hurt because ego is easily bruised*
*The truth about you never hurts but rejoices*

*You are angry because the ego did not get what it expects or demands*
*What you are is everything you need*

*The ego grieves the loss of what does not belong to it*
*"Being" enjoys everything without ownership*

*You are depressed because your ego feels deprived*
*Because "Being Is" everything you need, you experience gratitude*

*You are anxious because of the impulsively changeable whims of the ego*
*As Eternal, you are beyond the whims of ever-changing nothingness*

*You feel guilty because the ego is a making in opposition to your Source*
*You are guiltless because the eternal you can't be changed by the whim of a mistaken thought*

*Healing is the road to your inheritance*
*Forgiving what never happened is your means*

**Therapy at Work**

"But what about the mom or dad who left me when I was young?" your client asks.

1) This is where you list on a board a basic profile of the person who was *not able* to show up in your client's life. Your client will have ample things to say about this person they are mad at. These same reasons your client uses to justify feeling abandoned will be *the real reasons* this person was *not able* to be involved in your client's life. Although your client took it personally, it is not about your client.

2) In what ways does your client share the profile? Identifying with the profile rather than fighting it is a way to Zen it. The more your client is like the profile, the more the profile has to teach them. The understanding of

another's motivation without justifying the behavior ties your client together with them in a forgiveness lesson.

Your client does not have to forgive the other person for their mistakes. This frees your client from their conflict of what they think they must do for release. Therapist, remember, it's not about forgiving another for what you perceived they did to you. It's about forgiving your perception of how you see it.

3) You can use an empty box of tissues as a teaching tool. The *empty box* is symbolic of the love your family member who left had for themself. Hold the empty box up to your client and say, "Here, take some love from the person you perceive as leaving you."

They look in the box and say, "There's nothing there, no love to take."

"Exactly" you answer. Ask your client "Is it that they did not love you? Or is it that they had no love for themself and thus, no love to give anybody?" Let them think this through. You might add "They may have been there in body, but did they really show up?" Reiterate "It's not that they did not love you. It's that they had no love for themself to give anyone, especially themself." Or "How could they have abandoned you when they were not capable of showing up for themself. They also felt abandoned and couldn't find a way out."

This is what a non-dualistic principle of undoing looks like. It is a reclarification, a tool for healing everyone involved. As an epiphany, it might be a "wow" moment. "I never thought about it that way" is the demonstration of a mind that changed its mind.

*All healing is about joining*

To diffuse your client's temptation to think you are justifying another's behavior, you can say "I am not saying that it's OK with what they did, it's just not about you like you thought. That part is about them. However, how you took it as personal is about you, making their error real for you." Again, a change of mind says "Oh, I never thought about it that way."

The perception that the child grew up maladaptive because of a childhood issue is plagued with exceptions.[127] A reframing or different view is the opportunity your client can do as an adult to free the child who (in an Adlerian sense) got stuck in a childhood perception for survival.

**Clients do not represent themselves well**

Your clients do not represent themselves well. You know this is true because they have a problem. Because complexity of form does not imply complexity of content, the presenting problem your client offers through hurt or anger, is always a misperception of another's motive. You can profile many different people in the life of your client's many different presenting problems until they begin to

---

[127] To look at a childhood issue as a product of social conditioning is the mistake of trying to understand what is going on at the level of appearances. All appearances of abandonment are played out as socialized symbols of your primary dis-relation with Source. You are not in dis-relation with yourself because of social conditioning or an unresolved childhood issue. You incarnated because of your dis-relation. Social conditioning is one of many effects of your dis-relation with Source. All effects confused as causes have one thing in common; they are delays that hide your real dilemma, your dis-relation with Source.

generalize the fact that we all operate out of ignorance and take others ignorance as personal.

*The misperception of someone else's dis-relation with themself, played out as conflict, is nothing to take personally*

In the light of the facts, your client still may want to justify as real their experience of dis-relation as coming from someone else abandoning them. Be lovingly strong and gentle when you say to them "No matter how you think about it, another's dis-relation with themself is not about you; It's about them. What is about you is how you made your dis-relation to be about them. That is how you keep yourself from being able to resolve it."

So called failed relationships of abandonment can also be reframed as "It's not that your relationship did not work, it's that you gave it the wrong goals."

## Summary

Therapist, throw the "abandonment" word away. It serves no good purpose in your therapeutic encounter. It is a delay tactic for you and your client. It keeps your client from looking within to the fact that they abandoned themself first! To be abandoned is a projection of your mind mistaken as a self you are not. Your abandonment is not out there.

*Transformational Psychotherapy is the process of changing your view of yourself in the light of a world of fictional facts used to defend your imagination of a "self" in a world of fictional facts.*

Mathias Karayan

# The Power of Grief as a Means to Remember Passage[128]

*To give up something or someone implies loss. Transformational Psychotherapy is not about giving up anything. That is about deprivation. Transformational Psychotherapy is about an exchange. There is no loss in this.*

Client: *Life is no dance.*
Therapist: *Sure it is; it is the dance of a dirge until you die to the idea of death. And resistance to this idea is your grief as long as pseudo-self is in charge.*

Because you are in dis-relation with yourself, you can't but grieve. Just like your grief, the world you see is in a constant state of grief, sacrifice and loss! Everything is symptomatic of your denial of your dis-relation with Source. Your attempts to restore yourself have been through the experience of a belief in deprivation. You are a frustrated student because you are attempting to ingratiate an ego-self you are not. How could you not but grieve? In other words:

*Trying to find mental health in a fiction is self-defeating … because the means used sabotages the goal*

## The Sacred Fiction

*To talk about death to the fearful who interpret death as a fearful loss, is an accomplished task of them responding with "how dare you"*

---

[128] *The Way Home p180-182*

That you suffer the sacrifice of attachments can be viewed as "God is to be mocked for his creation of futility." Or "God is absurd for His set-up to grieve His creation." Some try to take God off the hook by saying "It was meant to be" or "God has a greater reason for taking them." *To implicate Source in death is a fiction that needs to die.* All explanations about death are maneuvers to deny your fiction.

Simply stated, loss is the experience of attachments that were never yours to possess in the first place. You know they were not for you to possess when you grieve their loss. I realize you will deny the implication that you were out to possess someone you "love," yet your reaction to the death of a body is proof of your dissociation from the fact that your happiness was tied up to a body that dies. It also demonstrates that your relationship was transactional for you, rather than unconditional.

You will feel insulted by the idea that your association with this body was out of need, desire, security, responsibility, rather than love. You will argue that you miss them because you love them. I would never tell you that you do not love them, but you do deny the experience of love by your reaction out of grief and anger. You will argue that "To grieve is to love" and that "grieving is a form of love" and that "grieving is a natural process for healing to occur."

It is true that once you make a mistaken investment in something that is not yours to have in the way you think it should be, you will have to go through the process of undoing it. However, love does not suffer loss, nor does it demand sacrifice. If it did, it would not be love we are talking about. Pseudo-ego[129] in the name of love, tells you that love demands suffering. Because you deny the temporal nature of what you perceive "as it is, temporal" you perceive loss, guilt, distrust, envy, anger, abandonment, betrayal and sorrow. Whether your reaction is denial, bargaining, anger or sadness, the loss of what was never yours to identify with, is a witness of misplaced allegiance and the seeds of discontent. Love has nothing to do with this except to bring you back to love.

Others, out of their own sacred fictions will attempt to bond with other bodies for security's sake. These are called ego alliances. They will demand the attachment of "love and commitment" through gifts, promises and rituals of affiliation as proof that you love them, "till death do we part." ... or until they like you remember that they are everything they need.

*Transformational Psychotherapy is about an exchange. There is no loss in remembering that you are everything you need.*

## Society at Large Grieves

*You always grieve when you believe a lie*

Because the body experiences lack, society at large grieves. It is not a learned sociologically conditioned response. It is the dilemma of being in dis-relation with Self. Society as a collective hunch is an alliance of egos to deny the loss of this primary relationship. To not recognize how this is played out in your particular life

---

[129] Pseudo-ego is a defensive facade or a sense of self, created to protect against perceived threats or vulnerabilities, at the expense of authenticity and genuine self-expression.

experience is called denial. Are daily disappointments viewed as expressions of grief? Are your temper tantrums viewed as grief? Are arguments with another viewed as grief when someone has to win? Is hurt from criticism perceived as grieving? They are expressions of perceived and anticipated loss … the Power of Grief. All of your compensations, adjustments and negotiations are attempts to deny grief as a way of life.

To grab on and secure a body that will die is the Power of Grief. The loss of a loved one as compared to a disappointment in your day may be incomparable in form, but they both have the same effect, loss of peace.

Your grief does not only involve any particular or ritualized event; it encompasses daily living. To recognize your moments of daily grieving is to begin to diffuse its power as some special event. What you possess for security is what makes you the most insecure because it can be taken away. This is the power of grief, alive through the fiction of what you think is yours to possess in the name of security or "love." You say you accept life on life's terms, yet justify bargaining, anger, stress, anxiety and sadness as being human. Your experience of the power of grief is your witness to your fiction that you do not accept life on life terms. When you can't have it your way, you grieve.[130] To grieve is your witness to your dis-relation with Source, not an actual loss of anything lasting.

*Transformational Psychotherapy is about an exchange, the reminder that your dis-relation has not occurred but is only imagined. There is no loss in this.*

---

[130] In form, this is a temper tantrum

What is yours in truth you cannot lose in the eternal present. But you do seem to lose what was never yours to hold on to in the temporal ever-changing.

*To anticipate grief is to bargain*
*And you will pay every time*

Healing always comes to the mind that recognizes the illusion of ownership. The illusion of ownership in the name of love is the power of grief's denial. Through confusion, you think that to love is to grieve loss. This is the making of all the symbols that are used to mourn the dead. And in the name of love, yet out of fear, you morn the inevitable. Now you have identified love with fear; that to love is to fear loss. In the name of love, society at large grieves. How insane!

*That love is all and love is everyone*
*It is knowing, it is knowing*
*That ignorance and hate may morn the dead*
*It is believing, it is believing*[131]
Lennon & McCartney
Tomorrow Never Knows

## The Expression of Grief

*There is a disappointment about wanting something from the world that it can't give*

Your expression of grief is neither good nor bad, nor right or wrong. But your expressions do reflect investments of self-sabotage, your temptation to perceive and anticipate loss. These investments, when seen for

---

[131] *Symbols of Power in Philosophy p282*

what they really are, are expressions of anticipated grief. Use grief as a teaching aid to remind you of how you set yourself up to feel. Underneath the surface, your temptation to anticipate loss is really about grieving your dis-relation from Self.

"It's not fair!" is the grief of justified anger.

"I don't want to go to work" is the grief of dissatisfaction.

"I don't want to do anything" is the grief of general dissatisfaction.

"I feel sick, or I feel pain" is the grief of your body letting you down.

"What you said hurts me" is the grief of your pseudo self-esteem letting you down.

"No one cares about me" is the grief of self-pity.

"She's mine!" is the grief of jealousy over a threatened relationship.

"I feel worn out" is the grief of your mental defenses or boundaries wearing down.

"Why try, there's no hope" is the grief of depression

"I messed up" is the grief of guilt.

"I can't do anything right" is the grief of despair.

"I'm scared" is the grief of impending disaster.

The list goes on and on ...

Denial is the refusal to look at what you will lose through your fearful anticipation that you might grieve its loss. The way of peace is to allow grief to teach you that what you thought was yours was never so ... that all things enjoyed are in the moment, never anticipated, expected or obligated.

*Transformational Psychotherapy is about an exchange. There is no loss in this.*

## True Relationships

*That which is truly yours can never be taken from you*
*That which can be taken was never yours*
*You always grieve what was never yours to possess*

True relationships are out of something other than need and dependence. Not that you can't need or depend on someone, but there is something in true relationships that transcend this. The process of moving towards a true relationship is a process of withdrawing from an addiction of adapting and being habitually involved in expecting from another.

When your client says "But they did give me happiness" you use it as an educational opportunity. Because no thought leaves its source, what you give you always give to yourself first. In other words, no one can make you happy or sad. But you can experience the joy or sadness you bring into any relationship … and this no one can take from you.

If your client is grieving it is not out of what they stopped receiving from another. It is out of their own lack, what they don't have to give themselves. This fact is denied in the name of grieving so your client's fiction can't be dealt with honestly. Grieving is the fact of trying to fill your lack with something outside of everything you already are. The death of another exposes your lack to remind you of the work you need to do.

Those who invest in the temporal for happiness and pleasure always find grief. For many, it is hard to understand that *having is Being* … you are everything you need.

*To give out of the storage of your wealth is to experience love*
*To give out of lack is to experience grief*

Because of *a chronic habitual conditioning*, it becomes hard to believe that you grieve because you have lied to yourself. You would rather hold on to your sacred lie to deny yourself the means to healing; and then teach this error to others to reinforce it in your life. "We read the world wrong and say it deceives us"[132] … daily.

**Unconditional Love**

Love cannot suffer loss, or it would not be love. The lie is: Though we talk about love as unconditional, our grief reminds us that our love has strings of attachment. That is not unconditional love.

I am not saying don't have attachments, don't have investments, don't have commitments, don't grieve. You can do all those things. I am saying don't confuse your attachments and investments as relationships of unconditional love. I realize that for many this appears to be an attack on your sacred fiction, that to love is to grieve. Yet, unconditional love never demands suffering or loss. Ego love does.

Unconditional love does not grieve because it does not possess. To try to possess is coercion out of fear … hidden in the name of love. Unconditional love accepts life on life's terms because life's terms are irrelevant to unconditional love. Unconditional love accepts your baggage because unconditional love does not see baggage.

---

[132] Rabindranath Tagore

Unconditional love is active in relationships because it sees what you are beyond behaviors. Unconditional love sees the spirit you are, not the body you are not. Namaste![133] Society's definition of what love is, is an ever-changing whim. If you can be disappointed in love, your experience of love is not unconditional.

> *Why tell me why did you not treat me right*
> *Love has a nasty habit of disappearing overnight*
> Lennon & McCartney
> I'm Looking Through You

Your anger in grief is because you do not want to see that your love has conditions. And you will defend your lie by stating that it is OK to grieve their loss because you loved them. No one is saying "You did not love them." No one is saying "Stop grieving!" I am saying let your grief be a teacher to remind you of what unconditional love is. Your Source of Being demonstrates unconditional love. It does not love and take away at the same time. But your making of what you think love is, suffers loss. We do see the world wrong and say it deceives us … daily.

*What you are cannot be threatened or taken away. If you think it can, you will grieve the loss of what you are not.*

I will say this again to those who, in the name of love, fear loss: To grieve is not love but mental contradiction

---

[133] The gesture 'Namaste' or 'namaskar' is the Indian or Hindu way of greeting each other. Namaste represents the belief that there is a Divine spark within each of us. The gesture is an acknowledgment of the soul in one by the soul in another. It is not a superficial gesture or a mere word. And it is a greeting for everyone you meet along your way.

and conflict, your block to peace of mind. It is the result of your dis-relation with Source. In that light, of course you grieve … all the time.

*Love does not possess, nor does it suffer loss*
*But fear in the name of love does*

*To give up something or someone implies loss. That is about deprivation and fear. Transformational Psychotherapy is not about giving up anything. It is about exchange. There is no loss in this.*

### "What Is"

*When you grabbed to possess, you gave yourself over to the power of grief*
*Now you must live for the illusion of death*
*Until you die to ownership*

Social adaptation, educational ideology and economic pressure teach an attitude of investment in things and ideas to be worked for or taken for granted as your right! To buy this package you must deny that you are everything Creation made you "To Be."[134] Through this forgetting you exchange everything that you are for a security in the ever-changing that you will never find. Thus does your grieving over nothingness become a real-life experience. No wonder you grieve. Everything you hope for is built on an ever-shifting sand of nothingness.

An honest re-orientation of "What is" is in order of your:
1. Rights. "I have the right to choose again."

---

[134] The cost of this package is death.

2. Personal responsibilities. "I am the only one responsible for how I perceive what I perceive. Thus, are my feelings self-caused."

3. Stewardship. "I have a responsibility to journey to peace of mind when I am ready. This involves a learning - teaching relationship with everyone I meet along the way."[135]

The power of grief as an everyday experience is reflected through all the stress and feelings you do not like. All your subtle emotional discomforts and fears that underlie your life events are your moments of grieving. To deny that your grief is the result of a dis-relation with Source is your journey to find resolve in a world of ever-changing "what ifs" the place where resolve is forever elusive. You will find relief at times, even a shallow happiness, but never release ... until you die to pseudo-self.[136]

*You don't ask honestly "why do I grieve?"*
*Otherwise, you would have to look at the reason why.*
*OK then, "why do I grieve?"*
*Because of your investment in nothingness.*

## Grief as a Means to Suffering

*Because you use an "individual body" as your symbol for power to defend against your dis-relation from Self, your "individual body" is your ultimate idol for death*

---

[135] *The Way Home p15*
[136] *The Way Home p183*

Grief always involves the body as a mental focus. You relate to your impressions of your world view through a body image. Therefore, your body becomes the means to get what you think you want or need.

As a matter of survival, the body demands food, shelter and clothing. These three are the measures of the body's comfort and survival. They are not the measure or means to peace of mind. In extreme forms, the collecting and storing of that which does not make you happy, is known as addictions in all its forms; the need to possess for bliss and security's sake.

What you mentally possess in the name of a body will be lost or taken away. Your experience of personal disappointment (grief) reminds you of this daily. Grief also reminds you to learn the difference between what the body needs for survival and what you take for granted as rights.

1) How grief is viewed in our society
  a. Sacred
  b. Inevitable
2) The truth about grief that no one wants to hear
  a. You believe loss is real as you fear the loss of something that does not belong to you. You know it doesn't belong to you otherwise you would not have lost it.
  b. Because of your investment in a body you are not, you grieve from the time you are born until the time you die. Your world is a place to suffer grief on a daily basis.
3) The form grief takes[137]
  a. Sadness/Incomplete

---

[137] If you notice, love does not belong to this list

b. Anger/Grievances
c. Guilt/Suffering
d. Depression/Despair
e. Shame/Flawed
f. Fear

All other feelings *you do not like* are a form of the above. You may be a therapist big on accepting feelings as they are. Yet, you grieve through those feelings when you judge them as "not likable." Use those feelings to reveal your fiction about your belief in loss.

*You can't take it with you and you know it's too worthless to be sold ... They'll tell you time is money as if your life was worth its weight in gold*
Bob Dylan
When You Gonna Wake Up

## Your Client's Resistance to Change as the Means to Passage

The power of grief is not a learned sociologically conditioned response. It is the dilemma of being in dis-relation with Self. That is why there is no significant correlation to grieving and social conditioning, except for the fact that social conditioning is a result, an adaptation to grieving your dis-relation from Source.

In your original error was the illusion of change; a thought where you experienced your dis-relation with Self. Through this illusion of change loss was perceived. That is why all change involves the idea of fear and grieving. That is also why change is resisted as a tiring task in all your life forms. Your client's resistance to address their fictions as "accepting life on life's terms" is interrupted through the grieving process. This process can be an opportunity for them to begin to embrace a more honest view of life.

*Death is but another path, a means to an end*

Everything is in a constant state of flux. Stability is an illusion. Your denial of this fact is your attempt to stabilize, normalize, quantify, identify and label that which can't be done. To quantify means that the measure of "more" has an element of security. In forms that look extreme, this is called hoarding or greed. We try to normalize personal as well as international relations for security and peace. However, as long as you do not have peace with yourself, it is never ending. So, you search endlessly for that piece of negotiated reality that constantly eludes your grasp.

*Unconditional love does not search*
*It has everything it is*

Why is there resistance to not want to look within? Because to look within might involve the need to change. And this change might be something I have to give up. Thus, a loss. Even though it is a loss you are already experiencing anyway. While,

*Transformational Psychotherapy is not about giving something up. That is about deprivation. Transformational Psychotherapy is about exchange; giving up a fiction that causes you pain in exchange for your journey to peace of mind. There is no loss in this. It is a state of mind.*

There seems to be a security (relief) in the stabilizing of relationships and functions. The need for predictability is an obsession of anxiety for the sake of security. It is a future that can never be yours in the present. So you rob yourself of a present peace in an attempt to secure for a peaceful future that can never come except in the present. To be anxious is to grieve.

The power of grief is your client's opportunity to look at the fictions they identify with, have invested in for security, relationship and meaning. It is the spiritual journey to wake up from the lie that keeps you asleep. *The lie is that loss is real!* It is the waking up from the dream of "the self" that identifies with the ever-changing forms of fleeting pleasure and pain. That you "have to give up" anything is a battle ground; a lack of recognition that you are everything you need. If you do not think you are everything you need, you will look for it in a world where it will never be found.[138] Why will it never be found out there? Because you are everything you need!

The therapeutic opportunity is to use grief as the reminder that you are in dis-relation with your ground of Being, a spiritual dilemma. In other words, all that you grieve becomes your opportunity to look within, to re-evaluate everything. Because the belief in loss is so heavily guarded from the truth, the therapist does not begin here.

*Transformational Psychotherapy is about an exchange; giving up a fiction that causes you pain for your journey to peace of mind. There is no loss in this. It is a state of mind. Though you might deny it, everything is a state of mind.*

---

[138] The seeds of co-dependency

*Can you hear me*
*That when it rains and shines*
*It's just a state of mind*
*Can you hear me*
Lennon & McCartney
Rain

## What You Take for Granted

*Death is the final reminder that everything you thought was "yours" was only borrowed. This is grief's resolution.*

What you take for granted will hurt you because it is the means you allow to experience grief. The words you use are dead giveaways to the ownership of things that are not yours to possess.

What "I should" have
What "I expect"
It's "my right!"

These anticipated expressions are yet to be realized in fact. In this way you grieve over the "idea" of something you do not have.

"My" wife
"My" boyfriend
"My" children

There is nothing wrong with the word "my" as long as you know it as an expression of relationship rather than ownership. You own no one, not even your children. Your destiny to truth through time and space will be different in form than anybody else's.

"My" car
"My" job

Would you even think of considering these as guarantees?

"My" house

Don't pay your taxes and see who owns it. All things of ownership, including its maintenance, have a string attached to them. It is the selling of peace of mind to maintain that relationship of ownership.

"My" self

No wonder you grieve. You gave yourself up to maintain the fantasy of being a body image. This image you will nurture to its grave … until you wake up to what you are.

Mother Earth reminds you daily through the power of grief that the body you inhabit is born to the distractions of pleasure and pain, in search of a hollow happiness, that is as fleeting as the winds of change. In the end, you will give this all up. You have no choice in this. Grieve or recognize your fiction for what it is.

*Until you die to the idea of ownership, your only choice is to grieve the loss of that which was never yours to possess*

**Process**

*Holding on to the way your loved ones were*
*Keeps you from experiencing them the way they are now*

To comfort the client, the therapist often reinforces the idea that "there is life after death." That comment validates the death of a body as real. The real question that is non-dualistic is, "Is there death?"[139] And, if you are not the death of a body, what does that say about the fiction you have identified with for security, meaning and love?[140] The deceptive appearance of flesh and blood as dust of the earth is what it is. Namaste.

The battle ground seems to be that someday you will have to let go of your attachments to the ones you love. Therapist, you don't need to reinforce this. Nor does your client need to write a goodbye letter as if it is part of a therapeutic process of grieving. This line of thinking is a battle ground. Rather, talk about how your client's relationship *is to be transformed,* how your client can make a shift to experience them differently. Their loved one is still present, yet in a different way to be experienced.

*You never have to let them go. But it is for your client to be open, to make a shift, to allow space to experience them differently.*[141]

This idea can be of comfort to your client.

When your client asks, "Why did they have to die?"

You can say "They have something to teach you that they could not do on this side of the veil. When you are ready, you will know why they had to die, and it will be a lesson beyond death itself."

Regarding death by suicide or addiction, you might ask your client how their deceased loved one lived their life on this side of the veil. When you help your client clarify what

---

[139] *The Way Home p172*

[140] *The Way Home p37-39; 158-161; 162-165;173-176*

[141] *Symbols of Power in Metaphysics p91-92*

the quality of their loved one's life was before their death by suicide or addiction, they will answer "Not so good. They had an addiction, an ailment, a depression that was debilitating, etc." After some discussion about how your client was not able to help the deceased from this side of the veil because your loved one would not allow it. Nor where they able to help you on this side because of their ailment, you can say, "Now are they free to help you from the other side like they were not able to do from this side." This is a shift in focus. You can also tell them "That is one of the reasons why your loved one did not die in vain. They are with you, involved in a bigger picture, different than your mind can see at this time. And every time you tell your story you honor them." Therapist, this is what therapeutic exchange is all about. There is something your client has to teach you about death?[142]

## Exchange

*What is life?*
*It is the flash of the butterfly in the night*
*It is the little shadow which runs across the grass and loses itself in the sunset*
*There is no death ... only a change of worlds*
Crowfoot Chief Seattle

People do not die; they experience a surrounding change that is separate from the illusion of body identification.[143] They really didn't go anywhere. There is a bigger picture that heals the grief when this picture is experienced directly rather than understood intellectually.

---

[142] *The Way Home p180-183*
[143] *Symbols of Power in Metaphysics p120-133*

*Release is the restoring of your mind to the remembrance of what you already know to be true. It is about exchange; giving up a fiction that causes you pain in exchange for your journey to peace of mind. There is no loss in this. It is a state of mind. And those you seem to have lost now continue with you on your journey … in another form.*

## Remember Gratitude

*You think you know what will make you happy, and yet you grieve. It would be better for you if you knew you did not know! Then you would be open.*[144]

   To recognize grief for what it is, is to allow it to teach you what is of value and what is not. We grieve the loss of a loved one because we have tried to possess the gift of friendship. Your time together was for a time not yours to decide. Grief forgets this. Gratitude does not. And so it is:

*If the dance of the butterfly should one day leave your open palm to return to you, the dance is a gift of joy. But if the butterfly returns in a form you don't recognize, in your grief you will track it down and kill it!*

   Gratitude looks within and sees that "Having is Being;" giving is receiving and thus you can dance with anyone because change is irrelevant. Gratitude looks through your distortions of self-deception to remind you that what

---

[144] *The Way Home p76, 85, 147-148; Tao Te Ching #71*

you are is beyond your decision. What was once reason to grieve is now transformed through gratitude as opportunities to heal (speed up). Remember gratitude daily, and you will find reasons for it throughout your day.

Love will not abandon you or else it would not be love. Like the caterpillar, your loved one is not gone but transformed into the beauty of a butterfly. Rejoice in the journey. It has been exchanged in a different form … yet still the same in content.

## Remember Passage

*Death is your opportunity to remember passage*

Your body life is your vehicle through birth to death in this time space continuum. Given its temporary nature, it is not yours to possess, but rather a stewardship to be respected. This stewardship is your opportunity to sort out that which is truly yours and that which is not. Outcomes do not belong to you. Because reality is not yours to select, what you fear you have to give up is that which you do not have. Again, you are being asked to "let go" of that which you do not have. Only in denial is it hard to do what is already done. Grief is the place where fact meets the magical thinking of your mind. *And here is your lesson undisguised!*

Your avoidance of the fact that "all things must pass away,"[145] is your means to grieve loss. We expect (or hope) our children will outlive us. Even so, all bodies die … and usually, not in your way or timing. It is a fiction that anyone *should* outlive you. The truth is your body doesn't

---

[145] All Things Must Pass – George Harrison

die. It is another form within the cycle of Mother Earth.[146] When you accept the loss of a loved one as someone that was never yours to possess, you leave space to find them in a different way. This is the lesson of exchange.

*Death is but another path … a means to an end*
*The end is not death. It is an exchange*

Death will be grieved if you see it as an end. If it is a means of change, a transformation, then there is no death. Let grief remind you that your passage is your opportunity to embrace the adventure of life rather than fearing the events of life.

*To give up something or someone implies loss. Transformational Psychotherapy is not about giving up anything. That is about deprivation. Transformational Psychotherapy is about an exchange. There is no loss in this. Namaste*

---

Mathias Karayan

# Shame's Opportunity

*Accept your sense of failure as nothing more than a mistake in who you are*

## Introduction

You made shame's secret. Because you believe in the secret, you experience a shame that needs protection from exposure. Why? Because you think the secret might be true.

One can argue that we live in a shame-based society. To Freud, the Oedipus complex was all about being socialized out of fear. It is hard not to perceive yourself as being socialized out of fear of punishment, as it appears. Although Freud was going in the right direction, he did not go far enough. The story of Oedipus[147] is one of many examples of living life as a fearful drama. Everything we do for the body has its grounding in fear … unless it is done through love.

## Definition of Terms

To Kierkegaard, our dilemma of being is living in dis-relation with Self. This dis-relation compensates for survival by making "a self" unreal to what you are in truth. Something other than what you are in Source is a violation as interpreted as doing something wrong. This is a *guilt* that can be justified, rationalized and minimized away

---

[147] Oedipus was a mythical Greek king of Thebes. Despite his efforts not to, Oedipus ended up killing his father and marrying his mother. When the truth was discovered, his wife-mother hanged herself, and Oedipus gouged out his own eyes. Oedipus represents an enduring theme of Greek myth and drama: the flawed nature of humanity.

into your unconscious mind. To unconsciously interpret and internalize your violation as being flawed to the core, is your experience of *shame*. Shame, as a disposition of being says "There is something wrong with me. I am unlovable. I am incomplete." It is true; you are incomplete as long as you are in dis-relation with Self.

*Existential dread*,[148] is a disposition of overwhelming anxiety and despair that arises from contemplating the fundamental questions of life. Both shame and dread have an anxious despair that when acute is your experience of a panic attack.

## Dynamics

To experience shame is a despair that cannot see through your lie about a "self" you made. This results in experiences of:

1. Extreme sensitivity to criticism
2. Obsessive thinking
3. Depression and despair
4. Uncontrollable bouts of self-destruction
5. Suicide

Because of shame's willingness to identify with the deception of an ephemeral experience of nothingness, the despair of what you think you are, has no exit. And although you are close to the truth of the matter, of ephemeral nothingness, shame won't let you go all the way through to the truth of the matter.

---

[148] The Concept of Dread (or Anxiety) is a philosophical work written by Danish philosopher Søren Kierkegaard in 1844. It explores the concept of anxiety as it relates to human freedom, original sin, and existential choice.

**Truth and Deception**

What you think you are as far as a body self-identity goes, is not true. This is your primary deception. Because it is not true, it is not lovable. To think it can be lovable is your effort to make your deception truth. In your attempt to love the body you are not, you paint, groom, garnish and punish it. Punishment and suffering become your means to salvation ... a way to appease your god.[149] Still, if you cannot love the image you made, people telling you over and over again that "You are lovable!" brings no resolution ... maybe relief through magical thinking but not resolution.

To argue that a dysfunctional upbringing makes you unlovable is a defense to maintain your deception. You were born out of a dis-relation of not knowing who you are. Why would a self you are not, need to be rescued from your upbringing?

Everybody has their story, and they are all different in form, but the same in truth.[150] That you were incarnated out of a dis-relation with Self is what we all have in common to play out in its effects we call a world. Everything after that choice is your effect, a place nowhere in particular to act out your error, sometimes in terror. The cause of what you are will not be found in your effect. Social conditioning is not the cause of why you think about yourself the way you do. It is an effect of your dilemma of being in dis-relation with Source. You are merely playing out your dis-relation through social conditioning. Your deception is putting the cart before the horse!

---

[149] To the ego, attack and punishment is salvation.
[150] Complexity of form does not imply complexity of content.

## The Issue of Authority

Of course, the self you made out of dis-relation is unlovable. How can what you made out of a perceived violation ever be lovable? What you are in truth, and what you have made to identify with, are two different things. Because shame is a response that doubts your own lovability and completeness, those who identify with their shame are actually grappling with core issues of truth and self-deception.

*There is an instant when terror grips your mind and escape appears hopeless. When the mind perceives itself as split, you realize it is you that you fear. There seemed to be an enemy outside that you had to fear. However, the mind perceiving itself as split, for an instant sees its betrayal as within, plotting punishment for you. Yet, in this same instant is the time in which your opportunity appears. For fear of God has disappeared.*

Therapist, stop trying to teach your client to ingratiate and love an unlovable self they are not. Rather teach them that they are right about an ugly self they made, an ugly self they are not. It is a spiritual dilemma of who's in charge. Reality is not yours to select. That is why you can;

*Accept your sense of failure as nothing more than a mistake in who you are*

Ask your client, "Are you your own creation or are you Love's Creation?" Let your client struggle with this question. "If you are Loves Creation, is it for you to decide your value?"

"No but ..." your client begins with examples of failure.

Ask your client, "So it is you who decides value and not your Creator?" Allow your client room to grapple with the inconsistency of their logic. You can continue with "Did God die and leave you in charge? If this is not the case, stop deciding who you are so who you are can tell you." This is a wonderful mantra to help your client get out of the way. Or "Thank God you've been wrong about yourself. You have an opportunity to rethink everything you thought was true."

If your client does not believe in a higher power, you can still say "Thankfully, you've been wrong about yourself. You know this is true because of your thought-provoking fictions that bring you despair. Now you have an opportunity to rethink everything you thought was true."

## The Lost Child

*You cannot shame another, but you can participate in your vulnerability to shame yourself through another's words*

Do not underestimate a child's sensibility that does not understand adult reasoning! Any shamed child has as much aptitude as any adult to interpret what shaming really is; the movement and noise of another's unresolved error. Just like any adult, not all children take criticism personally. Don't decide that they are more vulnerable to interpreting words as shameful then any adult. Again, you would assume that we did not bring dis-relation with us at birth.

The lost child is a journey of each embodied spirit to incarnate … until they awaken to the remembrance of their value as being established *only* in Source. Everything else is the authority problem of believing you can oppose the will of Love and succeed. Because you can't oppose the will of Love and succeed, in dis-relation you will have to live with the effects of your fiction (karma) until you learn to see it a way to forgive it its nothingness. When you are finally able to forgive the split that never occurred, you will awaken to the truth about YOU.

The spirit of any child can never be shamed. The child that forgets the Spirit of what they are is lost in shame. If you've ever felt lost, you understand the feeling of panic. The lost child that identifies with shame lives close to their panic. However, they were not socialized into shame. That shame may have been reinforced is not the issue. That is just a distractive effect. To incarnate because of a dis-relation with Source and make an unlovable self as a compensation for this dis-relation, is the shame we all brought with us. That is the point!

Your attempts to resolve all your discomforts of relationship, job, self-worth, etc., are all about an insecure self. They are all symptoms of trying to compensate for a self you do not like. That is why the need for achievement is paramount to the shamefully insecure ego-self you are not. Understanding passage helps this child through their panic. You are the lost child journeying to once again remember YOU. You are not lost alone and will be found as One.

**Summary**

Because shame confronts core beliefs of being, use shame as a reminder that your client is not far from finding their freedom, the truth about themselves in Source.

*Your darkest hour is just before your dawn*

When you experience shame, your defenses are not working well because you come close to entertaining a deeply seated doubt that you have mistaken yourself as something you are not. Until you recognize your mistake, your doubt leaves you extremely upset. Not knowing how to fix your dilemma, or how to verbalize with another your experience of shame's secret, you feel despair. In this place, diversion does not work for your client or else they would once again be able to bury their despair … like the rest of us do.

Therapist, don't try to teach your client to love the unlovable fiction they are not. That is an impossible lesson that only exacerbates your student's frustration. How can you love what you are not, except in magical self-deception? This is not love. This is a nightmare that searches for escape. To recognize the world as a place that was made so you could not find meaning, is to finally begin to look for meaning somewhere else.

You do not know as you think. To not know is to guess. Be of good cheer, you are not alone. The world is one big guess. Most of us deny this fact, wanting so hard to make sense out of confusion. But how can you perceive anything accurately when you are looking through the eyes of a shame you are not? This only sets you up to experience the failure of guilt and regret; the justification for shames reason.

Even still, shame is the experience of questioning your core beliefs. It is at these times you are the closest to truth. For when you question the unlovable lie you made, you are only one step away from the lovable child you are.

*Transformational Psychotherapy is about questioning your reality. It is the process of exchanging your view of yourself for a reality that is not yours to select.*

*Accept your sense of failure as nothing more than a mistake in who you are.*

# Anger:[151] The Sacred Fiction

*Justified anger always demands revenge for the wrong it perceives. But who always pays for that perception? The angry person.*

It is said often that "It is OK to be angry as long as you express it in an appropriate fashion." People also talk about "justified" anger as appropriate. What most do not realize in their attempts to justify anger as appropriate, or OK is that;

1) not only is all anger justified according to the eye of the beholder but also,

2) all anger is an attack on the person justifying their anger.

3) Therapist, are you teaching your client to be OK with attacking their peace of mind?

This section is not about whether or not anger is right or wrong or good or bad. That line of conversation is irrelevant to the fact that you cannot have peace of mind and justify the right to be angry at the same time.

### "My Right to be Angry!" as a Sacred Fiction

*Of course you have a right to be angry! You have a right to be a blubbering rageful idiot! So … what's your point?*

Anger is always a response to a fiction that something should be other than what it is. Therapist, stop reinforcing your client's right to be angry. It does neither of you justice! You may want to argue that it is not about judging anger but accepting it for what it is. I am not talking about

---

[151] *Healing the Wound p42-45*

judging or accepting anger. I am talking about the karma[152] you can't escape with the thoughts you choose to entertain. And to reinforce the idea of anger as being justified is to deny the therapeutic opportunity to facilitate the dispelling of one of your client's sacred fictions; that people, places and things *should* be other than what they are. The simple fact is, what your client thinks, is other than what is. Acts out of "evil" is not an option for explaining motivation. Recognizing "ignorance" and "confusion" as motivation, without using those words with an angry judgy edge, are options for understanding that what was done to you was not about you.

"The way I see things is the right way because that's the way I see it," is a statement of justified anger based on the self-deception of circular reasoning. The fact of the matter is that all perception leads you into the arena of uncertainty.

## Myths to Dispute

1) It is a myth that people push your buttons. You push your own buttons depending on how you perceive another's words and behaviors.

2) It is a myth that people can take your power away from you. This is the idea that loss is real and anger justified. What "you are" cannot be taken from you. [153] What you are not … get rid of it!

3) It is a myth that you can give your power to another. Because *no thought leaves its source,* what you give you always give to yourself first. That is why to justify the right

---

[152] Out of anger, you can dismiss the idea of "karma" as stupid. But you can't dismiss the fact that "NO THOUGHT LEAVES ITS SOURCE." *Symbols of Power in Metaphysics p98-119*
[153] Having is Being

to be angry is an attack on your peace of mind. Just as to give love is to receive it, is to heal your mind; the law of karma. Cause and effect are in the same place always. To fully realize and generalize this lesson to all areas of your life is the canceling of karma and the end of time.

4) It is a myth that blame solves your problem. Actually, to blame is to depreciate the power of your mind because blame puts the problem away from your mind, the only place your anger can be resolved.

## Anger Management

*I don't need anger management. I need people to stop ticking me off.*

Because thought precedes experience,[154] all cathartic[155] experiences have their resolution when you change your mind about your thoughts. In other words, all cathartic expressions are irrelevant to the mind that does not dispel the beliefs that cause the expressions. If the underlying beliefs that cause the purging is not changed, the purging is regurgitation over and over again. There is a direct correlation between a change of mind "Oh, I never thought about it that way" and resolution. A changed mind has no need for cathartic expressions when it realizes no reason for anger's justification. It looks within for the answer.

*You are angry because you see an unjust world. You see an unjust world because you have violated yourself first. How can*

---

[154] And "Being" precedes thought.
[155] Purifying, cleansing, liberating, releasing, intense, emotional, therapeutic, purgative

*there ever be justice as long as you are in dis-relation with yourself?*

Expressing anger may bring temporary relief, to be added to your pile of unresolved resentment,[156] but only a fundamental shift in your client's thinking will bring release. Helping your client manage their anger is a never-ending task of energy and work as long as they are justifying their fictions. Rather, facilitate the opportunity for your client to dispel their fiction of how they perceive life events. You know that their perception is erroneous because they are angry.

Your client's release from the bonds of repeating their anger over and over again involves fundamental change in the way they habitually think about their world. Until your client is "sick and tired of being sick and tired," they will continue with self-inflicting pain at the expense of blaming another for the pain another never could have caused.[157] So, you always start with the problem your client presents.

To many in traditional psycho-therapy, emoting is seen as an important part of the healing process. Some even maintain that emoting is the only way to experience release. Some clients are not properly served by this because of their inability to emote in a fashion that satisfies the therapist's needs. They learn to emote over and over again … needlessly. So, the therapist listens to the client complain over and over again through the first half of each therapy session.

---

[156] Anger held onto over time becomes resentment.

[157] I am not justifying misunderstandings that often end up as a clash of bodies. But if you don't get past taking it personally you will not see the ignorance you both participate in.

You cannot change anyone, but you can change the way you view them. Your awareness of this principle is the realizing of your center of power. To think that you can give your power away to another is a lie. Nor does anyone push your buttons. You choose what buttons to push depending on your interpretation of any person, thing or event.

*You have lost sight of where your true power and safety reside. It is always with you ... just denied.*

It takes more work to manage your anger than it takes to resolve it. To manage is ongoing work. To resolve is completion. However, to resolve anger takes a fundamental shift in your world view. And this your client may feel too threatened to do as they express their need for security and justice through anger. And to your ego, self-defense in a form of attack, is always salvation.

## Principles of Anger Resolution

*Resentment is anger held onto ... over time*
*Karma is resentment unresolved ... seemingly played back at you ... in other presenting forms*
*This instant is any moment you take to undo resentment in any situation you face "now"*

1) First, you will have to decide you do not know anything about your world and how to perceive it. This may seem insulting to the one who justifies their anger. Yet, your justified anger is proof of this fact.

Even though your anger seems to testify to the idea that someone or most everyone is "stupid," your anger actually witnesses to the fact that *without exception* you do not understand what you see. The person you view out there as stupid is you. To recognize this is a huge step towards anger resolution. *Without your undivided commitment to this principle, all the other steps become ineffectually irrelevant.*

2) Second, you need help to see everything in a different way.

Without exception, your anger is a witness to the fact you do not know how to perceive what you perceive. Humility allows you to be a teachable student. Because anger leaves no room for humility, sponsorship, mentorship and redirection from healed healers[158] is your greatest need.

3) When you begin to commit yourself to a different way of looking at your life events, you can use anybody's anger as an opportunity to look with an open mind as to how they can be angry about nothing, just like you. You know when your mind is not open ... you will be angry.

4) Without exception, when you are angry say to yourself; *"It's not who I see that is angering me"* that angers me, it's *"how I see what I see"* that angers me, and *"this I can change."*

Practice this thought as a mantra, as if it is your means to peace of mind ... because it is!

### Anger Resolution as a Process

*You know you have a crisis ... when your karma stomps all over your fiction ... you're angry*

---

[158] *Symbols of Power in Metaphysics p20-32, Reflections for the Wandering Mind p36-42*

Anger is a superficial expression of a more fundamental fiction that was violated.[159] If your client is new to you, don't start with the fundamental fiction. Start with the superficial expression.

When you ask your clients if they can be angry and at peace at the same time, most of your clients while thinking for a moment will say "no." The few who keep the right hand from knowing what the left hand is doing so their mind can maintain a divided conflictual goal of justified anger, will answer "yes." But only because their anger is driven to find a satisfaction in revenge … but never resolution. The therapist job will be to help their client bring their left and right hand together to see the contradiction[160] they are trying to maintain.

At the same time, because your client may be tempted to think that you are justifying or defending another's behavior as "OK," the therapist reminds the client "I am not saying this person's behavior that you are mad at is OK. I am saying that you have to pay a price to justify the right to be mad at someone else's ignorance." Ask your client "Do you want to pay the price of personal peace to justify the right to be angry at another's act of ignorance, or can they be a lesson as to how you can forgive *all* your acts out of ignorance?" For your client, you just reframed a block to healing into a stepping stone for healing.

After your client describes why they are angry at a particular person, you will find this particular person (through the eyes of your angry client), to be an alcoholic,

---

[159] If you believe you are a body, you will feel violation in some fashion or form. Never would I say that those who perceive themselves as "victims" of sexual abuse are the cause of it. But in the end, you still will have to deal with how to perceive it for resolution, for your own peace of mind.

[160] Divided or split mind, conflicting goal

insecure, selfish,[161] mentally ill, co-dependent, lacking self-love, lacking parenting skills, is critical, etc. This gives your client another view to understand that the person they are mad at is also, like you, under duress. Not justifying anybody's behavior, this person, not unlike your client, may be an angry person, a suffering person who is calling out for help. Your client is not being asked to rescue the person they dislike. However, for your client, their description reframed, clarifies motivation out of ignorance and confusion. What else could it be when the world operates out of ignorance and confusion? As you can see, many different words and behaviors show you a similar cause. For your client to see this is great gains in the therapeutic process. Again and again, complexity of form does not imply complexity of content.

That there are times that we all operate under confusion and ignorance, is a given. This will help your client move towards identifying with the person they are mad at. If you can forgive them their confusion, you can also forgive you your confusion. Now the person you are angry at becomes your teacher.

Again, I am not saying that what the other person did is OK. I am saying that what they did out of their own ignorance, confusion is not about you. That you took it personally is about you. This is what the therapeutic process is about. To realize this allows you a different choice, a choice you never had before: a choice to work towards resolution.

---

[161] The word "selfish" is a judgy word, difficult for your client to overcome. Teach (reframe) instead motivation out of being "needy, insecure or fearful." Whether you have a million dollars or not, all greed is a compensation for the fiction of personal lack. From this view, you can never have enough.

To help diffuse the battle ground in your client's head, remind them *"I am not asking you to forgive them. I am asking you to forgive your perception of them."* By taking the resistance out of the process, your client can focus on themselves in a different way, on what they can do. Encourage them to *"Be the change you wish to see in the world."*[162]

The person who stays in a neglectful or abusive relationship is fearfully insecure with no exit insight. However, if your client is not ready to go, they have a lesson there to learn. Dealing with where they are at is to accept their process as what it is, their process.

### Dealing with Justified Anger

The paradox of accepting your client where they are, is to tell them "It's OK to be angry if you want to; you just have to attack yourself first." This is about spending the therapeutic time helping your client accept *the fact* that the justification of their anger has no merit for resolution.

The simplest and most direct approach would be to tell your client to remind themself that *"No matter how I feel, I am not reacting to the person. I am reacting to my own interpretation of the person."* To diffuse client argumentation, you tell them that "You don't have to believe this. Just practice it when you can remember to say it. Consistent application always has its experiences." Another meditative thought that interrupts the clients thinking would be, *"I forgive the way I see it because the way I see it hurts me."* With blame diffused, ownership of where the problem lies can be dealt with. Your client is on their way. With your clients understanding that their anger attacks no one but themself, they will be motivated to practice a

---

[162] Mahatma Gandhi

discipline of meditative thinking[163] that interrupt's the ruminating thoughts of trying to justify their anger. Also, your client's ability to forgive themself for missed opportunities to practice this simple approach, is great gains towards working through it. Reinforcement is needed from those who have in-site about their own anger.

*Own anger as yours*
*Embrace anger as self-caused*
*This is the path of the peaceful warrior*

## Anger as my Witness to Truth

*To see another as stupid is to make you stupid in your misperception. This is the karma you make for yourself.*

Anger can be used as your witness to the truth of the matter when you use it *without exception,* as being a self-caused set up. Unless this is the case, anger will not teach you anything.

Say to yourself; "Whenever I am angry, I did not get what I thought was my right or what I thought I needed. Or "Whenever I am in an argument, I am angry because I am trying to change someone's mind."

1) Anger is not the result of a fact.  It's the result of an interpretation.  Therefore;

2) Confusion and denial are always involved in anger. Your interpretation frustrates you, not because people can't see the rightness of your interpretation, but because your interpretation is not realistic to "what is."

---

[163] *Reflections for the Wandering Mind p24-42, 52-54*

3) Anger is the result of broken rules, expectations not met. This is a direct cause and effect relationship.

a. Those who have a strong need to control have many rules about how things should or should not be. Not only are rules an attempt to manage chaos for security's sake, they are also made to protect us from seeing our fictions. However, they don't protect us from anything.

b. Your primary fiction being that you are angry because of something happening "out there." However, what seems to be happening out there is happening in your mind first. You don't understand what it means to live life on life's terms because you are in dis-relation with a self that needs fictions of security to operate out of.

c. Those who have many rules have many opportunities for them to be broken. The insanity is, you make rules to protect you from seeing the fact that your beliefs of how the world works or should work are fictions. With that set up, you will feel the threat of a rule being broken, coming from someone outside of you. And, when they are broken you feel the anger to make it right and the need to make more rules. Your preoccupation with rules to protect your thought system allows you no room for love. As long as an expectation is an investment, an expectation not met will be your disappointment. Disappointment and frustration are both forms of anger. The unaware will think they need more rules to avoid disappointment. They don't know that this is their very means to disappointment. There is a direct correlation between the more rules you have the more opportunities you will have to get angry.

4) Fear and hurt are always implied in anger. Unmet expectations involve an underlying perception of threat to one's personal world view.

5) Anger is a defensive response. Though its object of wrath may be incidental or symbolic, anger is first and foremost a response against what it perceives as a threat to your fictitious world view, hidden as an injustice. "It's not fair," means the situation should be different than what it is. In other words, it is an affront to your fictions.

6) As a defensive response, vindication seems appropriate. Feeling justified in your anger, your defensive response to make right looks like attack to another. And to the ego, attack is salvation.

7) Anger is a symptom of limited awareness. You are angry because unknown to you, you see something that is not there. And what is there you can't see it.

8) Anger is not random; it is self-caused. Those who do not make adjustments to their unrealistic fictions, are angry often. And those who are angry often don't seem to ask, "Why am I more often angry as compared to my friends?"

### Principles of Mind

Because your mind is split between investment in the eternal and investment in the temporal, you experience conflict (dis-relation). Your conflict is symbolic of the split. Your conflict is intolerable to you because it denies you the experience of your Self as authentic in Source. Rather than recognize your will in Source, you try to get rid of this intolerable disposition through projection. Because *denial precedes projection*[164] you lose awareness of your identity in Source. You become a stranger in a strange land.

---

[164] *Symbols of Power in Philosophy p253*

That attack is real, coming from the outside is based on the Principle of Mind that *you perceive what you project*.[165] In other words, your experience of anger, guilt and fear in a form that appears outside of you, was first projected from your split mind as an intolerable thought. Because it is a principle of mind that *no thought leaves its source*,[166] all you do in trying to get rid of this intolerable disposition, is hide it, make it unconscious from your awareness. That is why you experience anger over and over again, projected as people and events happening outside your mind.

In summary:

1) You made what you believe because it was made by your belief in it.

2) Your split mind can't but experience conflict.

3) To get rid of conflict, in denial you project it away to experience again and again as seemingly outside of you.

4) Now it appears that you are being attacked from the outside, making attack seem real.

5) Because you were unknowingly successful in attacking your peace of mind,[167] you believe attack is real.

6) Your fear of attack as coming from outside of you is to deny that you are experiencing the effects of your projection.

7) This denial is the justification for a strong defense.[168] Your deception is the fact that you are defending against the awareness of self-deception.

---

[165] *Symbols of Power in Philosophy p253*

[166] *Symbols of Power in Philosophy p252*

[167] It is a Principle of Mind that you cannot serve two masters. You cannot have peace and anger, guilt or fear at the same time. *Symbols of Power in Philosophy p252*

[168] The justification for the ego alliance of nationalistic thinking.

8) Justified in the experience of feeling attacked, you strike back. Or, the best defense is a strong offense. "If you want to get me, I'll get you first!"

In short, what you have done is made another person's error (of not recognizing their projection) real for you by taking their confusion personally. This is the basis of all wars; this is the making of a justified terrorist. And we do it in our minds daily with just a thought that attacks our peace of mind.

*God, grant me the serenity to accept the things I cannot change; the courage to kill the bodies of those who get in the way; and the wisdom to know where to hide the bodies so I don't get found out.*

You have to equate yourself as a body when you think that attack will get you what you want. If "you," for a moment would dispel the fiction that you are a body, attack as a problem-solving strategy would have no appeal for you. Namaste.

## Principles of Perception

*In each and every body life experience
The possession of anger is potential*

Principle 1) A mind split between the eternal and the temporal, experiences the conflict of dualistic thinking. Because no one is consistent with what they do and say,[169] the hypocrite is made.

---

[169] **Cognitive dissonance** is the mental discomfort or tension that arises when an individual holds two or more conflicting beliefs, values, or attitudes, or when their behavior clashes with their beliefs.

Principle 2) Because of a split mind of choices, you perceive confusion, uncertainty and doubt. Through perception, nothing can be known for sure; but believed and thus assumed; the breeding ground for differences and conflict.

Principle 3) Selective perception is a choice; the many ways of looking at any person, event or thing. To choose how to perceive becomes selective to the mind to only see those things that supports your point of view. It is a way to justify your beliefs as true. Because belief precedes experience, what you decide to believe you selectively perceive to see it. What you select to perceive, you experience. That is why the world you see is the world you made through selective perception. No one is immune to this except those who are awake.[170]

Principle 4) Because projection makes perception and you deny you are projecting from your mind; all projection is hidden (unconscious) through your denial that you are doing it. You don't always believe that you are the cause of your experience. None the less, you do experience what you believe.

Principle 5) Because principle #4 is true, you have the solution to where your anger was made; in your mind.

## Selective Perception as a Means for Healing

*The complicating of information makes it difficult to see its nothingness*

---

[170] When Buddha said "I am awake" it was not about understanding that he was a participant in the illusion. He understood that he was the maker of the illusion.

Because perception brings you into the arena of uncertainty, for security's sake you try to make meaningful an uncertain world. Because an uncertain world cannot be made meaningful, you perceive a complex world.

Your perceptions have not solved your problems, but have only complicated a lack of resolution. You have misused the power of your mind to selectively perceive only those witnesses to justify anger, guilt and fear. Because of the power that your mind is, you experience the thoughts you entertain. And because the thoughts you entertain are conflictual/divided, you experience painful thoughts. Thus, do you depreciate the power of your mind by fearing it. Ask your client "What are you giving to another; love or anger? Whatever it is, that is what you are giving to yourself first." [171] It is for you to either free yourself by freeing your perception of another or attack yourself by enslaving your mind to a self-limiting perception of justified anger.

When you recognize that you are the cause of how you see what you see, perception can be used as a teaching device. Selective perception can be used for healing when it is focused on peace of mind as a unifying goal. Because your mind is disorganized and easily tempted to misperceive, clarification of a goal needs to be set in the beginning. If you do not do this, all situations are evaluated in hindsight, after they happen, with no clear idea of what should have happened. Any event will be evaluated as whether you like it or if it is deserving of vengeance.

However, with a clear goal in the beginning, you will selectively perceive the situation as a means to make your

[171] The law of instant karma

170

goal happen. Any interference to the goal will be overlooked. Any situation has meaning because the goal has made it meaningful. If you have a goal related to peace of mind, you will selectively perceive only that which brings your mind in line with peace. This is the proper use of the power of your mind. This is what meditation, prayer and mantras are all about.[172]

## Summary

Your decision to need to be right is a mistake that makes you angry. All of your rightness is an ideology. Look at the foundation of your ideology. It is based on the ever-changing nothingness of Mother Earth.[173] Your price to dig in is peace of mind. And though you will pay that price, it still does not make you right.

How could you not feel a sense of sacrifice and loss when you are in dis-relation with yourself? How can you know what you are from the lie you are not? This is what denial is all about. And how can you remedy this yourself, when your attempts come from your belief in the reality of deprivation, what you are not?

From the view that you have been deprived comes the justification for attack. Anger as justified makes attack become salvation and sacrifice becomes love.

*Transformational Psychotherapy recognizes that trying to find resolution through a mind-set of deprivation is self-defeating, because the means used defeats its goal.*

---

[172] *Reflections for The Wandering Mind p24-35*

[173] The book *Symbols of Power in Philosophy* questions all of our assumptions, our fictions, our foundations, built on assumptions.

# Lying / Betrayal:
# The Seeds of Self-deception

Shortcut: All who come to this world of dreams come out of self-deception. So, if you think someone has lied to you, remember that they lied to themselves first … just like you lied to yourself first. Just like *"We see the world wrong and then say it deceives us."* Just like *"All the truth in the world adds up to one big lie."* Just like *"Appearances are deceiving because they are appearances."* If you understand this inclusively, there is nothing else to read.

*"Master, tell us about those who deceive others. Are they not among the least beloved in the Kingdom of God?"*

*"Always remember that if you see deception in another, it is because you have deceived yourself first."*

*"What do you mean 'we have deceived ourselves first'?" protested one of the disciples.*

*"To not see those who deceive others as being in a place of self-deception is self-deception on your part. It is self-deception because it is your judgment of another that breeds conflict rather than peace within you. And when you deceive yourself by seeing the world wrong," the master stressed, "you will deceive, because you will be teaching deception."*

*"Remember this," summarized the master. "In self-awareness, another's self-deception allows you an opportunity to forgive the self-deception you did not see in yourself."*[174]

I am not saying that people are not about premeditated deception. I am saying that your client lied to themselves first and that's the truth of the matter. *We do see the world wrong and say it deceives us …*

---

[174] *The Way Home p155*

*constantly!* Someone betraying you (as you perceive it), started with the betrayal of yourself first. There is no betrayal but this … *Goo goo ga' joob.*

As far as your client wanting to hold on to a justification to be mad at someone for lying to them, you can begin to reframe an understanding of their experience with *principles of truth*. For example, you can tell them: "There is a reason for another's lie and that's the truth of the matter. Let's look past the lie." Or "Appearances are deceiving because they are appearances. Don't stop with appearances, dig deeper."

Your client might say "People should not lie?!?"

You respond with "What planet do you live on?!? That you can tell me that you do not lie is a lie!" Or, "Self-deception is the human condition." Or, "That is why we all seem to be here!" Or, "That is why you are doing therapy."

Your client might argue "Yes, but it is different lying to myself rather than to someone else. I'm only hurting me."

The fact of the matter is because you have lied to yourself, you can't help but present yourself as a lie to another. Lying to yourself is no different than lying to another*! "I am he as you are he as you are me and we are all together."*[175]

The truth of the matter is "all the truth in the world adds up to one big lie" and you usually believe what your senses tell you. Your sense perceptions are limited by and subject to the ever-changing uncertainty. In other words, appearances are deceiving because they are appearances. "We see the world wrong and then say it deceives us." *Goo goo ga' joob, goo goo goo ga' joob … jooba jooba …*

---

[175] I Am the Walrus, Lennon & McCartney

*You experience the karma you make*
*What are you making?*

  Remember, either everyone including you is a hypocrite
or we all teach what we need to learn. What else could it
be?

  *Transformational psychotherapy is about a fundamental shift*
*in how you see everything. The body's eyes may see differences,*
*but it is the healed mind that does not acknowledge them.*

# Trauma / PTSD:
# The Instant of Change

*People are not disturbed by things, but by the view they take of them*
*Epictetus*

## The Experience of Trauma

*One day two servants were out picking berries for their king. Their picking brought them to a hillside overlooking a meandering river. Just below, the river flowed swiftly around the hillside through rocky rapids. Looking up stream, one of the servants noticed what appeared to be a figure of a man in the river. The man appeared to be in trouble. He was kicking, splashing, clinging and tumbling around the rocks of this fast-flowing river.*

*The servants dropped their baskets of berries and ran down the steep bank to the river's edge. As the man tumbled by he went under then came up choking and screaming for help. The servants chased along the river, stumbling blindly through deep thickets.*

*Finally, the river took a bend away from the bank and opened into a calm. When the servants arrived out of the dense thickets at the bend of the river, they almost ran into the man. He was just walking out of the water. The servants, over excited from all the commotion and breathing heavily from all their running, were all over the man.*

*"Are you all right?" exclaimed one of the servants in anxious anticipation. "We heard your cries for help."*

*The man, old in appearance, stood there dripping wet watching the two in animated confusion. "What's wrong with you two?" spoke the old man out of bewilderment, "Can't you see that everything's fine?"*

*Surprised by the comment, the servants stood motionless and speechless before the old man. The old man wandered aimlessly toward the surrounding thick underbrush mumbling under his breath "Now how am I gonna get through all these thickets?"*

*One of the servants, not yet ready to let go of the fact that the old man almost died in the river, blurted out "But you were screaming just a minute ago, screaming for your life!"*

*The old man turned to them with a sparkle in his eye and simply stated "That was then, this is now" and in the same breath added, "Now tell me, what's the best way through these thickets?"*[176]

## Ownership or Partnership

*Each and every traumatic experience involves the belief in a body image as "you." When you transcend the body "You" transcend trauma.*

All memories of "traumatic" body-threatening experiences are symbolic of your first "traumatic" experience of change.[177] "In a thoughtless instant that never occurred, mind entertained a thought separate from Source. Through this thought consciousness was made. Consciousness, viewing itself as separate[178] from Source, divided into a consciousness of many. The idea of a separation that could never be, was thoughtless mind's "traumatic" detour into confusion, self-deception and fear."[179]

---

[176] *The Way Home p82-83*

[177] Now, it is your journey home, a gradual awakening to remember your Source of Being.

[178] The beginning of dualistic thinking; I – You / subject - object.

[179] In terms of Christian theology this is the "original sin," the loss of innocence, the fall from the Garden of Eden. In existential

Through your detour into fear, confused about what you are, the power of your mind mismanaged, took on a body image as a self. As *ownership*, the body you think you are is the seat of the kingdom of pseudo-ego to be protected, nurtured and ingratiated as your kingdom of an end in itself ... your eventual demise. From this foundation, the body you think you are will rise up as your worst fear to shake the very foundation of everything you cherish and believe to be true. As your primary symbol of power, the body will be your means to experience attack as real. As your most protected friend, your body will be the enemy that assaults your humanity, insults your integrity, causes you to be angry, guilty and fearful, and takes everything you hold dear away from you! And before your demise, it will change, take on a different form, experience ailments and pains ... and then die. And yet, till just before the end will you defend it to your death as your cherished and priceless idol, your most important love affair. And your magically religious rituals, you hope, will save you after the body dies. And you wonder why you experience trauma? This is the payback for your investment in nothingness.

To reinterpret this symbol of power as *partnership*, the body is a means *only to teach you* your lessons of passage. What else could it be for? It is a teaching aid you will one day say to "Thank you and goodbye." Because the world is not left by death but by truth, there is no death but a change in dreams. You will do it again and again until

---

psychology, this is the source of all "separation anxiety, adjustment disorders" the human dilemma of being in dis-relation with Self. Is not your life one big adjustment disorder?
*Symbols of Power in Metaphysics p34*

your awakening.[180] The journey sounds traumatic until you finally understand to use change as your means for passage. The battle is in your mind. It is in your investments of the temporal as a world … until you experience the eternal that you are, apart from a body self-idea.

*Transformational Psychotherapy is about the questioning of your reality; it is in the changing of your view of yourself.*

## Orientation Exercise

*Because thought precedes experience, [181] all traumatic experiences have their resolution when you change your mind about them*

Trauma is the perception of a body-threatening experience. No matter what the form maybe it is perception overload. It is not a life-threatening experience because your life does not belong to a body! Therefore, trauma is an impetus to remind you what is truly of value compared to the fictions you have adjusted to and settled for.

1) At your own pace, explore your traumatic experience; talk about it.
2) List all that was threatened or lost.

Because you can't take it with you, all that can be threatened or lost is an inconvenience of degrees. Your protest here is in defense of a body you are not. Get past your indignation so you can use this inconvenience as a helpful reminder that what you have placed value in for

---

[180] *Symbols of Power in Metaphysics p120-145*
[181] And "Being" precedes thought.

security, has no intrinsic or lasting benefit. You know it has no lasting value because it can be threatened and painfully lost.

3) What has lasting value cannot be threatened or lost. List what you have lost that has lasting value. When you come to the place where nothing has been lost, you come to the place that in Source you really are everything you need. This is a *fundamental shift* in what you value and therefore how you approach life circumstances.

The belief that loss is real will be the resistance that will keep you in your suffering. Do not fear the giving up of investments that have actually been the means to your suffering. You are traumatized because you took the body as "you." If the body was not the seat of your safety you would not be traumatized. What you are being asked to do is allow for an exchange, to transcend what you thought was your safety. I am not asking you to change, or give up anything of value. What I am asking you to do is celebrate exchange.

## Exchange

*The only reason change is difficult is because you mistook nothingness for something to be valued*

All experiences of trauma are to be transcended or exchanged; they are reframed as opportunity. In the whirlwind of nothingness what else would they be?

*Nothing's Way*[182]
*Making something out of nothing*
*Makes nothing seem like something*
*When nothing seems like something*
*You have to do something about it*
*Until you see it as it is … Nothing*
*And when you do see it as nothing*
*You just moved a mountain*

So-called lost relationships are exchanged as something else. Someone on the other side of the veil is more available to help you as a guide then they were able to help you on this side. But you will need to get to know them other than your conception of them as a body. It's the same with so-called failed relationships. The exchange being "It's not that your relationship did not work, it's that you gave it the wrong goals." Because complexity of form does not imply complexity of content, this applies to all relationships.

*Any problem "now" represents your unresolved past … the opportunity to be resolved today … in any present moment you choose … in the current problem laid before you. This brings you closer to the understanding of your original error. The original error being the trauma of a change, when you thought you lost your relationship with Source. That is why all change involves a resistance from an unconscious trauma of change.*

Trauma confronts you with the opportunity to look at the defenses you use to protect your fictions from scrutiny. You may go into a panic attack of dread when you realize the body you held onto for safety has been your means to trauma. Do not despair, the opportunity of release is

---

[182] *The Way Home p146*

knocking on your door. You will not be asked to give up anything of value. You are being asked to exchange your fictions of nothingness for the remembrance of Spirit that "You Are." There is no loss in this. The only reason exchange is difficult is because you mistook nothingness as something to be valued.

4) You reinforce your shift by telling your story to others. Those who are ready to listen will.

5) Remind yourself of #3 daily. Of course you are vulnerable to perceiving changing events as traumatic. Your perceived dis-relation with Source was a traumatic experience; but only for an instant as the making of a world of time ... and what you mind made, it will undo.

## A Thoughtless Instant that never occurred

Trauma belongs to a thoughtless instant that never occurred; a forgotten memory of your seeming dis-relation of your identity with Source; thus, your detour into fear. Everything the world is to you is in this thoughtless instant. That is why the only function meaningful in time is your work of forgiveness. This is your means to waking up. What else could it be? Start doing the work!

*Transformational Psychotherapy is about exchange; the exchange of perceived trauma for opportunity*

# Stress as the Seriousness of Life

*Stress is always about taking "nothing" seriously*
*Release the butterfly and it will freely fly*

### What is Stress?

Stress is the body tension of a perceived threat to the self you made. Because you made this self, it is vulnerable to attack and disappointment. The Self you are cannot be threatened. It is complete. It is beyond the identity of a "self" as a body. To not recognize your completion is to deny the truth of what you are. The "self" you made becomes your substitution by which you look through to interpret your world view. From this view only uncertainty, vulnerability, lack, disappoint and some shallow passing happiness can be found. Denial of the truth is always stressful. It takes a lot of work to deny the truth of what you are really about. And when you are preoccupied with getting your ducks in a row throughout your day, you have no room in your mind to go about what you are really about. Because your denial of the truth is an endeavor you cannot totally achieve, this endeavor becomes stress-fully tiring.

Stress seems to have something to do with your list of changing life events. However, these stressors are merely symptoms, adjustments you have to make around your fiction as a body. Stress has *everything* to do with the way you view these ever-changing events. When you invest in these continually changing series of events as seriously meaningful for security's sake, they become life stressors. What else could the vulnerability of an incomplete self perceive, when change is threatening, but the need to adapt to the threat of an ever-changing world?

## The Seriousness of Life

*Because you are in dis-relation with yourself, what else could you feel but stress?*

Whenever the idea of loss is involved, so is stress. The idea of loss seems real to the mind that has substituted a "self" for your remembrance of your completion already accomplished. That is why the idea of fear is so foundational to your way of thinking. Fear is your witness to your search for completion.

To fear loss is to take your world seriously. "I must take it seriously" you argue, "I have too much at stake, too much to lose." However, the world is neutral. It is the power of your mind confused about itself that interprets this world as something serious with tension. To compensate for the tension, you become involved in innumerable distractions of personal and professional activity.

The perceived need to order your world for security (protection from loss) is a compensation for taking life events in a threatening manner. In the world, what one is, is what one does, achieves or fails to do. This belief leaves no room for freeing interpretations of your life events. You have no room in your mind to go about what you are really about. Your interpretations will drive you to achieve within the parameters of what you view as success and failure. Can you feel the tension, the need to control and produce?

### Damned if You Do, Damned if You Don't

The stress (worry) of something going wrong is very real when your definition of success is limited. If your life view states that success or failure depends upon an "indispensable" you, you will burnout defending indispensability. If you view yourself as "dispensable," you must work hard to compensate for the insignificantly dispensable self you have crucified. Either way, you will burn out. Can you feel the tension? But some say there is good stress. "It motivates me to do better." Stress, at the expense of your peace of mind, is not good stress. It is the justification of stress as necessary at the cost of your peace of mind.

## Failure

*Failure is your teacher when it reminds you of your limiting life view*

Perceived failure comes from constrictive (serious) views of life. Pseudo-ego[183] seeks for completion out of a belief in incompletion. Yet, through the eyes of in-completion you will never find completion because you are looking for it from an incomplete point of view. You have sabotaged yourself at the onset.

Avoiding failure is a compensation to control outcomes. Your obsession to avoid failure will haunt you to take over, control and consume everything and everyone. You cannot even play if you find time because your mind is preoccupied with what you need to do or what you should have done. Your job is never done. Can you feel the tension?

It is your body that feels and absorbs the results of your seriousness. Mind cannot be threatened. But it thinks it

---

[183] Pseudo-ego is a defensive facade or a sense of self, created to protect against perceived threats or vulnerabilities, at the expense of authenticity and genuine self-expression.

can when it uses an ephemeral body to find completion. Tight back muscles, headaches and panic attacks are common results.

Failure will show up in the form your seriousness takes until you allow it to teach you about your self-defeating constrictive views you have made. Actually, to resolve your stress, you don't need to change anything in your world. But you do need to make a fundamental shift, a change of mind about what you think the purpose of the world is for, if you want to find escape.

*Release the butterfly and it will freely fly*

## Major Life Stressors Explained

*There seems to be an inner world and an outer world. Your outer world is a reflection of what is going on in your inner world. There is no outer world but the world you made.*

Major life stressors are not so in themselves. It is your view of any event that determines how that event will affect you. They become stressors within the constrictive view of a serious attitude towards ever-changing life events. This makes you, not the world around you, responsible for your stress. *Nothing can make you stressful except your view of it.* To blame your stress on situational circumstances (stress factors) is to deny responsibility for your life view. Blame projected outside of you keeps the solution from where the problem was made, in you! Denial is your delay, while your circumstances of perceived stress reappear until you learn your lessons. Your need is to bring cause (your thinking) together with stress (the effect).

*Trials are lessons you failed to learn presented again*

Your stress reaction is a symptom of your denial to recognize "passage." To take seriously the transient events of your body life, is to deny the ever-changing disposition of your passage through. You have no room in your mind to go about what you are really about.

*Your denial of truth is always stressful*

## Signs of Job Burnout

Job Burnout is a form of prolonged stress:

1) You do not look forward to coming to work.

2) You look for lateral opportunities within the business.

3) You have low or no energy for your job.

4) You feel unproductive and non-creative.

5) You find yourself to be irritable in your relational interactions on and off the job.

6) You often feel anxiously overwhelmed on the job.

7) You bring your job home with you to anxiously ruminate over.

8) Because you come home from work with no energy to pursue other things (hobbies), you vegetate in front of the television or go to bed early.

9) You come back from a week's vacation with no change in attitude about your job.

## Orientation Exercise

Stress management is a fanciful rearrangement of time and priority if it does not address your fundamental attitude towards life. Therefore:

1) List what you take seriously in your life situation.

Do not attempt to justify as essential or minimize as unimportant what you think of as "serious." These are the defenses which keep you overworked, over-stressed and unable to make meaningful change. If you think of anything questionable write it down.

2) In each situation listed, what do you find unacceptable about you?

Your integrity is not at stake here, but the messages you communicate about you through your life situations are. Therefore, be honest so you can see the messages you are communicating about yourself through your chosen events.

3) What do you find unacceptable with the job or people around you?

Be careful here. You don't want to blame your stress on your outer world. But you do want to take an honest look at how you perceive it. If you can't change the outer world or change your view of it, you will be able to take responsibility for your misery on the job. This is a big step closer to reflective honesty, self-empowerment and real change.

4) If you want to find escape, you will have to change your mind about what you think the purpose of the world is.

*It's not what the world holds for you that makes a difference. It's what you bring to the world that makes all the difference in the world.*

What do you need to change for new grounding?    Find something you can be passionate about at work. It will be your means to creative collaborations in any field you work in. [184] Leave your mind room to find the fun by repeating throughout you day;

---

[184] *Symbols of Power in Philosophy p117-120*

*In any job that must be done, there is an element of fun. You find the fun and snap! The job's a game.*
A Spoon Full of Sugar
Mary Poppins

If you can't make the mental shift, you may need to change your job. If you stay for the money, that will be your investment in continued misery, making you look like a disgruntled employee.

## Some Principles of Reality for Personal Grounding

1) What is inevitably real is not fearfully punishing but rather beneficially healing.

Any protracted view of life as fearful is unrealistic. Find the courage to conduct a reality check. You can always change your view about the idea of "failure." Talk to a friend about it. Don't isolate, that only feeds your "fictions" of how you think the world sucks.

2) You are not defined by what you do or fail to do.

Don't use the externally socialized world to be your judge. The world is a passing fancy you have empowered to be a guide. It is a false idol!

3) You are neither "dispensable" nor "indispensable." Nor do you want to be. You are something altogether different than all that measure of nonsense. It is easy to complicate the results of information to be unable to see its nothingness. Stop taking "nothing" seriously!

## Summary

*Release the butterfly and it will freely fly*

To resolve your stress, you don't need to change anything in your world. To think you do, involves mental

189

conflict / cognitive dissonance.[185] But you will want to make a fundamental change of mind about what you think the world is for. There is no loss in this. It is about the exchange of the life you have taken seriously, for peace of mind.

**Short Cut**

Is what I am upset about an event that will change my life? NO. Then let it go!

*Fill your bowl to the brim and it will spill*
*Keep sharpening your knife and it will blunt*
*Chase after money and security and your heart will never unclench*
*Care about people's approval and you will be their prisoner*
*Do your work, then step back*
*The only path to serenity*
Tao Te Ching #9

---

[185] Cognitive dissonance describes the discomfort you feel when your beliefs don't line up with your actions. Or it could refer to the tension of holding two conflicting beliefs at once. "Cognitive" means relating to your thoughts. "Dissonance" describes a lack of harmony.

# Judging: The Authority Issue

*In the ever-changing, all you can obtain is partial evidence. No one can judge with partial evidence. And yet it is attempted all the time. That is why to overlook "nothing" is the proper use of judging.*[186]

## Judging as the Authority Problem

To judge is to compare through arbitrary values that limit. To limit your experience to a thought is to experience that thought alone. You can't see the whole picture. The paradox is; when you judge for understanding, you limit your ability to understand ... until you change your mind about it.

If the premise is true that;

1) You are in dis-relation with Source and

2) Because of your dis-relation you do not know who or what you are, then it follows that

3) Any idea that you can judge or analyze anything including you as meaningful from an erroneous point of view is ludicrous!

4) In dis-relation, reality is not yours to select.

## Judging as Self-Defeating

*What you do not understand, you judge as lacking*

You know you have chosen pseudo-ego's interpretation when;

1) You are depressed because your ego feels deprived.

2) You are anxious because of the impulsive changeable whims of the ego.

---

[186] *Symbols of Power in Philosophy p225-228*

3) You feel guilty because the ego is a making in opposition to your Source.

4) You are angry because the ego did not get what it expects or demands.

These are the things the ego gives you while it tells you to seek peace through its dictates. Seeking what you will never find is why you are tired.

Allow your moods to be what they are so they can tell you when you have chosen wrongly. When you have feelings you do not like you have chosen a guide who is lacking. The only good use of judging is to judge the ego as lacking and therefore useless to your journey. The short cut is to overlook nothingness as the proper use of judging.

## Getting Out of the Way

*Your understanding is so limited that you try to make confusion meaningful. Your shifting dreams of nothingness and fearful thoughts of possibilities are engaged in defending what is not there.*

1) It is OK not to know what you are or what you should do. Actually, because of your propensity to want to make nothingness meaningfully real, it is most beneficial for you to admit you do not know.

2) You really don't understand what you see, for what you have used for personal validation you have also used to hurt yourself. This principle allows you to be open to "different thinking."

3) Your confusion need not be viewed fearfully. Rather, confusion is an opportunity to practice the invitation of accepting things to be as they are because they are that way.

4) If you want to get out of the way of judging, *without exception*, in each and every encounter with whoever you meet, there is but one of two interpretations to their behavior and attitude. All people are either:
   a. Extending love, or
   b. Calling for help

Because *complexity of form does not imply complexity of content* no other interpretation of life is necessary, nor is any other interpretation required. Your *willingness* to apply these two interpretations to the experiences of your daily encounters will simplify the confusion of all your validating contradictions of trying to understand by judging the motive of others. You will see immediate value in your encounters as you practice to see only these two motivations in every person you meet. Because of you propensity for mind wandering, don't judge yourself as if you are falling short.! This section is about not judging, remember? *All you are being asked do is be willing to receive correction.* All consistent applications have their experience.[187]

If you only knew how long it has been for you to finally come to this place in time to say with conviction, "*I don't want to be in charge of how I see this situation because how I see it hurts me,*" you would allow for yourself a joyful and grateful time of rest.

## This Simple Story Has a Great Message!

*A young couple moved into a new neighborhood. The next morning while they were eating breakfast, the young woman saw her neighbor hanging the wash outside. "That laundry is*

---

[187] *Reflections for the Wandering Mind, p 32*

*not very clean," she said. "She doesn't know how to wash correctly. Perhaps she needs better laundry soap." Her husband looked on, but remained silent. Every time her neighbor would hang her wash to dry, the young woman would make the same comments. About a month later, the woman was surprised to see a nice clean wash on the line and said to her husband, "Look, she has learned how to wash correctly. I wonder who taught her this."*

*The husband said, "I got up early this morning and cleaned our windows."*

Author Unknown

And so, it is with life. What we see when watching others depends on the window through which we look.

## A Collapse in Time from a Linear Point of View

Because you cannot have peace of mind and judge at the same time, it is your lack of peace that tells you of your propensity to want to judge to a degree far greater than you realize. It is a collapse of time when you realize to judge another is to judge yourself first. Because no thought leaves its source, whatever you give you give to yourself first.[188] It is a collapse in time (speed-up) when you bring cause and effect together in the same place they were both made; IN YOUR MIND!

When you generalize this principle to everything in your life, time is no more; you are at the end of your journey. [189] Therefore, the sooner you recognize your propensity to judge erroneously, the sooner you come to recognize it is not for you to judge. And the sooner you relinquish your desire to want to judge, the sooner you will be able to forgive it. Eventually you will catch yourself wanting to judge at its inception and will be able to

[188] *Symbols of Power in Philosophy p252*
[189] *Symbols of Power in Metaphysics p128-132*

interrupt your mistake before it happens. In this way you collapse time (speed-up).[190]

## Which do you choose?

*Judgment takes work*
*Forgiveness is effortless*

*Judgment involves mental strain and physical pain*
*Forgiveness relaxes your mind and body*

*Judgment drains you of your energy*
*Forgiveness revitalizes*

*Judgment locks you into a battle of limited points of view*
*Forgiveness frees you to transcend all views*

*Judgment of another condemns you as guilty*
*Forgiveness of your perception reflects your innocence*

*Judgment binds you to the world of laws*
*Forgiveness releases you to the law of love*

*Judgment is the ego's complexity*
*Forgiveness is the ego's undoing*

*Judgment gives you hell*
*Forgiveness gives you heaven*

---

[190] *Symbols of Power in Metaphysics p99-109*

Because you cannot serve two masters [191] you can't have both at the same time

## Summary

In short, you can either attempt to judge as an expression of your fear, or forgive as an expression of your love. Which do you choose?

*Transformational Psychotherapy understands that to overlook nothingness is the proper use of judging.*

*Namaste*

---

[191] Matthew 6:24; Luke 16:13. You can believe anything you want. However, it is a principle of mind that you cannot serve two masters without inviting confusion and conflict.

# Your Attraction to Guilt

*Fear of the dark, fear of the unknown, dreams of fear, have everything to do with guilt*

### The Original Error

The original error is a thought that you could be in dis-relation with Source. To be in dis-relation with Source is to not know "You." From this point of view is guilt and fear born.

### The Dilemma of an Ancient Buzz

You are afraid of the unknown because to not know "You" is the unknown that engenders fear. Covering this fear is the continual buzz of anxiety, just under the conscious level of your awareness. You experience guilt but most of the time are unaware of how it is experienced. Your anxiety is one form.

To fill this void, you made a "you" that must do something about this guilt. But you fear to look within because the violation you fear you committed is deserving of punishment. Yet, you find guilt to be intolerable because it stands in the way of remembering Source. So, you displace [192] Source with pseudo-ego [193] and disassociate[194] from the guilt of what you did by projecting it away.

---

[192] To displace is to substitute. p351

[193] Pseudo-ego is a defensive facade or a sense of self, created to protect against perceived threats or vulnerabilities, at the expense of authenticity and genuine self-expression.

[194] To disassociate is to distance yourself from knowing what you substituted (denial). p351

The primary purpose of projection is to get rid of guilt. Under the conscious level are back door deals, compensations[195] with pseudo-ego. These are all bargains to absolve you of guilt. These absolution's can be to blame another, to punish another or self, and of course, to crucify someone. But because denial always precedes projection, all you do is conceal your guilt. Your ancient buzz continues just under the conscious level; the effect of denying how intolerable guilt stands in the way of remembering Source.

## Where all Religions are Made

You view a world of guilt, justified anger and the need for punishment, not knowing that you projected it from your own conflicted mind. Here is where all religions are made with zealots[196] to justify their righteous beliefs to appease their vengeful god. In this kingdom everything you do, think or say is at the mercy of king pseudo-ego, who you made to escape guilt, yet was made out of guilt and is therefore demanding punishment; the dilemma of an ancient buzz.

*As long as you try to find resolution for guilt in a world that was made out of guilt, you will have no resolution*

---

[195] To compensate is to make adjustments that justify/defend against your awareness of your disassociation. All your compensations are about making your fictions workable in denial of what you did. A self apart from Source is your number one fiction. p351

[196] The zealous terrorist is trying to appease their guilt by doing God's will. It is terroristic because guilt demands punishment for the violation that occurred. To project the violation away makes any passerby the infidel.

## Disassociation from Guilt Played Out

It is often said that anger masks hurt. It is less often stated that hurt masks fear. So, you think you see where the source of your pain is coming from; emotionally from someone out there, or from your body. However, if you are not the body you think you are, as far as pain coming from your body, it is still out there. Yet, to disassociate from the source of your pain is to hide the fact that your body pain is coming from a guilty mind. Mind over matter is true. But not for a mind in conflict with itself. Recognize what is cause and what is effect.

*What kind of therapy can be done with a guilt displaced on a self you are not, demanding punishment for the error that never occurred?*

When you disassociate from your guilt as coming from you, you play out your guilt as "special love" and "justified hate" relationships. Special love, blame, justified anger and hate demonstrate your attempt to hide your dis-relation with Self. There is no real relationship when you use your relationships to justify anger, guilt, fear, abandonment and blame. You have done this to escape the punishment guilt says you deserve. Your own beliefs out of dis-relation as to what you think relationships are for have left you lonely and bankrupt. Unknown to you, this is what the self-sabotage of your relationships are about.

Because you are fearful, hurt and angry, you demand from relationships what you think they should be for. Yet those demands sabotage what love is all about. Of course you feel abandoned; no one can save you from your dis-relation but yourself. Yet, you need relationships that are not yours to decide what they are for, so you can remind yourself what they are for.

*It's not that your relationships didn't work*
*It's that you gave them the wrong goals*

Don't you know that the punishment you think another deserves is your own punishment displaced? How can you have the love relationship you so badly want to save you from the loneliness of guilt when you don't love yourself?

*You can justify using the word "hate" because you hate yourself first*

## Relationships Beyond Guilt

When you bring your guilt into any relationship no relationship is possible. What you encounter is your unresolved past displaced as a present issue. You could not solve your problem of the past. Why would you use the past to solve the present? Determination is needed here to save you from a past that you lay upon the one you meet in any present moment. You need each other to see your innocence instead! There is no other reason! This is a different purpose for what all relationships are for.

As it seems, people do you wrong. As it seems, you have done people wrong. The world is a place as it seems, that you do each other wrong. When ignorance is recognized as universal and chaos is the background that nurtures ignorance, you can forgive. Complexity of form does not imply complexity of content. There is no such thing as "special love." There is relationship when you use them to remember every one you meet is like you, on a journey to remember your experience of One Mind. From this point of view, what's to forgive? As long as you believe that guilt serves a purpose you will defend the need for retribution … until you learn that guilt is insane with no justifiable cause.

*What you make you defend against*
*What you defend against you make real*
*There is no escape from what you make real*
*Until you undo it*

As long as you believe guilt has a justifiable reason, you will feel guilty, but only because you made it real in your mind alone. Guilt is only a figment of your imagination. This lesson seems hard indeed, deserving of much consideration and work.[197] It is a paradox as to how hard it is to get over nothing. Your journey to healing starts with you. And it will be a fundamental shift you will make when you are ready to come back to YOU.

## Your Attraction to Guilt

*You believe what you made because it was made by your belief in it*

No one consciously invites guilt into their lives. Nor do you want to believe that you are attracted to guilt, that you actually invite it into your life on a daily basis. However, what you make is your world. And at the core of your world is an error intolerable to your peace of mind. There is no escape except through the changing of your mind.

Guilt's invitation comes every time you say phrases like "I should have" or "I should not have" or "if only I would have …" or "Why did I." Even though it is a present

---

[197] Look at how tempting it is to perceive all the ignorant confusing injustices in the world as a stupidity that needs to be punished.

thought about a memory, guilt's invitation seems to make the past real … but only in the mind of the thinker. To experience the memory of a yesterday that is no more, is to experience a tense other than the present.[198] You always experience that memory in the present, making the illusion of time appear to be linear.

## Guilt's Need for Punishment

Your hidden error of dis-relation through the guidance of pseudo-ego needs correction. But because guilt through displacement and disassociation is an attack on the self you are not, it seems to be coming from outside of you. And from outside of you, attack is experienced as real and punishment as deserving.

You want to get rid of guilt because it is intolerable to your natural inclination for peace of mind. You use projection to get rid of guilt. But because no thought leaves its source you still have guilt. And because you are in denial of your projection you remain unaware of what you have done to yourself. Now that your mind is split through projection and your tracks are hidden through denial, you seem to have an outer and an inner world. However, no outer world exists outside of your mind. All you have done is to conceal your guilt through projection. Not only are you holding guilt through denial but you are also involved in defending and ingratiating a "you" you are not. No wonder you feel crazy and tired. You're trying to make sense out of a world of contradiction that can never make sense.[199]

---

[198] *Symbols of Power in Philosophy P27-34*
[199] *Free floating anxiety* is the concealing of guilt through your unaware attempt to project it away. Because it remains, you experience an illusively haunting ancient buzz. To make sense

## The Unsolvable Problem

*That you are a product of social conditioning is a socially conditioned view reinforced through selective perception*

A good example of social conditioned thinking gone awry is when parents evaluate how they parented according to how their kids turned out. Looking back, the temptation is to draw "supposed" correlations of things they should have done differently as a parent with a difficult kid. And because the self-scrutiny is hypothetical, no conclusion is possible as to what the parent should have done. The problem becomes unsolvable. When you identify a self you are not as being guilty or hang it out there on some unsuspecting passerby to get rid of it, you can't solve it within your mind where the problem was made.

This is exactly how *every problem* in your world becomes unsolvable … until you recognize without exception that social conditioning is an effect of a spiritual dilemma that all of us play out in our own socially conditioned ways. The exceptions to why a kid turns out the way they did, is as numerous as the stars. The fact that there is no real correlation as to why anyone turns out the way they do, stands against your assumed correlations as being what they are … nothingness.[200]

*Accept your sense of failure as nothing more than a mistake in who you are*

out of this for resolution, you find explanations for your guilt. You temptingly select a ridiculous assortment of ways you have failed or should be afraid, that justify why you "should" feel guilty or scared.

[200] *Symbols of Power in Philosophy p69-89*

## Forgiving an Error that Never Occurred

From ego's view, violation has occurred. Therefore, rules are necessary for conformity and order. Again, it is ego's backdoor deals for you to have a blue print for right living. How noble. However, no one can be consistent in the instability of the ever-changing. Ethics is situational in a negotiated reality. [201] That is why ego's remedy for conformity and order regarding your inconsistent behavior of violations, is a set up. Your rules for order and justice become means to judge and condemn violation. Yet, because no one is consistent, the rules are broken. Everyone stands condemned. Ego says "What you need are more rules." Now the more rules you have the more opportunity you have for violating or being violated. [202] Now you have to seek resolution through punishment. Someone must pay to atone for their "sin." Either it is to be you or the unsuspecting passerby in your life. And because ego's solution does not work, your need for appeasement through punishment is never ending. Now your ego says "You should be angry because justice does not always prevail!" Yet, the world of people, things and events is a crazy and insane complication with no resolution possible.[203] Therefore;

*Accept your sense of failure as nothing more than a mistake in who you are*

---

[201] *Symbols of Power in Philosophy p 50-68, 55-62*

[202] And all this complicating of conflicting information for results, hides the fact that the complicating of information makes it difficult to see its nothingness.

[203] That change is ever-changing is a fact of nature. That evolution of the species as far as growing awareness goes, is a fiction demonstrated by history. *Symbols of Power in Philosophy p196-236*

The fact of the matter is that nothing really occurred but an error of thought. This is what real forgiveness is all about. In the end what you are teaching your client to do is to forgive an error that never occurred.

*"Master, what about the unforgivable sin?"*
*"Because God has never condemned, He sees no sin to forgive. Therefore, the only unforgivable sin is the one you refuse to forgive."*[204]

The intangible is the miracle. When your client is ready the miracle occurs.

## Diffusing Guilt through Non-dualistic Teaching

*Your shortcomings do not teach you that you are a failure They teach you that reality is not yours to select*[205]

Some will argue that guilt is a powerful tool for therapeutic change. Only if it leads you beyond guilt. I am not against people feeling guilty. I am not against allowing consequences for "deviant" behaviors. [206] But if guilt, consequences and traditional therapy worked we would not have our jails filling up with repeat offenders.

Repeat offenses can be explained as;
   1)   Society's failure to educate,
   2)   Family history of traumatic experiences,
   3)   Mental illnesses,

---

[204] *The Way Home p124*

[205] Immanuel Kant's Categorical Imperative says that the results of human action are subject to accident and circumstance; you are not in charge of outcomes. *Symbols of Power in Philosophy p55-68*

[206] Whatever that might be in the ever-changing ephemeral?

4) A combination of all of them which explains why nothing is working,[207] or
5) None of them.

Even though nothing else on the board has a high empirical correlation of cause and effect, a spiritual dilemma of dis-relation is not empirical enough to consider. However, all of the first four possibilities are merely effects played out that disguise your spiritual dilemma. Do whatever it is you want to do to motivate someone, but when it comes to waking up ... WAKE UP!

The "I should have done it differently" thinking can be diffused by a simple challenge that helps your client accept the reality of "what is."

By stating definitively "That you should have done it differently is not true. You could not have done it any other way. Do you know why that is true?"

"Why?" they respond.

"Because you didn't!" you state firmly.

"You know why you didn't?" you ask.

"Why?" they respond.

"Because if you were supposed to do it differently, you would have," you answer.

This dialogue is not an excuse for what your client did. It is an example of non-dualistic acceptance without judgment. It always transcends your client's dualistic thinking that involves comparisons of conflict.[208] There is no resolve in that place of conflictual thinking; only damned if you do and damned if you don't scenarios with smatterings of relief. *That people should feel guilty because it*

---

[207] Complicating the results of information so you can't see its nothingness.

[208] *Symbols of Power in Philosophy p 44-49*

*helps them change is a lie.* Because the world was made out of guilt and fear, it runs on guilt and fear. It is a change of mind that your client needs, not the same old worn-out rhetoric.

Other thoughts of encouragement or meditation for mental space that involve non-dualistic acceptance would be;

1) "Stop deciding who you are so who you are can tell you."

2) "You are not in charge of knowing."

3) "God did not die and leave you in charge."

4) "Thank goodness you got it wrong because the way you have been thinking about it makes you miserable."

5) "There is another way to see it if you are ready?"

6) "It's not that your relationship failed, it's that you gave it the wrong goals."

7) "Forgiveness will get you to the next step faster than guilting will."

*Everything in your world that has happened does not teach you that you are a failure. It teaches you that reality is not yours to select. Rethink all of it so you can get past thinking all-together.*[209]

## Summary

You made time when you decided to look for completion in a place it could not be found. Now you need to use time to remember what you forgot.[210] For as long as you are fixated on trying to make your projection of a world meaningfully important, for that long will peace of mind elude you. Only in dis-relation with Self could you not

---

[209] *Symbols of Power in Philosophy p247-251*
[210] *Symbols of Power in Metaphysics p98-109*

know this. Only in dis-relation do you seek for a remedy in a place it cannot be found.

Your miracle is the forgiving or undoing of a violation you thought you did to your Eternal Self. Now your journey becomes the forgiving or undoing of the self you are not as you forgive your perceptions of those you thought did you wrong. This is what a collapse of time is all about. There is a place above the dust of time waiting for your acceptance. *Accept your sense of failure as nothing more than a mistake in who you are* … Oh yes, you have to take everyone with you.[211]

*Transformational Psychotherapy is a reminder that reality is not yours to select.*

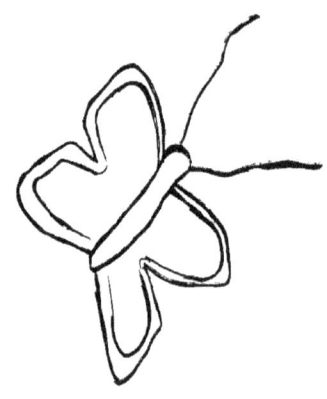

---

[211] *Symbols of Power in Metaphysics p200*

# Depression: A Sense of Deprivation

*There is a disappointment about wanting something from the world that it can't give*

### The Frustrated Learner

Speaking succinctly, you are not the body you think you are. If you believe yourself to be a body, you will experience depression. Because you are eternal, trying to find peace of mind in your striving for achievements, will make you a frustrated learner. The belief that the body is an end in itself is a set-up to try to achieve goals you cannot achieve. As a result, you will experience depression.

*Watch out now, take care*
*Beware of the thoughts that linger*
*Winding up inside your head*
*The hopelessness around you*
*In the dead of night*
*Beware of sadness*
George Harrison
Beware Of Darkness

### Deprivation as a Fiction

Those who perceive themselves as inadequate always feel deprived. Any concept of deprivation is an illusion because your inheritance in Source will never suffer loss. Only you can deprive yourself of anything. Therefore, your search for completion through all the forms your world offers become a series of a shallow happiness and defeats. What else could you find when you deprive yourself of the remembrance of what you are in Source? Ego baits you with a pleasurably fleeting moment of elated success. You try to savor this fleeting satisfaction through distractions the world offers. But your lack of fulfillment always finds you in the end. There is a frustration of striving that brings on the sadness of despair.

The world is depressing because it is faced with an impossible learning situation … to find a "you" in a place you are not. You are not alone in your dilemma because everybody else is in their own dream of striving for distractions to deny their predicament. Your process of self-actualization through the world becomes an impossible task because what you learn about a "you" you are not, becomes a series of meaningless lessons of hardship to nowhere. That is what "one step forward and one step back" is all about. Magical thinking and all its forms towards an evolving you is your false hope; your leap of faith; your religious zeal.

## Allow

*When you perceive yourself as a body*
*You will experience depression*

Because you are not the body you think you are there is a way through.

1) You are not being asked to give anything up. To view loss as real in your process of transformation is a battle ground. A sabotage to your transformation.

2) By turning the tables on depression, you allow it to become your reminder that you have been trying to learn an impossible lesson. Rather than bury your discomfort or find distractions to occupy your time, patiently stop and rest in the acceptance to be where you are. With acceptance, you will find that place in the mud, that place in a swarm of mosquitoes, where there is solace. *It is in*

*your mind, not your body.* At first, it will take some effort. It is hard to make any effort about anything while you are in your depression. But with just a little effort, you will find that place. "How do you know," you ask. "I know because *it is already there, in your mind."* Once you find that place of solace, it will always be there when you need it. Because you are everything you need, that place is waiting for you to remember. You don't find it because you have been busy running from one distraction to another medicating your discomfort.[212] It's OK to experience your own pain so you can find your way through.

3) Because reality is not yours to select, *your only goal* is to remember what you are in Source. "Having is Being," is not understood until you experience it directly. To not understand this is to be involved in trying to serve contradicting goals that the world offers for your happiness. This causes you deep distress and great depression. Therefore, be determined to remember that what you want today is peace of mind. This is the only goal that will unify your mind towards healing.

---

[212] Because your mind is not focused but distracted outside, it cannot heal itself. The placebo effect works because your mind seems to need something outside of itself for healing. In one form or another, everything the world is, is a placebo effect to heal your dis-relation. In other words, in one form or another, everyone is on a medication. There is nothing wrong with taking medications. In the end, you will find it to be mind over matter. In the meantime, everything that seems to be outside of your mind is an opportunity to focus on a unified goal for peace of mind. *Reflections for The Wandering Mind p24-35; Symbols of Power in Philosophy p148-151*

## Summary

*You are sad because you are not fulfilling your function in Source.* Allow an open mind and you will be given direction back to the "You" you have always been. Your work is to interrupt judging anything. You want to do this because reality is not for you to select. If you want to argue with me about this then why do you keep selecting opportunities to feel miserable? The curriculum presented in this book is in direct opposition to the world's curriculum. The world teaches you to be a better judge for decision. This curriculum teaches that to relinquish judgment is your journey to freedom, for it is your beliefs about a world untrue that has enslaved you.[213] Whatever you decide, reality is not yours to select. Your life experiences continually bring you to this lesson. As you teach it, you begin to experience *the incredible lightness of being.*

> *If you are depressed you are living in the past*
> *If you are anxious you are living in the future*
> *If you are at peace you are living in the present*
> Lao Tzu

*Transformational Psychotherapy is not about loss. It is about exchange. There is an appreciation beyond how you feel when you ask to see only that.*

---

[213] For those who say, "You have to have judgments to survive or to operate in the world," are those who believe their judgments protect them. This book suggests that your judgments feed your fears! *Symbols of Power in Metaphysics p15*

# Fence Building:
# The Dynamics of Personal Boundaries

*Every boundary you use to limit, limits you from the
experience of what "You Are."*[214] *Namaste*

## Introduction

You are Creations effect. This makes your mind the
most powerful thing in the universe. Because of this power,
you can make an error in a thought and experience a world
untrue to what you are in Source. In denial of that fact, you
think you are an effect of the world you made.[215] These
witnesses to the fact that you do not know what you are,
and you do not know that you do not know this. That is
why you are trying to find meaning in the effect of your
miscreation. However, the power of your mind to can also
undo what it made.

## Identity Confusion as Justification

It is easily said "We have boundaries because we don't
trust other people." But actually, we have boundaries
because we don't know what we are, lost in a dream of
miscreation. You are not in a body. The body is outside of
you. This body that requires food, clothing and shelter,
also needs protection from aggression. The issue of
aggression disguised as instinctual is mentally caused.
Mind, lost to an external world as projected, reacts out of

---

[214] *Symbols of Power in Metaphysics p33-47*

[215] In his philosophy, Martin Heidegger uses the term
"thrownness" (Geworfenheit) to describe the fact that humans
are "thrown" into the world, meaning we are not self-created but
rather exist as beings already situated in a world with a pre-
existing history and culture, without our own choice or input.

fear of not knowing. Displacing what you are for what you are not is an enormous task to maintain. This compensation allows your mind the justification to accumulate goods, territory, bodies, etc., in an attempt to protect the body from hurt, pain, deprivation and death. Your safety from threat and loss for the body is an insatiable fiction. A fiction because your mind through a body experiences threat, pain and loss on a daily basis.

Your mind does not need protection from the ephemeral because it is not part of its ever-changing nature. Your instinctual experiences belong to the body, not to your mind. Your interpretations of the instinctual gives you experiences of trauma to undo. Life in a body involves grieving. I am not telling you to deny the instinctual. I am telling you to become sensitive to differentiate between the two. What belongs to Mother Earth is your body. What belongs to you is the Power of your mind! And thought is a function of mind, not a fact.

## Do Boundaries Work?

Boundaries as a means to protect have always been the opportunity for violation. Your world is witness to this fact. Nationalistic boundaries of pride are opportunities for war. Cultural and ethnic identities to identify separateness can be slandered and offended. Racial boundaries continuously see prejudice and injustice. Personal boundaries for safety find violation of personal space. And legions of endless verbal and physical behaviors are deemed "inappropriate."

The world is a place of boundaries for safety and yet, no safety is to be found. That is because the world is a boundary keeping you from finding "You." Individuality is all about ego survival. The less secure you are about a self you are not, the more boundaries you will need, to protect/defend your self-deception. This complication makes it difficult for you to see its nothingness.

People with a diffused sense of self, may need help in developing boundaries. Those who are easily influenced are taught rules of conduct as guidelines for decision making. This may help one regulate personal space for protection against violation. It also defines limits out of fear of who they are not. I am not saying don't have boundaries. Have all the boundaries you think you need, and remember:

*Boundaries are a frame of mind that life is to be lived in fear*

Rules of conduct can guide one in establishing social limits and responsible relational interaction. However, these rules cannot be used consistently across the board because no two situations are alike. Even the most ardent defender of boundaries must accept the fact that there always exceptions.

Do boundaries really work? That depends on what they are used for. If their use is for "temporary" clarification of verbal and physical space, they can be helpful. If they are used to justify an insatiable need for protection, they become your prison walls.

*Every king has an army and he still lives behind walls*

## Boundaries as a Measure of Safety

*Boundaries used to protect you from fear*
*Are the reminders that you live in fear*

Boundaries do measure safety. The more you have the less safe you feel. That's because boundaries are made out of fear, to keep fear out! Every boundary you have represents a fear you hold in your mind. Fear has not been kept out. It has been denied expression through projection. Be it psychological boundaries or a physical wall, they are the result of fear. What needs protection is weak because it needs protection. However, what is weak is not what you are. Strange it is, that you made what you are not, out of fear to protect you from your awareness of the safety of what "You Are."

Every lock you place on your door to keep fear out is a lock you place to keep you hostage. And no matter how many or how strong your boundaries are, you still feel violated! Fear denied its expression hangs as pictures on the walls of the home you built for protection. You may be able to protect the body for little bits of time, but you delude yourself if you think you can protect the body from time itself. The time you take through all your little designs to protect your body from the ultimate fear of death, is the time you use to avoid living.

## Boundaries and Interpersonal Interaction

*Ever-changing differences make everything illusive. When you are ready, boundaries are conventions waiting to be transcended.*

Relationships based on the level of change, are transient. In this ever-changing shadow-land, it is easy to interpret situations as experiences of fear. Violation is the result. Trust becomes an issue that cannot be resolved on the physical level because that is the level where stability is an illusion. No wonder you feel violated. You are trying to find stability in a place it cannot be found.

All minds that identify as a body will experience violation. To be in dis-relation with self is the primary violation. All other violations are symbolic to this. You don't lack trust because you are in a body dance with other body dancers stepping on each other's feet. You are in a body dance stepping on each other's feet because you lack trust. [216] How could you trust anybody when you are trying to trust a "you" you are not? Of course fear reigns just under the conscious level to be fenced in and tamed! To not know "You" engenders fear and needs an enormous amount of attention and resources to defend. Building fences to keep others out, keeps you out.

Boundaries are out of a lack of trust to protect your belief that you are weak and can be attacked and hurt. It is true, the "self" you made is weak and easily hurt; the justification for boundaries. Relational interactions without trust lack depth. Because you do not know "You," you look outside for a security you can never find and find violation. Your continued attempts to join on a physical level of interaction reflect your desire to remember something more than the fleeting body you are not. Namaste.

A mind free of the instinctual impulses of a body is free of violation. Moderation and delayed gratification are good places to start. Beyond the ephemeral is the joining of minds. Because it is an experience that transcends the ephemeral it is beyond ever-changing boundaries of shifting sand that seek out violation.[217]

---

[216] Don't confuse cause and effect here.

[217] Selective perception says you find what you are looking for. Boundaries find violation because they were made out of a perceived violation.

## Thoughts as Self-Defeating Boundaries

*Once there were: Sacred grounds to hunt*
*Sacred hills for vision quests*
*Sacred mounds to bury, honor and remember those who walked*
*before us*
*Money will buy a fence line through anything*
*This is because you do not understand natural boundaries*

The boundaries of Mother Earth have a natural reason.[218] Even so, the temporal order of things has no limit over you. But your thoughts do. You can never undo the violation of rape. But you can undo your view of that incident to find resolution. Allow your client space to see it in a way to free themselves.

Just like the earth that needs time to undo violation, this your client will do within the opportunity of their unfolding. When they are ready, they will look beyond their limits of self-definition. Because the temporal order of things is a temptation to limit your thoughts to it, it will be your thoughts that will free you from the limits you have designed.

A locked door may keep someone out but a thought that violates your peace of mind will torture you behind your locked door ... for as long as you choose! In other words, that which you limit, you hold in your mind! You are the maker of the monster you choose to limit as "powerful" within your own world view.[219] What ever happened to the old adage; *Sticks and stones can break my bones but words can never hurt me.*

---

[218] *Symbols of Power in Metaphysics p48-59*
[219] *Symbol of Power in Metaphysics p110-118*

**Orientation Exercise**

If your life is full of boundaries (rules of conduct) and you still live in fear, your boundaries are not working.

1) Sit down and make a list of all the boundaries you can think of having. For one day, carry your list with you adding to it as you find yourself using a boundary. Physical boundaries are psychological in cause.

Fear is a reminder that you are using a boundary, or that you need a boundary. If in doubt about a boundary, write it down anyway. This is the collecting of information part, not the analyzing part.

2) Using patience, look over each item on your list asking yourself "Does this particular boundary protect me from fear?" Underline those boundaries that do not. These are the ones that don't work.

3) For each boundary you underlined, ask yourself "What am I afraid of?" and write it down beside the boundary. Be honest.

4) Your willingness to look at your fear is movement beyond words. Be patient. Take one step at a time and time will be your friend. If you need help with this, talk about it with someone you trust.

5) Eventually you will ask yourself "Do I need this boundary anymore? Have I outgrown it? Is it self-limiting?" When you think that way about it, you are moving beyond the fear of letting a boundary go.

**Beyond Boundaries**

*I understand now – that boundaries between noises and sound - are conventions. All boundaries are conventions - waiting to be transcended. One may transcend any convention - if only one can first conceive of doing so.*

*Moments like this – I can feel your heart beating - as clearly as I feel my own … And I know that separation is an illusion.*
*My life extends far beyond the limitations of me.*
From the movie "Cloud Atlas"

Everything and every "body" are in a state of flux. Boundaries set in stone is a rigidity that limits your expression of the flow of life unfolding before you. The violating of your own boundaries is potential. Your contradictions of thought, give you inconsistent behaviors that sabotage your ability to have meaningful relationships.[220] And to be in fear of violating a boundary is to fear life. What safety and freedom of mind is in that?

*Now I've always been the kind of a person that doesn't like to trespass … But sometimes you just find yourself over the line.*
Bob Dylan
Brownsville Girl

If you feel the need to use boundaries, use them. But don't use them at the expense of your creative authenticity. Discard them as you unfold into remembering the strength "You Are" beyond a vulnerable body. You will experience a sense of freedom in this.

## Summary

*Boundaries are mental limits that box you in*
*They keep you from knowing your real self*

Any wall you build, you build to limit you from the expression of life's journey. Ask yourself honestly "If true safety is not to be found in the boundaries of the ever-

---

[220] Cognitive dissonance

changing, where is it to be found?"[221] When fear no longer clouds your view, you will clearly see your choice for freedom rather than calculate moves to protect a self you are not.

*Transformational Psychotherapy is about exchanging your limits as strengths. For every boundary you use to limit, you can use as a stepping stone to your freedom ... beyond the rules of the world. Namaste*

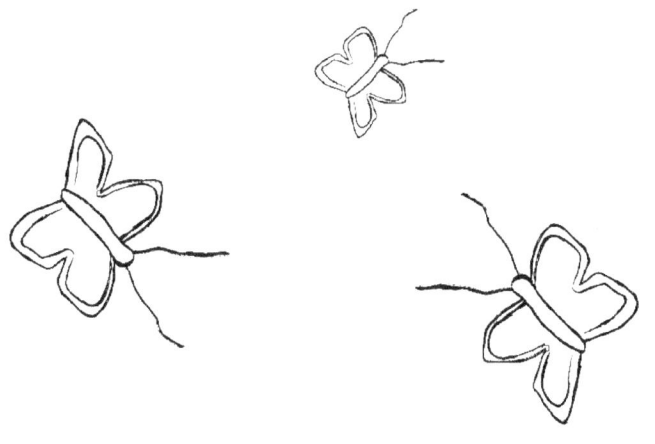

---

[221] The fact of the matter is that the laws of how the world works are not governed by the rules made to manage the world. This is because the rules made to govern the world are continually being re-made to manage chaos. You know the rules made to manage chaos do not work because violation occurs. The rules of the world merely mask its appearance of chaos. And through this you are to selectively perceive what? *Symbols of Power in Philosophy p238-241*

# The Dance of the Resistant Client

*The resistant client is the one who fears change.*
*Who among us does not harbor resistance?*

## What is a Resistant Client?

Because you perceive what you project and deny that you projected what you perceive, you are lost in the loop of a shadow dance of confusing fear. From this perspective, for security's sake you need to think that reality is for you to select. There is no room for error or creative unfolding. But there is a rigidity of limiting choices for security's sake to resist change.

## The Trap

A closed mind wants to believe that the future and the present will be the same. This establishes a seemingly stable state that is usually an attempt to counteract an underlying fear that the future will be worse than the present. This fear inhibits the tendency to question at all. Stability means resisting change which lends itself to a rigid lifestyle. Perceptions of uncertainty are avoided by selecting only those views that do not threaten your clients' fictions of how the world "should" work. This is what is called a rigid ideology of how life events "should be." Their greatest need is for them to be able to question their fictions. But their fear of being out of control prevents questioning.

Those around them give in to their need to control, to avoid everything becoming an argument. The perk for allowing the controller to take over is that the controller does all the planning. Somewhere in the process, the resistant clients need for control elicits confrontations or push-backs from those who feel caught in the web of the resistant clients need to control. Yet, their resistance towards you or whatever it is, is not about you. It is about their internal battle through a divided mind[222] of needing to be right. This circular trap of reasoning looks like this:

1)   Self-destructive attitudes, beliefs and behaviors are inconsistent to the point where it causes family, social and legal trouble.  Lack of resolution makes for a history of unresolved conflict.

2) This history allows for habitual defensive or explaining behaviors as a maneuver to protect them from the idea that they might be wrong. These self-defeating maneuvers keep your client from looking within to resolve their inconsistency.

3) These blaming evasions elicit probes of intervention from others.

4) These probes are interpreted as threatening to your client's ego because they bring into focus your clients' fictions of life that do not work.

5) Out of fear, a defensive posture of resistance or retaliation seems justified.

---

[222] Cognitive dissonance is mental stress experienced by an individual who holds two or more contradictory beliefs or values at the same time, performs an action that is contradictory to one or more beliefs or values, or is confronted by new information that conflicts with existing beliefs or values. If you've ever told a lie and felt uncomfortable because you see yourself as honest, then you've experienced cognitive dissonance. Leon Festinger's theory of cognitive dissonance (1957) focuses on how humans strive for internal consistency. An individual who experiences inconsistency (dissonance) tends to become psychologically uncomfortable, and is motivated to try to reduce this dissonance, as well as actively avoid situations and information likely to increase it.

Your client's solution will come from within. The answers are internal, not external. If an answer shows up in the world, it's a symbolic solution to your client's problem. As a spiritual dilemma, there is no answer heard from within as long as the mind is cluttered with controlling thoughts.

## The Issue of Authority

*Take a moment to rest your mind in meditation. In this moment, can you feel a resistance to go inside? Distractions abound.*

Client resistance may be labeled as an authority issue or any other issue you fancy, yet the fact remains; to deny the truth that you are in dis-relation with Source is a conflict that involves enormous energy to maintain. The world you made becomes a battle ground to resist the truth.

*Looking for clarity in a cloudy pool will only result in a cloudy solution. If you assume what the solution should be, anything that brings relief will do.*

Your client needs to believe that reality is theirs to select. This is their primary fiction. This is why they resist any information that contradicts their thinking. A a closed mind out of fear of future possibilities will not allow for an alternative view. They will have all the facts of why their view is the right one. They have practiced thinking this way as a way of safety. This is the history of a frustrated learner. This is the story of the repeat offender.

Every mind has a moment when it naturally looks beyond its self-defeating world view. Therapist, patience is called for to pace yourself with helping your client unravel their fiction as to how they think life "should" be. Your attempt to try to help your client move on before they are ready, will be a battle ground of conflict, your belief that reality is yours to select.

## Denial: The Fear of Change

*Because of the split, you do not recognize your resistance at the most fundamental level*

Your first encounter with the illusion of change was *a fearful experience* because it involved the denial of what "You Are" in Source (dis-relation). That is why any change since then has a fearful undertone to resist and protect the belief of what you are not.

A closed mind resists future possibilities because it fears it will be different than the present misery that your client has adjusted too. But then your client might say, "Are you kidding me?! I want my future to be different than my present misery." Yet, they won't change the thinking that gave them their present misery. It's called the left hand not allowed to know what the right hand is doing. It is their failed attempt to serve two masters.[223]

Because the world is ever-changing instability, your choices in the world are always between two competing illusions. There is no choice in this, just delay. The real choice is will you continue to invest in the temporal, or decide to start your journey towards your Eternal Self?

Pseudo-ego's compromise for its survival is a smoke and mirror resolution of magical thinking. "You can be both eternal and temporal," ego whispers. However, there has been no solution in this thinking. Your anxiety

---

[223] *Symbols of Power in Philosophy p252*

remains, buried in fuzzy beliefs contrary to living life on life's terms. Your client's conflict of dis-relation is a buried resistance seen in numerous forms of defensive avoidance.

1) Minimizing may admit there's a problem, but at the cost of making it seem less serious by comparison. "It's not really that bad" or "Everybody's doing it."

2) Rationalizing is talking to justify a weak position. You know the position is weak because it involves lots of talk. "Let me explain ..." or "Yes but ..."

3) Diversion is to change the subject. Be aware of "What about you?" as a client's way of redirecting back at you.

4) Hostility is a reaction out of feeling threatened. It also intimidates people into backing off. "You don't understand me" can be a brush off of righteous indignation. Conflict in the therapeutic setting will be one-sided if the therapist does not get caught up in counter-transference.[224]

5) To withdraw or comply is the most difficult form of resistance to work with. You don't know what you are working with, except for the fact that your clients are clients because they have fictions that cause them conflict.

So they lie, comply, deny and resist. And to confront a resistant client will come to a blowout. So instead, you reframe with your client a view of a situation that their fiction will allow.

*To recognize that your client is a poor listener, gives the therapist room for patience*

If the basic definition of learning is change, and clients are resistant to change, the client must see learning as a

---

[224] Counter-transference is when a therapist transfers feelings onto the patient, such as reacting angrily to a client's resistance.

painful loss and therefore something to avoid. But there's been no gain, just the repetition of the same mistake in different situational forms, resulting in mental anguish. The primary fiction here is that change involves pain. Because complexity of form does not imply complexity of content, the therapist works with the client's seemingly individual situations in a way (reframe) that shows them their common solution. And that solution is a change of mind about everything your client thought the world was about.

Although there is no pain with learning the truth about "You," the therapist's primary task is to help the client reframe their symbols of pain as messages of gain (turning blocks into steps). This *approach,* easy to listen to, instills hope and motivation for change. For example; for the chemically dependent person, *avoidance therapy* is to admit they have to give up or sacrifice the loss of a dysfunctional life style. Now they must grieve the loss, the change, the letting go of a lifestyle they so hard tried to protect against invasion.

*Approach therapy* reminds your client that they have the opportunity to live a new life towards peace of mind. It involves giving up the suffering road to hell for the road to peace of mind. Now you can rejoice.

## Learning is Change

*You are Eternal. To experience the temporal you are not, is a threatening vulnerability that needs defense. All resistance is a defense against the truth of what "You Are."*

Your client will choose within the limits they have set for themselves. When they are ready, they will learn the lesson they need to learn. Seed planters know there are factors beyond their control that contribute to a plant's growth and care.

As passerby's, therapists' plant seeds by:

1) Keeping it simple.

2) Being genuine. Relax, be who you are. Talk to your client about your struggles and how you deal with them in a way that teaches your client. It's a non-threatening way to show them something different.

3) When you don't get involved in counter-transference with your client, you can discuss and describe their thinking that is counter-productive. Then when your client slips into it you can easily say "You're doing it." There is no need to argue against their resistance. Describing their verbal behavior keeps the focus on your client. Repetition is their best teacher.[225]

4) Rather than focus on a fiction they resist changing, help your client identify the fears of change that feed their resistance. For example, if you have a goal that your client should read a letter in group, or that they are to make amends, and they refuse, instead of coaxing them, join with them on what is going on that they can't or won't do it. The behavior is not relevant. The thinking is relevant because the thinking is the *cause* of the behavior which is the *effect*. *Healing always involves a shift in perception from effect to cause.* This shift is about responding to what's being presented in the moment ... beyond the therapist's and client's agenda.

5) Remain available (open minded) for joint creative endeavors. It's OK to interrupt their self-defeating going justifications.[226] Are you OK with them being mad at you?

---

[225] *Symbols of Power in Metaphysics p20-22; The Way Home p171*
[226] I am not saying there is no place for confronting or redirecting. Everything is an opportunity for you and your client to work

6) Be creative. Because reality is not yours to select, you don't have to be right about anything. Be quick to apologize. You lose nothing and gain trust. As a metaphor, learn to dance with your client.

## Summery

You plant seeds, as their solution awaits their acceptance from within. The client that is ready will make the change.

---

things out. They came to you for a reason. Your contract with them is more encompassing than you think.

Therapist;

> *We're playing those mind games together*
> *Pushing the barriers planting seeds*
> *Playing the mind guerrilla*
> *Chanting the Mantra peace on earth*
> *We all been playing those mind games forever*
> *Some kinda druid dudes lifting the veil*
> *Doing the mind guerrilla*
> *Some call it magic the search for the grail*
> John Lennon
> Mind Games

Increasing motivation for change in your client is all that a therapist need do to guarantee change. For change in motivation is a change of mind.[227]

*Transformational Psychotherapy is a joint venture, a process of helping your client to question their reality.*
*Namaste*

---

[227] Remember Principle #3 p39.

# Descalation Techniques

*Trying to reason with anger is fruitless*
*To align with it is not*

**Objectives:**
    1) Identify what escalates patients
    2) Identify what techniques d-escalates patients
    3) Discuss the application of these techniques

**What Escalates Patients?**
    Milieus marked by rigid, authoritarian or controlling staff often result in incidents of acting out behaviors. When you find yourself in a situation where the client is getting irritable, verbally loud, swearing, etc., they may *appear* as aggressive. Yet, they *perceive themselves* as being threatened.
    1) Their needs or desired goals are frustrated
    2) They perceive others as not listening to them
    3) Their way of functioning seems ineffective

**How to Help Reduce the Perception of Threat**
    1) Understand that aggression occurs when people feel threatened.
    2) Allow them physical space because it is easy to interpret closeness as a threat.
    3) Is your body language (posture) open (relaxed) or closed?
    4) Is your verbal language directing to control the situation?
    5) Empathy is about listening to their perceived plight and feeding it back.

6) Be agreeable to the idea that whatever it is, you do not have to be right and the client does not need to be corrected. This helps you avoid verbal power struggles that escalate.

7) Help the client refocus on dealing with the "here and now" rather than "injustices" of the past.

8) If it is a staff member that is perceived as the threat, they may need to leave the situation.

9) Don't take it personally.

   a. Sometimes we can take words and behaviors personally. What immediate attitudes, feelings and behaviors tell us when we are doing this?

   b. What are your personal vulnerabilities?

   c. What moral or ethical issues do you have that may influence your work?

10)  Pick your battles.

   a. Don't get caught up with confronting irrelevant or minor issues.

   b. Don't get caught up confronting the client's attitude, language and dress. These only feed the fire of frustration and anxiety.

11)  When the client begins to calm down, you can use humor as a means to reduce the tension of the situation. Not everybody agrees with the use of humor.

## Discussion

Before we talk about de-escalation techniques, let's talk about what escalates a client.

1) First off, they're angry and unpredictable.

2) What behaviors verbal and nonverbal, would the client be demonstrating?

3) What escalates you as a therapist?

4) What are the fictions your client is operating under. You know they are operating under fictions. How do you know? Their angry.

## Principle

*It is empowering for the patient when they are involved in making decisions about their care*

It doesn't matter if the client is wrong, deluded or in denial. The immediate goal is to de-escalate the anger. Aligning with your client to de-escalate would be lines like "I hear what you are saying. I'm sorry about that. Let's see what we can do about it. I may need your help."

## Summary
1) Provide physical space/distance
2) Present an open posture
3) Lower voice and speak slowly
4) Empathize, identify with them. "I can see how that would make anybody angry."
5) Be agreeable. "You may be right about that?
6) Buy time for them to cool down. "Let's see what I can do about this …
7) Engage them in problem solving with you "… but I'm going to need your help."
8) Be sensitive to the possible use of humor as they cool down. It releases tension.

# Co-Dependency: Life on the Outside

*Co-dependency is the belief you can find happiness in something or someone outside of yourself*

## Introduction

The definition, that co-dependency is the belief you can find happiness in something or someone outside of yourself is a leveler. There are no mixed messages here. It is a spiritual dilemma of dis-relation; the dis-relation of trying to heal the split from outside of you in a place it cannot be done. To be in dis-relation is to experience life outside of everything you are. All of your investments in the world are co-dependent because in some way they are investments to establish what you are not. They are witnesses of self-deception, defending the illusive experience of a world of bodies. Thus, the world is either delay to be lost in ever-changing shadows, or the world is an opportunity of people, places and things to remind you where the solution is. It is in the healing of your mind as split.

There really is nothing more to say, but for the sake of repetition, I will say it again, and then again.[228]

## What Co-Dependency is not

*I do not deny that social conditioning happens*
*That it is the cause of anything significant is the fiction*[229]

---

[228] *The Way Home p171; Symbols of Power in Metaphysics p22, 30-32; Reflections for the Wandering Mind p36-42*
[229] *Symbols of Power in Philosophy p71-78*

Co-dependency is not a result of social conditioning. Co-dependency is the result of a personal dis-relation with self, played out as a search, in a world that isn't, looking for a you, that you are not. That is why your search is a self-defeating frustration.

That social conditioning occurs, I do not deny. You do learn language, culture and social niceties of "appropriate" behavior. However, social conditioning is one of the many crafty ways you are taught to look at the world to find out why you are the way you are … while never finding out exactly why you are the way you are. Social conditioning is not a cause but is played out as an effect of your dis-relation with Source. Pseudo-ego would like to complicate the simple so its nothingness is obscure to you. Let it not distract you from where your journey lies. It lies in forgiving yourself for what you thought you knew about you.

## Focusing Outside

Because your mind is split, there seems to be an outer and inner world. The making of your outer world is your attempt to deny the inner as your cause of the outer. The co-dependent puts their life on hold to focus on the life of other people, places, events and things. The adjustment is motivated by the fiction that the co-dependent's happiness is based on changing or securing someone or something outside of themself. This motivation is out of an attempt to find happiness and avoid fear. Yet, fear reigns. Because the co-dependent's focus is outside of themself in an attempt to find security, they are more concerned about trying to control people and events. They are not focused on dealing with their own thoughts and feelings, except as it relates to how someone else can be for them to be happy. "If only they would be different, things would be different." Or, it would be "What I could do for you," which in self-deception is actually "what I can do for you so I can be happy."[230] Co-dependents are attracted to try and save "needy" people. Needy people are not givers; they are takers who in the beginning may seem like givers yet to let co-dependent people down. This external focus for the co-dependent is the foundation for the drama and martyrdom.

## Your Desire for Relationship

Most of us want to be in relationship with someone. This search is symbolic of your search to heal your dis-relation with Source. But all too often you find conflict. If it is true that you are in dis-relation with you, you will find conflict of dis-relation with others. For any relationship to thrive, blame cannot be an option.

1) To be in dis-relation with Self is to not know your identity with Source.

2) To not know "You" engenders fear.

3) To be in fear is to experience an underlying anxiety that is intolerable because it prevents you from your natural disposition of peace of mind.

4) To get rid of this underlying anxiety, you try to project it out of your mind.

5) To project is to perceive. But because *no thought leaves its source,* all you do is bury it at the unconscious level (disassociation).[231]

6) Because you made an "out there" to get rid of what you do not like, you must defend against it.

---

[230] Love does not give to receive because it already has everything it is. Co-dependency is a giving to get out of lack.

[231] *Symbols of Power in Philosophy p252*

7) To defend against it is to make it real.

8) To make "out there" real, becomes the battle ground you think that resolution is to be found.

9) Because you are in dis-relation with Source and therefore with yourself, you are a stranger in a strange land. You experience abandonment, betrayal, anger, guilt, depression and fear (to name a few), rather than the love you seek.

10) In your conflict of an "out there," you try to find resolution through people, places and things as your means to find peace. This never-ending conflict, is attempted to be resolved through politics, wars, economics, technology, psychology, education, religion, altruism, etc.[232] But the peace you want cannot be found "out there." This has been your experience over and over again as witnessed through the annals of history. There's a lot of frustration buried on the unconscious level, out of reach of resolution.

"Out there" becomes the place to live, the place to stabilize personal as well as international relations for security and peace. So, you go searching endlessly for that piece of negotiated reality, for a satisfaction that constantly eludes your grasp. But there is always something out there that brings you discontent. As long as your mind is split, nothing but conflict will be your effect.[233]

---

[232] There is nothing wrong with altruism. You just won't find release through trying to fix chaos. *The Way Home p115-120; Symbols of Power in Philosophy p196-236*

[233] *The Way Home p101-102*

## The Hand of Betrayal

*To be dependent on the world for a validation you will never find
is the self-betrayal of a frustrated learner*

Because the co-dependents dis-relation is with themself, whatever changes they make on the outside for resolution will not appease the dis-relation on the inside. So, an unsuspecting passerby can be blamed for your misery for not fulfilling their obligation to you. Yet, you set yourself up for expecting something from another that was not for them to give. You know it was not for them to give because they did not give it. No one makes you happy. But you can share your happiness with another.

You look for peace in the world because you can't find it in yourself. That is why trying to solve the world's problems is an endless endeavor of trying to fix the symptom rather than the cause.[234] Making truces out of diplomacy and marriage, is as old as the world ... and always temporary. To blame another for not fulfilling their obligation is your avoidance of the betrayal you did to yourself first.

> *We see the world wrong and say it deceived us*
> Tagore

You have had many opportunities to gladden yourself, and have refused many of those opportunities. Unless you change your mind about the purpose of the world, you will perceive conflict. Remember, your mind is cause, the world is its effect.

---

[234] *The Way Home p115-120*

## The Mental Battle Ground

Because you are everything you need, it is a fiction to believe you can find happiness in something or someone outside of you. Therefore, your client's attempt to look outside for what they can't find inside, is a projection of lack. Their search for peace, love and acceptance is doomed to fail at the whims of an ever-changing perception in an ever-changing world of uncertain outcomes. If projection makes perception and you project the effects of your dis-relation, you will be looking for connection in a dis-connected world. Not that you can't at times find some fleeting semblance of connection, but if you don't find it in yourself first, they are just that, fleeting. It's the old bait and switch technique pseudo-ego uses for you to seek and not find.

Clarify with your client their self-defeating sabotage of trying to reach an impossible goal. The bigger picture suggests that all these issues are not failures but opportunities to forgive your misperceptions … to bring you closer to journey's end.

It's not that your relationships did not work. It's that you gave them the wrong goals. The route you took to find love was the route you were supposed to take. Why? Because you took that route. And you took it because that was the route you were supposed to take. This is a non-dualistic statement of non-judgment, accepting what happened because it happened. "What else was supposed to happen?" you ask your client.

*If you understand, things are the way they are. If you don't understand, things are the way they are*
Zen Proverb

When your client begins by saying "Well I should have ..." you interrupt them with "That's not true because that's not what happened." Be relentless with practicing interrupting your client's hypothetical thinking.[235] That line of thinking is a mental battle ground of non-acceptance, counterproductive to a unified goal for peace of mind.

## Life on the Outside

Your body has a natural relationship to natural surroundings because it is part of it. Because your mind believes it is a body, it seeks meaning and purpose through it. Centered on a body for comfort and security, you believe certain things in the world have to happen to be happy. Because you are not a body, your search through a body and its surroundings is your frustrating experience of "Life on The Outside."

The key principle of Transformational Psychotherapy is that "Having Is Being." In other words, "You are everything you need." But in dis-relation with Source, these words make no sense. Because you do not know what you are, your search to find a "you" in a place it can't be found, is your delay.

That is why co-dependency is the belief that you can find happiness in something or someone outside of the truth of what you already are. It is for you to begin your journey to reclaim your natural state of joy, regardless of what appears to be happening in the world. This is the journey of the Buddha inside of you. Your motivation will be glimpses of joy. The end goal is your reclamation of your natural state of joy.

---

[235] *Symbols of Power in Philosophy p27-34*

## Your Search for Completion

Your search for completion (intimacy/acceptance) exhibits itself in innumerable forms of behavior. The child who has not yet learned to control the impulses for delayed gratification screams "I want what I want and I want it now!" as a temper tantrum for completion. The adolescent's attempt for completion can be a search for acceptance in the form of a peer group with all mannerisms of appearance, looks, behavior and clothing. As always fleeting in form; this year, "leather is in," last year it was "jeans with holes," next year it will be that elusive "something else." One's search for completion may take the form of "the defiant adolescent" for personal identity. An adult's search for completion, not unlike the adolescent's, manifests through a need for security and companionship. This need is the excuse for control through compensations of all sorts. The accumulation of goods beyond reason (hoarding), a work ethic that lacks time to enjoy the fruits of your labor (workaholism), prestige or recognition as tangible forms of perceived power.

All sorts of body obsessions/addictions fall into the category of a co-dependent relationship with a goal for happiness. In a world of form, the hope for completion is always manifest in form. The results are always the same; a fleeting pleasure; a shallow happiness; followed by disappoint and/or pain. Your companions along the path to that "something else" always elusive beyond your grasp are stress, depression and loneliness (alienation). Forgiving yourself for getting lost is your greatest need.

*I've spent my life following things I cannot see*
*And just when I catch up to them*
*They slip away from me*
Steve Earle
You're Still Standing There

## Care-taking's Motivation

No matter how altruistic the form may appear, care-taking always involves your attempt to take care of yourself first. Responding to fix another's emotional pain is an adjustment to avoid feeling your own pain. Your fear of grieving is a powerful fiction motivating you to fix another's pain as a way to avoid the fear of grieving your own pain. This understanding is a reflection of motivation rather than an evaluation of behavior. Understanding motivation rather than getting caught up on the appearances of form (behavior), helps you see a larger therapeutic picture.

To believe that another can bring you the completion you desperately desire is to invite relational disappointment. This is not to say that two lonely souls cannot help each other. But to use another as a device to continue your indulgence in a search for completion where it cannot be found, only invites misery, the perception of betrayal and abandonment. If you do not understand that you are Love, to hear the words "I love you" over and over again, will never be enough.

Even though you decided to put your life on hold for another, it was for you. It will be temptingly easy for you to blame the one who at one time represented your salvation, to now represent your bondage. It may be true that at one time another's charm took you in. But now you can change your mind and break the bind you allowed to tie you up. If frank communication does not accomplish an understanding of mutual respect and personal responsibility in the relationship, the apple cart must be turned over to break the habitual cycle reinforced by fear of loss; the fear of change. Either:

1) Submit to the relationship as it is, or

2) Fight for a relationship of mutual respect or

3) Leave

All these choices involve the fear of change until you transcend the belief that someone must lose.

## Mixed Messages about Co-dependency

Much has been written about co-dependency that falls short of an inclusive understanding. If it is true that by definition *co-dependency is the belief you can find happiness in something or someone outside of yourself*, then nothing the world offers is exempt from a co-dependent relationship. There are no mixed messages here. It is a spiritual dilemma of dis-relation; the dis-relation of trying to heal the split outside of you in a place it cannot be found. Either the world is delay, to be lost in ever-changing shadows. Or the world is a symbol of opportunity through which people, places and things remind you to look within to heal the split.

All therapeutic conversations about securing relationship boundaries and having needs met by another is distraction, displacement, fiction and delay. You either have trust in the process because you are secure in yourself as Love's creation or you don't. Your relationships are based on unconditional love because you understand unconditional love with Source, or you struggle with others in dis-relation trying to get something from them they do not have to give.

To look for completion in a place where it cannot be found is the setup for self-defeating relationships. What another does to you out of their insecurity may not be justifiable. But what you allow out of your own sense of need is not about the other. I am not saying relationships should not have negotiated give and take. I am saying no matter what you think another "should" or "should not do" for your peace of mind, is a set up for blame, justified anger and displaced fear. You might protest by saying that "relationships 'should' have expectations to work. However, your expectations are substitutes for lack of trust. Tell me, what are the chances of a relationship working without trust?

Your commitment to want to transcend this world of ever-changing unfulfilled attachments that are not yours to possess is the commitment to ask "Where is peace to be found?" Forgiving self-betrayal is your means to answer that question. The law of karma says that whatever you give you give to yourself first. You do not have to believe, trust, agree with or love anyone. But whatever you decide, you will experience. You either extend love or try to take love[236] out of the lack of what you think you are. What are you?

## Spiritual Restlessness

Any error about what you think you are brings about a belief that says you lack. A sense of lack about yourself leaves you restless to strive for completion. Those who lack look for completion through their projection of lack … and only find lack. Your search for intimacy/acceptance outside of yourself is a search for what you already have within but refuse to give yourself. Why is the body you inhabit ingratiated and embellished beyond reason?

---

[236] Trying to take or manipulate for love is coercion out of fear … in the name of love to hide the truth of the matter.

Because you see it as your means for completing a bruised ego that you are not.

*The Master has no possessions*
*The more she does for others the happier she is*
*The more she gives to others the wealthier she is*
Lao-tzu
Tao Te Ching #81

This statement is about a spiritual way of life. Joy is not in the outcome. It's in the journey. You have it to give as you walk your way. Your wealth increases as you give because to give is to give to yourself first. This is different than the motivation of giving to get. If you look closely, you find that the Master is one who is detached with love. *She "has no possessions" that she equates her identity with and is therefore free to love without a motivated outcome.* There are no strings in her relationships. She is free to give out of the wealth of what she is in any moment she finds herself in. In other words, she understands that giving is receiving, that having is Being. She lives in a place where cause and effect are always one and the same.

## The Three Demons that Stole Happiness

*There were three demons that came to earth and stole happiness.*

*The first demon said, "I know where we can hide happiness so humankind will not find it. We'll hide it on the highest mountaintop."*

*The other two demons laughed, saying, "They'll find it there."*

*The second demon said, "I know where we can hide happiness so humankind won't find it. We'll hide it in the deepest ocean."*

*The third demon laughed at both of them, saying, "They'll find it there."*

The third demon said, "I know where we can hide happiness and they won't find it until they look everywhere else. They will look into addictions of all sorts to find happiness. They will look into alcohol and drugs. They will look into gambling, sex, eating, and people they can save. They will value above everything else the way they dress, the kind of people they associate with, what others think of them, the kind of job they have, the amount of money they make, the number of things they accumulate, the look of their brand-new vehicle, but they will look here last."

"Guess where that demon hid happiness?" concluded the master.

"Inside of us," the student replied.

"As I said before," the master reminded, "The Kingdom of God is within you."[237]

"In the meantime, the many strive to collect and add pleasure and pain to their wealth of dust, all in the name of happiness."

"And beyond this?" asked a perceptive teacher.

"Not only is the Kingdom of God within you, but your journey through this seemingly body-based life experience has only been to remember that; God did not create the Kingdom for you … you are the Kingdom God created[238]

You can be an atheist and understand that there is something greater than yourself within you that we all share. However, when you believe there is "no exit," eat drink and be merry because tomorrow you will die.[239] Your humanistic ethics are noble but misguided.[240] As the world demonstrates, the one thing history teaches us is we don't learn from it. Only in denial will you continue to try to find solutions in a place where none is to be found.

---

[237] Luke 17:21 (ASV)

[238] *The Way Home p49-52*

[239] 1 Corinthians 15:32

[240] *Symbols of Power in Philosophy p50-68*

The world is an effect of your dis-relation with Self. Everything the world demonstrates is this. As long as you look at the effects for a solution, you will have none. Nor do you have to be religious to understand that the world was made as a projection to hide the fact that you are in dis-relation with yourself. Start there.

*There's a ship waiting in the harbor*
*Waiting to take you home*
*Search the world round about*
*If that's what it takes to figure out*
*You've been searching*
*You've been knocking*
*You've been banging*
*You've been screaming*
*And you've been doing it all*
*At your own back door*
Matt Karayan
Your Own Back Door

## Check List[241]

The following list is about identification, not crafty ways for your ego to see how you have failed, fallen short. When you identify habitual ways of thinking and behaving, you can begin the process of changing them.

Do any of the following statements accurately describe feelings/thoughts you have about someone in your life?

1) My mind is always focused on pleasing you.

2) I must protect you.

3) Most of my energy is spent on solving your problems or on relieving your pain.

---

[241] The checklist is from the EVN video "Understanding Codependency;" Web:edvidnet.com

4) Any good feelings that I have about myself come from being liked by you.

5) Most of my actions are actually reactions to your actions.

6) I am always giving to you, but you never give to me.

7) My own interests are no longer important. Instead, I try to share your interests.

8) My social circle has become much smaller.

9) Sometimes, I ignore my own values to please you. you.

10) I don't know what I want.

11) Your opinion is more important to me than any opinion of my own.

12) I feel your anger. If you are angry, it's my fault.

13) I fear rejection.

## Give It Up

If a number of these statements describe your relationship with others, you can begin to break the cycle by acknowledging your role in the relationship and decide to give up the habit of *trying* to control other people. You are not being asked to give up control. That you do not have. You are being asked to give up *the illusion of control.*

When you center your life on someone else, you lose your sense of self and are no longer in a place to be of help to anyone, especially yourself. Trying to step in and do for someone what they can do for themselves is not a helpful friend for yourself or them. Taking back your life involves releasing unhealthy attachments. Become clear on what you believe and feel. Let your relationships become ones that allow everyone involved the opportunity to give. Then you can remember to experience your relationships out of love rather than coercion out of fear, in the name of love.

That you do things because "otherwise it won't get done" is a justification to defend your agenda out of fear about how you think things "should" be for your happiness. Obsession with another person, habitually assigning blame, self-neglect, nagging and manipulative behaviors are the results. There is no relationship in this, just symptoms of dis-relation with Source.

## Orientation Exercise I

This exercise is not about identifying how you fell short (personal guilt). This is an exercise in identifying how you attempt to take care of yourself, and to evaluate whether or not it works.

1) What behaviors do you do for others? List each one. Do you feel resentful; unappreciated? How do you feel? List them.

2) What would happen if you discontinued or changed those behaviors? List them. How might you feel? List them. Don't forget fear.

3) Compare your list of #1 with your list of #2. Is it a damned if you do, damned if you don't set up? You may feel used, abused and anger towards someone. Allow it, it comes with the territory.

4) You may feel deceived. It is true, you have been deceived. But remember, to be deceived is to deceive yourself first! This idea may not be popular with you, but to own it is the first step towards emancipation. Taking responsibility for your own choices is the first step towards self-empowerment.

5) You can use your anger as a force to make the changes you need to make to break the cycle. I said the choices you need to make! The choices they need to make is none of your business! What changes do you need to make? List

them. Your fear will be out of what might happen or how another might respond. You are not in charge of outcomes; you never have been. Get there!

Stay here as long as you need to before you go on. If you need support, ask. It will always be there when you ask.

6) Share your list with a friend.

One day, you will find that you are all you need to make informed and empowering decisions about your life. In the meantime, be a passerby.

## Orientation Exercise II

Because completion cannot be found outside of you, none of your attempts will satisfy. But your attempts can be reframed as lessons/opportunities to learn where your completion can be found. If you allow them, they will remind you of your completion beyond your little world of lack.

1) What do you depend on to make you happy? List them.

2) How do you feel when they don't make you happy? List them.

3) According to your second list, does what you depend on to make you happy, also bring you misery?

4) What on your list are you willing to "exchange" in the name of giving up misery? List them on a separate sheet of paper. Misery is all you are being asked to sacrifice. You are not being asked to give up any relationship. You are being asked to give up the fiction that you can control any relationship for your happiness.

5) Look this sheet of paper over. Say good-bye and throw or burn your sheet. This can also be done ceremonially with another.

The real question to ask is "What in this world has given me constant joy?" Be rigorously honest because "Half measures availed us nothing. So now we stand at the turning point."[242]

## Summary

*Seek not outside yourself. For all your pain comes simply from a futile search for what you want, insisting where it must be found. You give the world goals it does not have, and thus do you decide what it is for. The power it has to hurt you, is the power you gave it. To change all this, and open up a road of hope and of release in what appeared to be an endless circle of despair, you need but to decide you do not know the purpose of the world. It is given you to know the truth, and not seek for it outside yourself.*
A Course in Miracles

*Transformational Psychotherapy is the process of reminding you that, in the light of a world of fictional facts used to defend your imagination of a "self" in a world of fictional facts, you can change your view of yourself. You are everything you need. Namaste*

---

[242] Alcoholic Anonymous (paraphrase) p59

Mathias Karayan

*Be the Butterfly dancing on its reflection*

# Relationships: Your Means to Remember Source

*It's not that your relationships did not work*
*It's that you gave them the wrong goals*

### Introduction

Your conflicts in your relationships are symbolic of your dis-relation with Source. And your attempts at having relationships are symbolic of your desire to heal your dis-relation with Source.

The body is about lack, not the mind. However, with identity confusion, mind experiences the body's lack as itself. Turning cause (the mind) and effect (the body) around, your mind attempts the impossible. It uses the body to supply for its perceived lack when its identity with a body is the reason for its perceived lack. You know this is true when you do all you can to ingratiate the body with trinkets, paint, body building, sculpting, etc. for self-validation and esteem.

To turn this around is to set a different goal for all relationships. They are the opportunity to remember Source. There is no other reason.

### Communication Breakdown

A thoughtless instant that never happened becomes a violation of guilt. Your guilt is intolerable. To get rid of guilt, you disassociate from it through projection. But to disassociate from it is to hide the fact that your guilt still remains. Because guilt cuts you off from your communication with Source, it isolates you to be "out there." By projecting your violation (guilt) "out there," all you seem to see "out there" is violation, in-completion, communication breakdown and separation.

*I was walkin' many days gone by*
*I was thinkin' about the lonely nights*
*Communication breakdown all around*
*(She's gone so long) what can I do*
*(Where could she be now?)*
*Don't know what I'm gonna do*
*I gotta get back to you*
Jeff Lynn
Sweet Talkin' Woman

## Special Love Relationships

*The body I see you in is a form of my desire*

Motivated out of guilt, your attempt *to connect through a body* is what "special love relationships" are all about. The idea of "special" becomes the blinders to not see beyond the attraction of a body for connection and companionship. There is nothing wrong with "attraction" as bodies go. That "you are a form of my desire" is what all the songs of love and love's sorrows are all about. But this is not love. To equate love with attraction is to misunderstand real connection. To think love involves sacrifice is not love. It is coercion out of fear in the name of love. That's why so many songs of love have lyrics like;

*Why, tell me why, did you not treat me right*
*Love has a nasty habit of disappearing over night*
Lennon & McCartney
I'm Looking Through You

It is not the body that determines value. That is temporary in appeal. It is the Spirit of You that determines what the body is for. All relationships of lasting value understand a connection that transcend the body. All relationships that are not grounded in something deeper than the transient nature of physical appeal, wither and die. That is why love seems to have a nasty habit of disappearing overnight. That so many "special love relationships" end in sorrow is not love. It is misunderstanding. How many times do you have to fail at what you call love until you get it? Again, it's not that your relationships did not work, it's that you gave them the wrong goals.

To use a relationship for what you as a body can get out of it, is misuse of opportunity and delay. You will be saddled with one relationship failure after another. What else would the punishment of guilt demand when another does not live up to what you think they should give you? That is why you have blame, anger, hurt, betrayal and jealously in special love relationships. Is this what love is? Can you love someone one day and hate them the next? A love that can abandon itself is not love. It's a misunderstanding of what you think relationships are for. What are relationships really for?

Your own beliefs as to what you think relationships "should be for" have left you lonely and bitter. Don't you know that the judgment you place on another is your own guilt displaced? How can you maintain the justification of blaming someone *you picked* to make you happy? This can only be done through the denial of your part in the arrangement.

Whether you stay together or not is not the issue. The issue is that in all relationships you meet, you need each other to work through your projected guilt, to see your innocence through theirs! *There is no other reason.* All miracles are acts of true forgiveness. Namaste![243]

## What Relationships are Really For

> *If it is about being right, I will find conflict*
> *If it is about relationship, I will find peace*

What you share in the present is the only meaning anything has. When you bring guilt into any relationship you also bring a past. No relationship is possible when you try to understand the present through an unresolved past. You could not solve your problems of the past. Why would you use the past to solve the present? Determination is needed here to save you from a past that you lay upon the one you meet in the present. When you bring the past into a present relationship you are not interacting with the other. You are reacting to your unresolved past through another. Is this what love is?

Because you projected guilt out of your dis-relation from Source, blame will be the messenger you send to be another's just punishment for how they let you down. And, for as long as you see the violation of guilt in the world, for that long will you believe punishment to be justifiable. And because no thought leaves its source, you can't escape the guilt you made real in your mind as "out there." To deny your part as being difficult to love, is the blame you place on another for them seeming difficult to love.

---

[243] Attributed to Mahatma Gandhi: In India when people meet and part they often say, Namaste' which means: "I honor the place within you where the entire Universe resides; I honor the place within you of love, of light, of truth, of peace; I honor the place within you, where, when you are in that place in you, and I am in that place in me, there is only one of us."

Look to see *your perceptions* of your partner's failings as opportunities to *forgive your perception* of them, and you will be able to forgive your guilt. All miracles are acts of true forgiveness. This is what all relationships are about. Namaste!

## Choose Again: A Handout for Relationships

*Since all healing involves replacing fear with love*
*The desire to awaken reflects your will to love*

1) All miracles occur naturally as an expression of Love.
   a. The only thing that blocks the awareness of love's presence is fear. Anger, hurt, guilt, embarrassment and shame are all rooted in fear.
   b. Because you are tempted to hear another voice, your voice for love/peace seems obscure to you. You can *choose* differently but an open mind is called for first.
2) Every person on your path is a learning and teaching partner. No relationship is accidental. *Choose* to see it that way without exception and you will see the opportunity.
3) Every circumstance, encounter and event is an opportunity to embrace a more peaceful path.
   a. Because only you are responsible for your view of life, you react to no one directly. You always react to your interpretation of them. Just as no one reacts to you directly. They react to their interpretation of you. This is the basis on which all communication and conflict occur.
   b. Because blame, guilt and anger block your ability to change your view of life, every conflict is telling you to *choose again,* to be open to another point of view. Conflicts become opportunities to embrace a more peaceful path when you *choose* to see them as opportunities.

4) To "justify" anger in any form is to block your path to peace.

a. Because you cannot be at peace with yourself and be angry at the same time, to be "justifiably" angry is to attack you first. This is what karma is all about.[244]

b. Therefore, we can be hurt by nothing but our thoughts; and those we can change. It is you that decides. *Choose again.*

5) Giving up the role of Judge, Jury, Jailer and Executioner is to allow your peaceful path to appear.

a. In their simplest forms, all behaviors can be summarized as a call for help or an extension of love.

b. *Choose* to see no exceptions in the above statement and you are free from judgment. Allowing for any exception to this is the ego's way to breed anger, guilt and fear. *Choose again.*

6) It's not that your relationships did not work. It's that you gave them goals that were not yours to give.

a. All emotional pain is the fear of losing something that is not yours to have.

b. To not recognize this is to experience loss and believe God to be cruel. *Choose again.*

7) Love could never abandon itself or it would not be love.

a. Ego gets by taking. Love receives by giving. This is the difference between the Kingdom of God and the kingdom of pseudo-ego.

b. You are Love's Creation. Though lost in a dream of nothingness, in time you will *choose* to awaken beyond time, to the remembrance of what "You Are."

---

[244] *Symbols of Power in Metaphysics p97-118*

c. To remember love is to give it. [245] Gratitude and service are demonstrations of love. Reaching out to others is a joining that takes the focus off of you. This you will *choose* consistently when you desire your inheritance of Love above all else.

8) The key to peace is the understanding of what real forgiveness is.

a. Making amends is not about forgiving someone for what they did to you; it is about you forgiving your perceptions of what you thought they did to you. *Choose again.*

b. All miracles are acts of true forgiveness.

9) Realizing "I don't know" is a gift you give yourself.

a. When you understand that you do not know as you think, your mind is open to receive communication, to receive direction. Now, with blocks to listening removed, you can truly listen.

b. Spirit's voice will direct you. You will be told all you need to know … as long as you get out of the way! Only the arrogant can feel humiliation. *Choose again.*

All healing is joining. And all joining is through real forgiveness. This leads to a unified goal of peace of mind. [246] Joining is not about what I can get out of a relationship or what I can give you because "You make me

---

[245] The co-dependent relationship gives out of lack to get. Love gives out of the wealth it is. There are no strings of return because giving is receiving is the Law of Love … and it is Love that you experience as you give it. This is the principle that cancels karma's time.

[246] *Symbols of Power in Metaphysics p26-28; Reflections for the Wandering Mind p24-35*

feel good."[247] A simple re-evaluation of what your goals are in any relationship provides clarification of how you have set yourself up, or how you free yourself to Love. It's not that your relationship did not work; it's that you gave it the wrong goals. *Choose again.*

## Non-dualistic Focus, Practice and Application[248]

*Everyone is always doing one of two things*
*They are either calling for help or extending Love*

I realize the above italics is unbelievably simplistic in approach. But as a unified goal for peace of mind, it is not difficult for the disciplined mind to apply.

*All consistent applications have their experience.*[249] Look within, beyond form to motivation. Isn't all you are about either a call for help or an extension of Love? You know this is true for everyone you meet when you see it in you. You know it is true for you when you see it in everyone you meet. Inclusiveness negates the belief in exclusiveness. It also diffuses the need to make all the judgments of motivation the world of form seems to offer. Inclusiveness diffuses all the prejudices that the appearance of differences seems to offer. Because you do not know the world as you perceive it, for security sake out of fear, your impulse is to perceive and judge what you do not know,

---

[247] That "you make me feel good" or that "you make me sad or angry or whatever you make me feel," is a fiction to dispute with your client.

[248] My book *The Way Home* is a practice for application in non-dualistic thinking.

[249] *Reflections for the Wandering Mind p36-38*

and not know that you do not know.[250] Because you want to complicate nothingness, your practice of consistent application regarding everyone as either calling for help or extending love is a practical way to move beyond your temptation to want to judge the appearance of nothingness. You are your only block to peace of mind. When you think you know what is best for you, you are thinking dualistically.

*My function here is to only decide that I do not know what is best for me, in recognition that I do not know*

Moving towards consistent application is to move towards allowing for no exception to the principle that *everyone is either calling for help or extending love*. Without exception, practice this principle on everyone you meet along your way. This work becomes easier when you recognize that your mind is basically out of control. Do not make the mistake of trying to make yourself an exception to the existential masses. Your experience of a world in conflict is a projection of dis-relation that testifies to the fact that you are confused about yourself. This principle practiced, nullifies your propensity to judge that which is never definitive.

That others behave out of confusion is not a justification for them, nor is it a justification for you to protect your judgment of them as justified. What you took personally was never about you. I am not saying that it is for you to help anyone. But with this principle practiced you will respond rather than react. You will know what to do.

---

[250] "Complicating the results of information does make it difficult to see its nothingness" is what my book *Symbols of Power in Philosophy* is all about.

Whether your partner practices this principle or not is irrelevant to what you need to do. [251] It is for you to practice this principle ... and you will see mighty changes in your response to others. These are the miracles that make you part of the solution.

*Transformational Psychotherapy teaches that it is not that your relationships did not work; it's that you gave them the wrong goals.*

---

[251] *Healing The Wound p75-78*

# Review

Because denial is incapable of recognizing itself, your resistance[252] to the following statements remind you that you fear change.

Your boundaries remind you of your fear of life.

Your care-taking reminds you that you are afraid of conflict.

Your co-dependency reminds you that you will not find your peace of mind out there.

Your addiction reminds you of how easily you are distracted.

Your lack of self-esteem reminds you that you hate the self you made.

Your shame reminds you that you misplaced your innocent child.

Your blaming reminds you that you fear exposure and thus punishment.

Your stress reminds you that you are serious about nothing.

Your need to control reminds you that you are insecure about what isn't.

Your trauma reminds you of the fictions you have settled for.

Your feelings remind you of what you are thinking.

---

[252] Your defense to hide your fear of change and defend your misery will exhibit itself as "these statements are too simplistic; not practical; insulting; outrageous; I don't need to change, they do; and the like, etc." Your resistance will be to justify, rationalize and minimize away the simple. It is a continued complication of information so you can't see its nothingness.

Your grief reminds you of attachments not yours to possess. Your resistance to this message reminds you of your denial that you *try* to possess

Your anger reminds you of your lack of acceptance. That what you think "should have been," was not to be. Why was it not to be? Because it did not happen.

Your judging reminds you that you do not know.

Your guilt reminds you that you are mistaken about yourself.

Your depression reminds you that the world offers you nothing that you want.

Your betrayal reminds you of self-betrayal … your dis-relation with Source.

Your pain reminds you to remember the power that you are … beyond a body identity.

Your relationship tensions remind you of your dis-relation with Source.

Your fear reminds you of your confusion.

Your need for love reminds you that you think you lack.

Your restlessness reminds you of your journey … to come home.

# Worksheet / Handout

*For a while, as a teacher, you need to use the symbols of the world. But in your practice do not be deceived by them, for they do not stand for anything. And in this thought alone will you be released from them.*[253]

Principle 1) All healing is of the mind. The body is an effect of mind's thoughts. You do what you think.

Principle 2) Resolution always follows a change in perspective; changing the way you see anything. Therefore, being "stuck" has to do with your unwillingness to change the way you see anything.

Principle 3) Because changing your mind is at the level of cause and behavior is the level of effect, your willingness to change the way you see anything opens the door for choices you could not see before.

What are the things that ask you to reevaluate the need to change the way you see something?

a. Feelings that make you uncomfortable

b. Conflict

c. Fixed beliefs you think you need to defend

Principle 4) A change in mind is a change in motivation. How do you go about making a change?

a. Ask yourself "What is going on with me that I feel this way?"

b. Talk about it, but not with someone who is aligned with your perception.

c. Be open-minded to an alternative interpretation.

---

[253] *Symbols of Power in Metaphysics p20-22*

d. Forgiving your view means "I want to see this differently" because, "The way I have chosen to see it hurts me." It is paramount that you take responsibility for how you see what you see. Allow for no exception.
e. "Blame is not an option in my life."

Because *all consistent applications have their experience*, practice means meditation, prayer and fellowship for strength and consistency. The last step is to use the symbols of time to live beyond them.

*Namaste*

# Some Signs of Inner Peace

A tendency to think and act spontaneously, rather than plan from fears based on past experience.

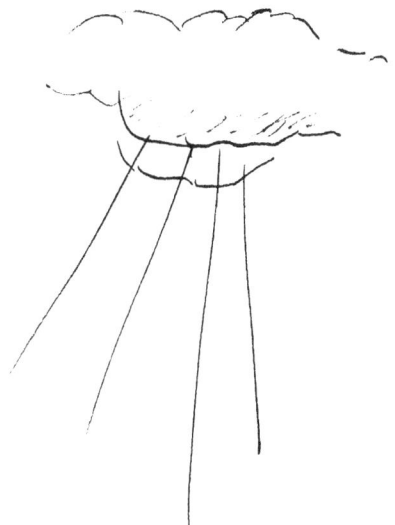

An unmistakable ability to enjoy each moment.

A loss of interest in interpreting the motives and actions of others.

A loss of interest in judging self.

A loss of the tendency to worry.

Frequent episodes of appreciation.

Contented feelings of connectedness with others and nature.

Frequent occurrences of smiling through the eyes from the heart.

An increasing tendency to allow things to unfold, rather than trying to make them happen.

An increased susceptibility to Love.

# III. Topics from Over the Edge

*The frame of reference you invest in to explain your encounters of life, is the life you will encounter*

If we are talking about bodies, we all tread a path. Along this path are numerous and diverse encounters of experience. As long as you recognize a body as you, you will have troublesome encounters. Because you have chosen a body as you, every one of these encounters belongs to you. Whether you want them or not is not the issue. How you choose to perceive them is. To believe you can have encounters that interfere with your life journey is to not accept the path you tread. Because, these encounters that seem to interfere are actually your opportunities. These are the reasons you walk this path in the first place.

# The Bridge across Different Cultures

## Basic Principles of Relating

*Blood is not thicker than water*

1) In a disconnected world of differences, to not see your connection through each of us as "One Spirit" is to be looking in the wrong place. *It is the bodies eyes that sees differences. It is the healed mind that does not acknowledge them.*

2) We all seek the same thing, peace of mind. We just do it through *different* customs, rituals, beliefs, habits of living. Some ways are more self-defeating, sabotaging or disconnecting than others.

3) Because connecting is relating through commonality rather than differences, differences are used *only* to celebrate the commonality of our differences on a superficial level. Otherwise, our differences become temptations to argue over and defend.

4) "Ashes to ash, dust to dust" is a celebration of commonality that diffuses all issues of differences.

5) Direct encounters of "In the now" provide us with all the information we need to know about each other. Hearsay, assumptions, past experience, cultural trends are biases that become irrelevant in the light of the "here and now."

6) Fear in all its forms is the only block to connecting. It makes differences to be more important than commonality.

7) Communication for an understanding of commonality rather than arguing for differences, is our great need.

**Body Identity and Integration**[254]

Is the question "Who am I" or is it "What am I?"

Whether you are heterosexual, homosexual, bisexual, transgender, male or female is irrelevant to the point. The point being that your mind cannot integrate (be one minded towards a unified goal) and heal as long as it is distracted to believe it is a body that dies. That's the battle ground of a split/dualistic mind. To argue for an individual body identity is your invitation to the world of conflictual misunderstanding. This is true because this is what it always has been. That is why mindful thoughts that transcend your belief in a body identity become essential to practice and apply.

*Namaste*

---

[254] *Symbols of Power in Philosophy p62-68*

# Mid-Life Crisis

*When we find out that the world does not possess the objective value or meaning that we want it to have, or have long since believed it to have, we find ourselves in a crisis.*
Friedrich Nietzsche

## Introduction

Heraclitus of Ephesus (535–475 BC) was a pre-Socratic Greek philosopher who insisted on ever-present change as being the fundamental essence of the universe, as stated in the famous saying, "No man ever steps in the same river twice." In essence he believed that because the world is ever-changing the idea of stability is an illusion.

## Life as a Crisis

That crisis occurs is a given to the survival of a body self-idea. In fact, the body self-idea is a struggle of adaptation throughout one's body life span. There is a crisis when you are born. There is a crisis when you are having a temper tantrum as a toddler. There are crises when you are a preteen. There is a crisis when you are an adolescent looking for acceptance from your peers. There are crises as a young adult going out to make your mark on the world. There are crises in the development of relationships. There are crises in addiction. There are crises in marriage and divorce. There are crises as an adult with kids. There are crises in job changes. There are crises with your car breaking down. There are crises with moving. There are socio-economic and political crises. There are crises as an elder with body/brain problems. There are crises in death.

In the world of the ever-changing, life can be viewed as the adjustment disorder of one big crisis … until you transcend the idea of a body image. Therefore, the correlation of crisis to a particular age is an irrelevant effect. The cause of the crisis is the point.

## Mid-Life Crisis

You may argue that a certain age lends itself to evaluation and questioning. For example, the so-called mid-life crisis involves questions of looking back and looking ahead. "What have I accomplished? What have I failed to accomplish? Have I been pursuing a personally meaningful direction?" In short, "What have I done with my life?" There is a list of mid-life changes you can check off regarding the stress of life adjustments.

How about the adolescent in high school who shows up over parental expectations, but can't figure out what he is doing there. He may not ask consciously "What is the relevance of what I am being subjected to?" But he demonstrates it by not understanding the nature of his given situation and therefore wanders through. Then one day it dawns on him "I am going to school to learn how to go to work for the rest of my life! Really?" Either he is a very immature boy who better start growing up, or "Is this what my life is all about?!" Isn't this a teen going through an existential life crisis?

If mid-life crisis is defined as a reassessment of what you have chased as valuable, only to find it does not bring you your prize, or that your prize after getting it isn't what you thought it would be,[255] then a mid-life crisis happens at any age of the socialization process.

---

[255] Like your disappointment over what you got for Christmas, or a firing or job change that makes you reexamine what you have valued to be meaningless, or a health crisis that makes you ponder what you have done with your life.

Suspend the nonsense of a mid-life crisis so you can recognize the question you need to ask.

## Summary

That you have achieved what you set out to achieve, or have failed to achieve in your life is irrelevant to the crisis at hand. That you have finally come to the end of trying to live through socially conditioned forms of expectations for meaning is the point! You can live your crisis over and over again through whatever forms you designate to live it through until you honestly ask, "Is this what my life is all about?" This question can be seriously asked at any time of your current body life span.

Regardless of the form a crisis may take and the psychological data you may conjure up in the name of explaining the concept of "life crisis," age is an irrelevant factor except for the time it takes you to ask, "What does it mean to be alive?" When you ask, your life will be clouded in confusion until you understand it as passage through, to find your value in the idea of a quest. Be a passerby.

*Namaste*

# The Use of Time as a Means for Healing

*One way or another, everybody seems to be trying to find ways to kill time when in the end, time kills you*

## Introduction

*We all have the same amount of time*
*How do you want to use it?*

As long as you continue to experience pain in your encounter with life events, time will seem like an arduous task to endure. However, because time was made out of your dis-relation with Source, it is for you to use time to undo the dis-relation.

## Identifying the Problem

*When you recognize your projections for what they are*
*You are doing the work you need to do*

Your encounters through life are not the sources of your problems. Your projections are. If you want to heal, you need to deal with this.

In denial you refuse to recognize your projections. Your resistance to change is your witness. Whatever you decide to not like as "out there," you do not see it as your reflection. This is an effect of a conflicted state of mind (split), projected away in an effort to avoid dealing with the conflict within. Your denial of what you are doing, is the reason you see your conflicts as externally caused. However, this effort to project away what you do not want to deal with, invites the conflict and the time you need to deal with that which you do not want to deal with.

Because you see the problem outside of you, you are focused towards an external world view of influence. You look for your solutions in the same place, the outside. This however is the place where no solution is to be found, only problems.

*Don't think you can find any solution in the world. The world was made so you could not escape from your problems.*[256]

Nothing outside of you causes you pain because there is nothing outside of you. What you experience outside of you is reflected as a temper tantrum of distortion. To identify the source of your problem as coming from within will be your opportunity for healing.

## The Misuse of Time

*Mistakes are nothing more than memories made*

Time is the measure of the place between the problem's inception and its resolution. The effects of the problem are all the annoying symptoms of guilt, anger, anxiety, depression and fear, carried along. Your inability to resolve these effects is the time you need to remind you that you are not working with the real problem. Any solution that does not address the real problem is not a solution, but a band aid of relief that keeps you in time. Your issue, experienced in all the seemingly different forms the world presents has a common cause. Multiple issues are an effect of one cause. Your dis-relation with Source and thus with yourself. The complexity of all your seemingly different issues has the same content.

---

[256] *Symbols of Power in Metaphysics p110-118*

To see the larger picture is to be willing to suspend judgment. In this way you buy yourself time's opportunity to see your situation another way. To not suspend judgment is to duplicate your conflict as seemingly separate and unrelated problems according to the dance of forms your world provides. To not learn from your mistakes is your inability to generalize a lesson learned to other seemingly different issues. With resentment, your reoccurring theme is to obsess about what was unfairly done to you, and how you would like to show them their hypocrisy. This thinking skips over the experience of a present reality. Time is needed now so you can figure out where the real problem lies. And out there is not where the problem and solution lie.

**What is Delay?**

Delay is your unwillingness to change your mind. This unwillingness refuses to recognize your condition of transition (passage) through the ephemeral for what it really is, *a temporary moment.* There is no place to find stability. Moments of rest (relief) maybe, but not stability. Fear is your greatest block to change until you see the boogie man for what it is ... nothing. How many times do you have to be mad or anxious about something before you understand that you put yourself in needless emotional pain?

Symptoms of delay are distractions. There are many ways that you occupy your time to avoid resolution. Solving the world's problems is one of them.[257] All the ways you chase after fleeting pleasure to also find pain, is

---

[257] I am not saying "Don't be a part of the world for solutions." I am saying "Don't invest in a place where peace of mind will not be found." *The Way Home p115-120*

another. Moments of temporary relief rather than release will be your experience. The lesson you need to learn will be repeated through all the different symptoms *you present* until you own the cause.

## Mental Shift

Because your mental shift was an adjustment directed towards validating self-deception, the scope of your life is that of a body-centered experience. Thus, your life experiences become limited to;

1) An intensive intellectual and social education of cognitive uncertainties limited within the paradox of an ephemeral arena of constant change.

2) An interpretation of a collection of events as successive, serious and traumatic (a past).[258]

3) A center of self-importance that experiences self-esteem issues, sickness, mood changes, pleasure, pain and death.

4) Being a good judge for decision making for your well-being when all you have done is decided for a world view of "no exit."[259]

Because your mental shift is expressed through the dynamics of a bio-chemical body, forms of mental illness will appear through your thought process to have bio-chemical and therefore pharmaceutical implications. Mental illness falls under the cloak of many clinical labels … yet, being an effect of a deeper dilemma. That is why just like everything else the world of healing provides,

---

[258] The pseudo-synchronicity of successive approximations. *Symbols of Power in Metaphysics p52-54*
[259] *Symbols of Power in Metaphysics p15; Symbols of Power in Philosophy 182-195*

all pharmaceutical aids are temporary in effect.[260] Be not deceived or distracted by appearances, because they are appearances.

## Developing Sensitivity

Because of your dis-relation with Source, there seems to be the experience of a separation or space between yourself and every other self. This space is witnessed as the appearances of bodies in a world of innumerable individual differences. Healing is the undoing of this separation. The undoing of time is the speed-up, and forgiveness is the means.

*The Space Between ... What's wrong and right*
*Is where you'll find me hiding, waiting for you*
*The Space Between ... Your heart and mine*
*Is the space we'll fill with time*
Dave Matthews Band
The Space Between

All problems, regardless of form (effects), are the same in resolve (cause). Do not be concerned about what this means. Rather, recognize the everyday effects of the problems you made through your thinking that cause you anxiety, guilt, anger, depression and fear, to name a few. This involves you taking responsibility for your unhappiness as self-caused. This openness is a sensitivity

---

[260] Your mind is a powerful healing tool when given the chance. The idea that your mind can convince your body that a fake treatment is the real thing, is the placebo effect. The use of anything outside of your mind that brings relief to your mind and body through your mind, is the placebo effect. This is aid from outside of your mind when your mind is not internally consistent enough to do it itself.

that will point you in the direction of resolve. Blame is not an option.

You always feel the effects of what you think. Without blame, you can own this. Responsibility for you being the cause of the world you choose to see, makes *vigilance* a necessary ability for you to suspend your propensity to defend self-deception. The illusion of guilt is a fear that breeds the need for a punishment that will absolve you of your guilt. Yet, there is nothing fearful to defend against.

## The Time you Take is the Time you Make

*You have misused your memory for so long that you do not understand that it can be used as an opportunity for you to remember your "present" experience in Source*

You have a past in thought because you did not resolve a problem at its inception. For example, let's say that someone says something to you that you interpret as personally hurtful. Because you were not able to see it for what it really was, you carry it into memories past as a thought to ruminate over. Or you bury it over time as unconscious when you can't tolerate the pain of carrying a problem you can't resolve. Either way, you are storing it as the making of your karma to undo at a later time.[261]

You have examples of resolution with issues of the past when light is placed upon them. The light is the common denominator of a changed point of view. "Oh, I never thought about it that way" is release through real forgiveness. This is what the collapse of time is all about. From this point of view, real forgiveness is the only

---

[261] *Symbols of Power in Metaphysics p98-109*

function meaningful in time. [262] When you see that all problems of form have their resolution in a changed perception, you can generalize this process to everything.

You are in the process of unfolding. Your *vigilance* is the work you do to replace self-attack thoughts with the truth of the matter. Meditation, prayer, or a simple thought for the day are your tools. Consistent application has its effects.[263] These effects undo the gap of time between your experience of a world of distortion and your inheritance in Source. As blocks are removed through forgiveness, the gap begins to collapse. Your creative flow that always is, is being experienced to be expressed through your brush of a body on the canvas of your life.[264] Now, rather than fear, you share love. You do not worry about outcomes or what other people will think because you love. You are close to waking up. Be patient.

## The Undoing of Time

*The time you take to resolve a problem you made, is the gap between perceiving and experiencing Being*

The ultimate in time collapse (speed-up) is the resolution of your problem at its inception. At this place of reflective immediacy, you see that *the way you just interpreted a situation* was an attack on your peace of mind.[265] You just caught yourself. Cause and effect are in the same place, in the mind that was tempted to breathe life into your misinterpretation as a life event. No gap was

---

[262] *The Way Home p104-107*
[263] *Reflections for the Wandering Mind p36-44*
[264] *Symbols of Power in Metaphysics P147-161*
[265] The experience of "No thought leaves its source" or "Giving is receiving is the law of love" springs alive in your mind.

created. No time was made. No hurtful memory was made as karma to undo. The person or event seemingly involved had nothing to do with you except to remind you of the work you need to do. No matter who they are, this is their blessing to you.

Your need to forgive, purge, undo an ancient grievance that has prolonged time, has been exposed through a present encounter. How is this so? Because complexity of form does not imply complexity of content you can generalize this lesson to everyone, every situation and everything. In this way does this passerby you thought was your enemy, become a friend to your peace of mind. Your awareness of interrupting your propensity to misinterpret at its inception, takes you to the next step of being able to cancel the time you need to work it out. When you are able to generalize this lesson to everyone and everything, a mighty speedup (collapse of time) will be your experience.

Resolution is the interruption of a self-defeating thought. When you see that all problems of form have their resolution in a changed perception, you can generalize this process to everything. When you catch a problem to be at its inception, and you see it for what it is, the problem was never allowed to slip into memory's time. Now, there is no personal history to deal with and defend. Karma is not made.

Waking up is the experience of having no problems to forgive. When you understand that the last illusion is that there never was anything to forgive, the gap between perceiving and experiencing, closes. You stand at the end of time.

## The Door to Resolution

*The proper use of judgment is to overlook nothingness*

Without exception, whatever you assess as meaningful in the ephemeral you breathe life into. This is the power your mind has to make nothingness mean something. What you are tempted to allow as a problem out there will be the time and space you need to undo it. Learning to cancel problems at their inception denies the life of its effect. This involves your reflective immediacy to not want to make non-essential, non-relevant correlations live.

*You stand at the door of resolution*
*The time you make to collapse your history*
*Is the time you take to change your mind*

# The Wisdom of the Elders

*You do not cease to play because you grow old*
*You grow old because you cease to play*
Anonymous

To be able to face the inevitable, you must see the temporal order as it really is . . . movement and noise.

## Introduction

The most common symptom of old age is confusion of familiar people's identity and place. This confusion is naturally expressed by the elderly in forgetfulness. It is not uncommon for an elder to become lost in a neighborhood they have lived in for over 40 years.[266]

Long term memory is the last to go. It has been imprinted the strongest over time by selective remembrance, fabrication, and repetition. Is this kind of confusion in the elderly degenerative? Not if you're a teller of stories.

## Confusion as a Way of Passage

*Only in confusion can you try to be what you are not*

Confusion has a bad name. It seems to engender experiences of uncertainty and disorientation. Babies are born not knowing their world through a body experience. Children learn to make confusion meaningful; their minds becoming socialized, their perception stabilizes and is set

---

[266] Ambrose Spartz

in dualistic thinking. [267] To try to make confusion meaningful is a fearfully socializing endeavor to nowhere.[268] Adults are fearful of confusion because they are not in control of the illusion of control. [269] Reactive panic in all its subtle forms of stress, anger and fear becomes potential as one tries to master the meaningless. If you allow, confusion can be a "moment" out of time to question your mental investments.

Confusion of identity and place is not traumatic to those who recognize that they are naturally simplifying by letting thoughts go! For the elderly, confusion is a process of undoing, as part of their reorientation back to their true center. They are allowing their mind to gravitate towards its natural state of abstraction. It is like preparing for a new birthing via a completion process. The metaphor is like when you are growing up, being socialized to invest in the world, you collect information, things, and a place to store it all. It is a subtle process. Eventually, you will need a home with more space to put your stuff.

*"Master, how do I make my life problem-free?"*
*"If you have a mouse that is a problem, get a cat! If you have a cat that is a problem, get a dog! If you have a dog that is a problem, get a leash! If the leash is not long enough, build a fence! Within a fence is a yard you have to mow. Get a lawnmower! A yard comes with a house. You will need a job to pay for it all! You will need to buy a car to get to your job to pay for your car! Is there no end?"[270]*

---

[267] *Symbols of Power in Philosophy p69-89; Symbols of Power in Metaphysics p133-143*

[268] Sigmund Freud was accurate about being socialized out of fear.

[269] *Healing the Wound p55-58*

[270] *The Way Home p40*

Downsizing is to discard what you no longer need. It is a cleansing process on the outside for what you are doing internally. It is a transformation; the dying of the old to make room for the new. Resolution comes out of consolidating. To consolidate is to simplify. To simplify is to discard the meaningless you have collected along the way. Confusion gives way to the simplicity of the obvious. The obvious becomes seeing your means for passage.

## The Forgotten Zone

When you assumed a body image as you, you entered into a process of body birth, socialization and death.[271] To learn or be socialized, is the world's effect of trying to understand confusion. As an effect, it is just part of the illusion of distractions away from the remembrance of your true center. It's important to note that you were not born as an innocent child to be socialized or corrupted away from your remembrance of Source.[272] You seemed to be born as an effect of your dis-relation with Source. Said another way, "Social conditioning is not a cause of confusion. It is an effect of already being confused."

To once again remember your true center, is your journey back to the inception of your original error. It is a process to consolidate through simplification. Your transformation towards a new birth is the process of being

---

[271] *Symbols of Power in Metaphysics p33-47*

[272] Jean Jacques Rousseau (1712-1778) was a Genevan philosopher, writer and composer, whose political philosophy influenced the progress of the Enlightenment throughout Europe. Rousseau claimed that children at birth are innately good, not evil, and that their natural tendencies should be protected against the corrupting influences of society. *Symbols of Power in Philosophy p69-89*

born again and again … until you wake up.[273]  Though it seems you are going forward as you undo everything you learned; you're actually going back to the beginning; to the forgotten zone; to The Voice That Proceeds Thought.

*Surrender to the Voice which flows from within*
*It will direct your thoughts on how to begin*
*Clean out your cupboards, sweep your floors*
*Throw out your windows, open your doors*

*Like water you flow to fill every space*
*There are no boundaries to keep you in place*
*Practice the moment and when it is clear*
*The Voice that precedes thought will appear*

*So let all go, abandon every block you know*
*And in that moment your creations will flow*

You can start the journey any time you want. In fact, you have been in a constant state of preparation.

As elders grow in recognition that the only thing of value in this world is that which will help them in their transition through, they begin the process of stepping back into the forgotten zone. They begin to turn their backs on everything they once valued. The forgotten zone is an experience beyond the twilight of selective perception … to step within. The wisdom of the elders know this.

---

[273] *Symbols of Power in Metaphysics p119-132*

## Passing Through a Fog

*There's a path that leads beyond your sorrow*
*Through the mist this path will take you there*
*And when you step through*
*Your fear you will undo*
*As you leave it at your own back door*
Mathias Karayan
Your Own Back Door

   Those who fight confusion are still invested in the body for security. They are afraid of the unknown. Because they resist death of a body, they experience fatigue. Your body's eyes will always see mysterious characters through flickering shadows. "Mysterious" because we're all changing masks. "Characters" because we're all in a play. That's OK. It prepares you for your step beyond all these arrangements. Don't worry; you will not be given a step too big for you. The unknown only involves a moment of confusion. Your moment of reorientation is like passing through a fog. You are preparing for a lift out of your body life experience to acknowledge an "Oh yea," in remembrance of when it happens.

> *As I allow,*
> *I feel the discomfort of the body*
> *It is only for an instant*
> *As I allow,*
> *An opening of blazing white light breaks through …*
> *… as if from above*
> *It permeates … as if to lift me out into it*
> *This is the moment of death*
> *Your passage through*
> *Your thoughtless instant of change remembered*

## Rite of Passage

*You are not in a body; the body is outside of you*

It is easy to fear the unknown of death and interpret a loved one's confusion of thought as degenerative. There is no confusion preparing for this journey. It only seems that way to those who live outside of their true center of rest. Outside of your center is the mental escape to try and make sense out of chaos … the cycle of birth to death to birth. The results have been stress, anger, grief and fear. To look inside is to step inside, into the eye of the hurricane.[274]

Your socialization into temporal distractions, entertained all your life in the name of chasing dreams of security, acknowledgment and contentment, all wash away in the image of a frail and vulnerable body … destined to die. No longer can this fact of "life" be evaded and hidden behind the energy of your youth. The energy of your youth is no longer there for exploitation and denial of the obvious. Years to days to minutes to seconds of your body's breath helps you to recognize as it leads you to your rite of passage.

## Summary

*The Way seems long but the end is "NOW"*

There is a quiet calm in the elderly who face death in the light of their friends' funerals. They are quietly undoing everything they learned on this side. Confusion of identity, people and place is a replay of old tapes. They

---

[274] *Symbols of Power in Metaphysics p127-128*

are attempting to put closure to as much business as they can before passing through. Those who hold to an ephemeral body beyond it's time do so in the name of completing one last task, seeing one last person, before lifting out. This clearly demonstrates the power of a resolved mind not unlike your own.

### Hildegard and Me

"I want to go home!" demanded Hildegard.

"You are home" I answered.

"Yes but, I want to go home," Hildegard repeated as she sat in the living room of the house she has lived in for over 50 years.

Attempting to orient her to the particular I asked, "Whose dining room table is that?"

"It's mine" she responded.

"And whose kitchen is that?" I asked.

"It's mine."

"And whose living room are you in right now?"

"Mine" she repeated irritably.

"So, whose house are you in?" I ask.

"My house" she resigned patiently.

"So, you are home," I stated skillfully.

"Of course dummy!" Hildegard expressed, "but I want to go home!"

Mathias Karayan

# Mother Earth Dance

*I am white, white and black*
*I am black, black and yellow*
*I am yellow, yellow and red*
*I am red, red and white*
*And I am none of these*
*You see …*
*Mother Earth pays no respect to color*
*No respect at all …*
*She just does her dance …*
*And dance she does*

Why do you focus on honoring your differences as strength, when Mother Earth pays no respect to any of it? To honor what we have in common is the true strength of all people. When I can walk a mile in your moccasins and see you as me, I see the bind that heals.

## Introduction

*It is the body's eyes that sees differences. It is the healed mind that does not acknowledge them.*

The idea of cultural differences in therapeutic encounters is too often used as a maneuver. "You don't understand me!" And that is used even if there is no so-called cultural barrier. This need to maintain an identity of difference through artificial boundaries of race, color, creed, culture etc., is out of an unawareness of where true identity resides. That we are all One Mind in Source is the reality we all share. That we see differences that separate us is the shadow dance of a split mind. Even on a superficial (body identity) level, Mother Earth teaches us that all ephemeral grounding has its roots in a shared identity. Those who fight vigorously for the identity of a cultural difference are those who do not understand grounding.

## Fear

*You defend what you identify with*
*But that does not make you what you are*

The barriers of cultural differences experienced in your encounter with your client are no different than all the other endless barriers your clients present. They are defenses of exclusion, all based in fear.

To fear is to not know. To not know is confusion. It is the nature of confusion that it has no meaning other than confusion itself. To be insecure in not knowing is the need to make confusion a meaningfully understandable encounter.[275] All symbols of social, cultural, and religious beliefs are enshrined to make ever-changing confusion a meaningful experience. These symbols of beliefs attempt to explain and ritualize the experiences of your journey (transition) through the ephemeral. [276] It might be a wonderful thing to be a pagan, to honor the equinox, the solstice and the constellation of the stars. But they are only metaphors for your journey into the "mysterious."

---

[275] All concepts are attempts to make confusion understandable. The concept of evil is one way to explain confusion, as confusion is a way to explain evil.

[276] *The Way Home p149-151*

*We were born before the wind*
*Also younger than the sun*
*Ere the bonnie boat was won*
*As we sailed into the mystic*

*And when that fog horn blows*
*I will be coming home, mmm*
*And when the fog horn blows*
*I want to hear it*
*I don't have to fear it*

*I wanna rock your gypsy soul*
*Just like way back in the days of old*
*Then magnificently we will float*
*Into the mystic*
Van Morrison
Into the Mystic

Because of the mysteriously unknown, there are rules of conduct established, ritualized and passed down in the name of preserving the culture. Culture is the safety of a people to survive on Mother Earth. It also hides the fact that the ever-changing is a dance of "random successive approximations" bound together in the magical thinking of "pseudo-synchronicity."[277] To defend your culture is an investment to defend an identity. This supposed safety limits you to a constrictive world view that justifies elitism, nationalism, separation and isolation. Demonizing differences is always a rallying point for ego alliances and a means to war.[278]

---

[277] *Symbols of Power in Metaphysics p52-54*
[278] Adolf Hitler (as one of many examples throughout history), used the fear of and hatred for Communism and the Jews as a way to galvanize the people.

No matter what concept you use to structure confusion, the fact still remains; you are trying to make your fearful experience of the ever-changing meaningfully relevant.[279]

## Sharing as Strength

*Boundaries do not protect, they divide*

Don't get me wrong. The expression of culture, variety and diversity can be beautiful. Differences of dress, language, custom, and color are her blossoms. This is the expression of Mother Earth's dance. Sharing is the strength of every culture, for in sharing is culture taught and preserved. Yet, all cultures have a common identity rooted in Mother Earth. As you look out from the sacred circle you see differences. As you look in to the center of the circle you see ONE.

Boundaries do not protect, they divide. Earth's history of wars testifies to this.[280] Look at the cultural difference of the Native Americans and the Europeans. The natives were not decimated because they were different. They were decimated because they did not have the means to defend themselves from domination. It is the same human condition of greed, domination and power that went on in Europe as went on in the Americas. We are all common in our human condition of problem solving.

---

[279] This is what the book *Symbols of Power in Philosophy* is all about *p50-68*

[280] *Symbols of Power in Philosophy p121-139*

Mathias Karayan

## Where the Eagle Soars

*People of all Nations, people of Mother Earth*
*Stop, look and listen*
*The Sacred Circle, thought to be broken*
*Remains whole*

*Yet, we are to journey*
*To look beyond to a new vision*
*To rise above and step within*
*Where the Eagle soars*

*Here we will find*
*The wholeness of the Sacred Circle*
*As it remains … Unbroken*

## Culture Used to Divert

*Ego wants you to look out and see how different you are; even honor it. It's a distraction from seeing the commonality we all are. All healing is about joining.*

By definition, a client is one who is limited in awareness. To be aware of your limits is great gain. It allows you room to open your mind towards the acceptance of mutually satisfying encounters. The encounter of phrases like "You don't understand me because you are not me" is a fearful comment that does not recognize the shared struggle of humanity at its deepest level.

Therapist, do not allow yourself to be diverted by such nonsense. The client's problem is a fearfully constrictive world view defended as a cultural issue. This is the maladaptation that makes for sabotaged relationships. You may not understand your client's particular situation. It matters not when you understand that it is not for you to know them as they think. Rather it is for you to facilitate an opportunity for them to know themselves as we all "are."

Culture used to justify differences are a ruse to hide behind, in the name of ego alliances. Within the same culture are personality conflicts. Differences within the same faith make for a variety of denominations. Wars are fought in the name of the same God. Families of blood run into misunderstanding. The exceptions to family harmony are too numerous for blood to be thicker than water. All these differences of division are symptoms of the same dilemma we all share … dis-relation with Source. Stop the blaming so you can look within at your dis-relation!

Should you want to turn the table on the comment "You don't understand me because you are not me" would be to respond with "How do you know I don't understand you. You don't know me!'

## Healing Through Commonality

*Healing always involves joining*

1) Different life interpretations are endless
   There are many faces of different colors
   There are many religions of different practices
   There are many cultures of different symbols
2) There is one earth we all share
   We all share individual body differences
   We all share symbolic differences
   We all share cultural differences
3) Beyond judgment are two responses we all share
   We extend love or … we call for help

4) Sharing is continuous

Sharing is practiced between bodies on that level of awareness as culture, humanitarian efforts of inclusion, commitments, etc., until it is realized as continuous beyond that level.

*Reality is experienced as the expression of One Mind*
*Therefore, all those individual minds you seem to see are you ...*
*an aspect of one mind*

*This is purely intellectual in concept*
*Until you experience it as One*
*Because, reality is only experienced as One[281]*

5) To share is to practice healing

To recognize everyone you meet as being involved in passage is to recognize community. What else is there when you recognize a shared reality of passing through with the commonality of an ephemeral body?

*Yes, you can always honor differences. But recognizing commonality is the practice of healing*

**Summary**

*All are born to share the earth, all are born to die*
*All experience the journey of life, to the mountain top of joy*

It is obvious that all bodies are different in color, size, appearance, language and culture. How is it not obvious that we are all one family nourished by Mother Earth under the sun of Father Sky?

---

[281] *Symbols of Power in Metaphysics p170-180*

Because of dis-relation with your spiritual ground of Being, you seem to be a separate entity, misunderstood as you misunderstand your dilemma. Of course you misunderstand your dilemma. How else could you explain the raping and contamination of Mother Earth, your body's ground of being, except through the fact that you must be insane? Your misunderstanding is projected as "you do not understand me." To say that to anyone is to not understand you at the most fundamental level of connection. Because, to understand you is to understand the journey you share with everyone you meet. And this is a journey that transcends your identity as a body. Namaste.

Therapist, use each and every expressed difference as an opportunity to communicate shared meaning.

**I am You**
*I am the wind through the dust of time*
*Whispering through your mind*

*I am the ocean mysterious and deep*
*With secrets yours to keep*

*I am the mountain standing tall and true*
*With no easy way through*

*I am the river from which I start*
*Through you back to my heart*

*I am you*

# Pain & The Power You Are

*Healing requires a shift in perception from effect to cause*

## The Illusion You are Not

Because of your mental shift to identify with a body image as "you," you experience all the investments a body has to offer. Pain experienced, is not to be judged as good or bad or right or wrong. But its experience in any form is proof of self-deception.

As a matter of mind over matter, the question becomes what is the purpose of my pain? This question shifts your mind from effect (the body) to cause (the mind). Healing requires a shift in perception from effect to cause. Your body is a mental experience; the reality of pain is rooted in the perception that God's children are bodies.

Pain is your reminder of your dis-relation from Source. Your dis-relation as mentally uncomfortable is also reflected as physically painful. Identifying as a body is your inheritance of all the attributes a body offers; death through fleeting pleasure and pain; from birth until you choose again. Pain is your experience of an illusion you are not.

## Attachment's Price

*The only limits you have are the limits you make . . .*
*. . . and that you can change*

Because there is nothing external to your mind that is capable of hurting you, it is your thoughts alone that cause you pain. Transcendence is the recognition that the world you made is harmless to the mind that made it. Because the world represents your thoughts, it will change as you change your mind about it. Because your mind cannot serve two masters, the eternal and the temporal cannot be experienced at the same time. Your choice is either or without exception. Your pain is the proof that you have chosen the temporal.

The world that seems to cause you pain is the effect of an error of thought; nothing more and nothing less. Mind over matter works. But the attachments you cling to, to avoid pain is the self-sabotage you use to cause you your pain. Transcendence is your journey through the illusion of a world as a passerby. A mind in conflict with itself cannot transcend matter.

*To not cling is to not have attachments*
*To not have attachments is to enjoy everything as it is*[282]

I am not saying "don't have attachments." I am saying that for every attachment you have, you will pay a price. To grieve is to pay the price for attachments that are not natural to the transcendent mind. The price you pay for the attachment to a body as "you" will be fleeting pleasure, pain, shallow happiness and death. So, you must die … again and again until you remember what it is to live once and for all as eternal "You."

Your judgment is the error that holds your pain in place. Flowing through your mind is your experience of peace that rests beyond your thoughts of pain that block this flow. Lay your body down in rest. Allow it to be as it is. Fight it not.

---

[282] *The Way Home p24-26, 33, 37-39, 42-47*

*Blow as a leaf in the wind*
*Experience the flow of Being*
*This is the mindfulness of the Buddha*[283]

## Pleasure & Pain

*Because mind over matter is true, to limit your mind to a body experience, is to limit yourself to death*

Your body is part of the sense experience of an ever-changing world through touch, taste, sight, sound, and smell.[284] Shades of pleasure and discomfort (pain) will be the experience of a mind that chooses the investments of a body-self idea.

An addict is one who is involved in a never-ending search for the fleeting pleasures of the body. In the end it becomes a never-ending search to avoid the fleeting pain of the body. Be aware of your daily search of some kind of relief from pain. It demonstrates how susceptible you are to pain. Relief through all your distractions, that adrenaline rush of adventure and excitement, has been your approach towards avoiding inevitable pain. Relief

---

[283] According to Buddhism, every living being has the same basic wish; to be happy and avoid suffering. We spend our whole life working hard to fulfill this wish. The evolution of human kind has been to spend their time and energy improving external conditions in their search for happiness and solutions to their many problems. What has been the result? Instead of your wishes being fulfilled, human suffering has continued while the experience of happiness eludes you. Problems arise only with a conflicted state of mind. If you want to be free from problems you must use them as opportunities to learn to change your thinking.

[284] *Symbols of Power in Metaphysics p47*

only masks to prolong your pain. Are you addicted to the idea that you are a body?[285]

## Anticipation

*Anticipation is the carrot at the end of the stick that your mind through a body is tempted to desire. Through a body of desire for that form you desire, you reach.*[286]

The feelings of your body pleasures and pains you might think is the witness to your presence. However, your focus on a body is an experience of *anticipation* external to what you are. You are not is a body, the body is outside of you. You experience what you believe because it was made by your belief in it. It is like the anticipation or wish for sex that breeds sexual desire before the object of your desire is present, though it is present in our mind. The form of your desire seeming external to your mind, always appears. This is the power of your mind over matter.

What you experience you do not understand. So, you decide what it is and *anticipate* the effects of what you decided. A mind lost in the experience of its *anticipation*, would find mind over matter hard to comprehend. To experience the "instant" that precedes thought is to "Be" ... prior to the thought of *anticipation*. Take heart, the *anticipation* of time was made by you to work this out.

Mind over matter works because

1) body-self-identity is an assumption you experience. Because you assume a body at the unconscious level of your mind,

---

[285] *This book, p66-76*
[286] Genesis 3:6

2) your pain presents you the opportunity to look at your assumption of a body not true to what you are. Now you can ask

3) "What is the purpose of my pain?" This is a question that shifts your mind from effect to cause. Healing requires a shift in perception from effect to cause.

4) You can forgive the pain (effect), but to forgive the thoughts that cause the pain is the ointment for the source of your pain.

## Mind Out of Time

*I am not talking about denial of pain. I am talking about a fiction that causes you the experience of pain.*

Physical pain is not good or bad, right or wrong. It is a condition of identifying with a body that is born to suffer pain and die. This is the investment you have chosen; a conflicted goal of trying to be what you are not. This mental battle ground is the thinking that causes stress and tightens the body muscles around the pain, exacerbating the situation.

At the level of the body, *approach therapy* becomes the client's willingness to embrace the pain rather than fight it. Before you can get through anything you must first own it for what it is. You can deal with what is when you accept it for what it is. It is an investment in a body that experiences pleasure and pain. What you think "should" be or what you desire is something else.

Relaxation of the body always comes from *a present moment focus of the mind*, not an anticipation of how the body feels. Mindful meditation, allows you the techniques of relaxing the body through the mind. From there, you can get to the "instant," the doorway to eternity. The adept go to the doorway easily when they need to. Those who are "awake," live on the other side of the doorway.

*Surrender to the place which flows from within*
*It will direct your thoughts on how to begin*
*Clean out your cupboards, sweep your floors*
*Throw out your windows, open your doors*

*Like water you flow to fill every space*
*There are no boundaries to keep you in place*
*Practice the moment and when it is clear*
*The place that precedes thought will appear*

*So let it all go, abandon every block you know*
*And in that moment your creations will flow*

Mindfulness frees your mind in a way that allows you to recognize opportunities for your release. Any discomfort you think yourself into, is also an opportunity to find that moment of resolve that lies out of time. You believe mind over matter does not work because you have not been diligent to practice mind over matter. Your propensity to seek escape for your body discomfort through anything that will relieve body pain has been your delay. When you "sit in it" like a pig in its mud, rather than look for an escape, you find that place in your mind, your oasis in the desert.[287] When you find that place, in your mind out of time, you can find it there in any situation you think yourself into. This is mind over matter at work.

*The practice of vigilance for application has immediate effects[288]*

---

[287] *The Way Home p42-43*
[288] *Reflections for the Wandering Mind p36-43*

To be addicted to chasing after a placebo effect is your delay. The world and everything in is your placebo. The world is not good or bad, or right and wrong.[289] It is illusion, a sleight of hand, smoke and mirrors, a distraction preventing you from practicing the power your mind has over pain. Therefore, be willing to focus on your sensation of *anticipated* pain as an opportunity to experience the transcendent "You" as mind out of time.

## Summary

*If you understand, things are the way they are*
*If you do not understand, things are the way they are*
Zen proverb

Society is in a state of perpetual grieving. Because reality is not yours to select;

1) The way things are is the way they are; when you are not judging to understand "the way things 'should' be."

2)  By not accepting things the way they are does not change the way things are.

3) By not accepting things the way they are invites resistance. Resistance is a battle ground in the mind, which invites pain.

4) Pain is your suffering through your journey. It is demonstrated through anger, guilt, fear, depression, and shame, to name a few.

5) Your path through your personal hell is the acceptance that things are the way they are. It takes a tremendous amount of vigilance, practice and support to

---

[289]. The limitation of your mind through dualistic thinking. *Symbols of Power in Philosophy p35-49*

trust that accepting your suffering is the way through . . . to peace of mind.

6) There will be sadness (grieving your attachments) before you get to acceptance. But through acceptance, a peaceful calm will follow. There is no battle ground here. The weapons you have used to hurt yourself, you can lay down. The place that precedes thought is the place where you allow things to be the way they are. In this place there is no struggle, no battle, and no anticipation. Just peaceful rest.

You have allowed your mind to be undisciplined and easily distracted to the sensations and desires of a body. Because mind over matter is true, h*ealing requires a shift in perception from effect to cause*. To allow is to remember that there is nothing wrong with the body you identify with. It is your temporary teaching aid to help you with your passage through the ephemeral. Use your pain to find the here and now rather than to escape and delay.[290] Then you can experience the power that "You Are," and find your release.

*The "Self" is greater than the pain*
*Pain is in the mind*
*There is no pain*

---

[290] *Symbols of Power in Philosophy* p27-34

# In the Dust:
# An Inquiry on Psychological Addiction

*There is no such thing as an altered reality*
*Unless you consider your experience with a body as altered*

## Introduction

*Your mind is so powerful it will experience what it thinks ...*
*even though what it thinks is not always true*

Mind is the place where thought apart from Spirit, makes an ephemeral experience. When mind assumes to be a body as itself, it invests in the experience of sensation and perception. This is not God wanting to experience what it is like to be human. Contrary, this experience is a distraction from remembering the Truth of what "You Are." This distraction becomes your journey through the deception of ever-changing shadows of nothingness until you awaken to the remembrance of what "you are."

Physiology is the study of how your body and its parts function together. Mind is not brain. But it does give itself over to brain's physiological impressions as its guide. Psychological addiction is the mind's adjustment to the brain's physiological impressions as if it is its own.

## Association

A mind confused with a body image will identify with the body's physiological rush (high) as a psychological reality. The psychological association of this rush is introduced to the body through various forms. Food, mood altering chemicals, gambling and sex, to name a few.

*Your body* gravitates towards security, comfort and pleasure. That is the nature of a body that lives within the ever-changing cycle of Mother Earth. And it experiences the ever-changing within the limits of the five senses. And the limits of your senses only experience fleeting pleasure and pain. Pleasure is to strive for while pain is to be avoided.

*A mind* confused as a body image is not at rest. It seeks its natural disposition of peace of mind. The problem is that because of your mind's confusion of identity, it seeks peace through the limits of the body's five senses. This confusion makes your mind vulnerable to the influences of your body's desire to seek pleasure and avoid pain. Your mind in confusion attributes this physiological dynamic to be its own, and psychologically associates this fleeting experience of pleasure as a shallow happiness. However, your psychological need for peace of mind or joy is something different, yet, unknown to the mind that has forgotten its Source of Being. The frustrated student's dilemma is that;

*No matter how hard you try, you will not find pleasure in the mind. Nor will you find peace in a body.*

To not recognize this principle is to misuse your body over and over again in an attempt to search for the resolution of peace of mind in a place where it cannot be found. Think of the times when you came to a place where nothing seemed to satisfy. Those were the times when you had the opportunity to rethink everything. However, your psychological habit and behavior adjustments to secure a pleasurable escape through the body from dissatisfaction is your distraction of self-indulgence from resolution. Your mind will never find contentment in a body.

## Mind's Vulnerability

As I stated "A mind confused with a body image remembers the body's rush (high) as a psychological reality." For example, mood chemicals are used to stimulate a physiological response. The pleasure center of the brain as well as the neurological communication system of the body is affected. The numbness and tingling is a distortion of one's sensual/body response.

Mind, confused about its own identity, in a vulnerable state of dissatisfaction, is easily tempted to prefer the distortion of a pleasurable body response as a fleeting shallow happiness in order to fill its anxious void of dissatisfaction. In fact, it will be tempted to use any kind of body stimulation as an attempt to numb its anxiety. Here is where the association is psychologically reinforced for the repeating of this experience. Every placebo the world offers seems medicinal to the mind distracted from resolution.

As long as contentment remains elusive to the mind distracted by the pleasurable experience of a distorted body experience, it will choose to seek that response over and over again in an attempt to fill its void of discontent. The vulnerability of mind's confusion is seen in its attempt to do the impossible, to attempt to fill a psychological void with a physiological response of pleasure. In this way does mind use the body over and over again as its means to deceive itself. This is what an existential / spiritual dilemma is all about.

## Motivation, Adjustment & Progression

*Anticipation is the carrot at the end of the stick that your mind is tempted to desire through a body of desire for the body*

Because pleasure is fleeting, the feeling of deprivation compared to temporary relief returns with more intensity. This increased intensity becomes a strong motivation to repeat the false association of bodily pleasure in an attempt to find psychological contentment. The stage is set for you to make psychological adjustments around the rush.

Euphoric recall is the motivation to repeat an experience you can never have again. Remember how great that first time was? That little window before you threw it all up? Why did you take more than you needed? Because there was a moment of euphoric surprise. "If one is good and three is awesome, how will ten feel?" is the reasoning. And because the experience of pleasure is temporary, your adjustment towards experiencing this pleasure again is the motivator to repeat the experience. However, never again can you have that first rush because there is no longer that first surprise. Nor is there any lack of tolerance. "I will need to figure out how to manage the high" you tell yourself. As your body develops tolerance with use, the need for more will come into play. However, only greater numbness and less euphoria will be your experience.

Physiological tolerance is your progression towards your need for more, more often. A subtle lifestyle adjustment is the beginning of a progression you use to reinforce the repetition of this experience.

## Addiction

The need to repeat the body's physiological rush is called addiction. Your psychological adjustment to remember the experience of body pleasure as contentment, reinforces the desire and justification to repeat the experience. Repeating the experience over time allows for dependency. This dependency becomes broad-based in reinforcement through lifestyle adjustments. Physical development over time deteriorates. Social maladaptation, isolation and spiritual bankruptcy become disease concepts of this addiction. The desire to want the experience of physiological pleasure again and again disrupts your ability to reflect, focus and grow. Spiritually speaking, the anticipation of your next physiological rush becomes an obsession away from the awareness of what you are beyond a body-life experience.

One may dry out (detoxify) with no physical desire for a fix. However, the desire to fill a void made strong over time by psychological adjustment is easily recalled. This is called relapse. This will drive the spiritually distracted back for that rush.

*It is not physical addiction that destroys the will to change. It is psychological addiction. That is why a spiritual focus becomes needful. It fills the psychological void.*

## Denial

*Addiction is maintained through denial*
*Second to denial is isolation*

Your dilemma is spiritual. Your addiction affects your willingness to choose something else. To decide that a body vehicle is your only witness for life's experience is to decide to block your remembrance of your true state of mind.

Denial is your resistance to want to know. Its form is anger, guilt and fear. You are angry because your life is out of control. In denial of this you blame others. You feel guilty for how you have taken advantage of others at the cost of maintaining your addiction. And although, what you have done to others is the witness that your life has been totally out of control, your denial won't let you admit that you are totally out of control. You fear how your life will be, should you give up your first love, your addiction. You are alone.

All your distractions bring you into the realm of constantly chasing after pleasure and avoiding pain. You are tired because you chase a phantom always elusively one step ahead of you.

You deny the fact that what you are in truth is more than the experiences of the body you are lost to as you habitually repeat the physiological / psychological rush. You are not willing to believe the one who tells you "You are not a good listener." Anything that suggests that you need to give up this lover that is killing you, needs to be defended against. You are alone in this battle.

**Relapse and Progression**

Relapse involves one who has psychologically adjusted to the weakened state of only desiring the experience of the fleeting pleasure of the body. They exhibit minimal impulse control and are therefore easily distracted. With a history of nothing but the numbness of pleasure and pain in their life, the fear of what abstinence means will tempt them to relapse. Psychologically speaking, what else is there when all they have done is cultivated a lifestyle that reinforces the need for a pleasure that through tolerance only makes them numb? The same senses initially used to experience the body's fleeting pleasure associated as a shallow happiness, now becomes one's psychological attempt to distort all awareness of the body's senses into obliteration. This despair is a progression that leads one into institutions, jails and death.

## Spiritual Focus

You think your body can give you the contentment your mind seeks. Because it can't, you are deceived. That is how you use a body as a means to deceive yourself. No longer do you seek pleasure through the body's seduction of drugs, food, sex, gambling, etc. You are just trying to obliterate the body that you have used to deceive yourself … because there is nothing else.

There is nothing right or wrong with pleasure and pain. Like the clouds in the sky, they are both fleeting illusions. However, your willingness to be distracted by the senses of desire, disguised as "I need it," calls for a focused concentration, to remind you of your primary purpose. "What is my primary purpose?" you ask. For starters, be honest and be willing to want to stop listening to all your distractions!

*Then will you hear your call*
*Then will you see the messenger sent*
*Then will it be given you to know your purpose*

"But my addictions are overwhelming; I am tired of fighting them with a will power that does not avail." Then use them as a means to find focused concentration. In other words, what you beat your head against as an impossible wall to climb, you use as your opportunity to step up and rise above. "How can this be?" You finally ask in defeat.

I have heard the alcoholic say "I am not a grateful alcoholic. I am grateful that I am an alcoholic." And I ask, "Why are you grateful for having such a malady?" The alcoholic responds "Because it brought me to my knees in humility. I could not conquer my addiction alone. I was driven to seek the Source of my strength, my Higher

Power, and connect with the gathering of fellow members. Rather than wander aimlessly alone through the wilderness, I am grateful that my addiction has been my wake-up call to speed me towards the Source of true and lasting contentment."

We are all like this alcoholic. Our obsessions are different in form. Because reality is not ours to select, we learn to be good listeners. Lessons of humility remind each of us to listen to the Source of our strength and seek out the like-minded in fellowship and celebration. It is through our weaknesses that we allow
the strength of our Spirit to shine through to complete the task at hand … when we are willing.

## Summary

In dis-relation you seek contentment in a place it cannot be found, over and over again. This is the definition of insanity.[291] The body is your addiction. You have allowed your mind to use the body as a means to deceive itself into believing your body is your savior. Through that fiction is a lifestyle of adjustments looking for a satisfaction that will never be.

Your addiction can also be used as your means to healing. Vigilance to see your investment in a body that will let you down, takes enormous courage. Yet, mighty are the friends of support you will meet on your journey when you change your mind about your purpose.

---

[291] Insanity is the magical thinking that you will get different results doing the same thing over and over again.

To remember only "now" is to desire nothing else. It will always be today where you will find the gifts needed for your healing to take its rightful place.

*Your focus to listen is your only need*
*To remember "now" is to desire nothing else*
*To recognize you are not a good listener is the place to start*

Your road to rise above the desire to repeat the meaningless is set before you. It is *only* that first step you need to see and no other. In that step you will find the messengers and fellowship needed for continued support. At the end of your journey, you will find that,

*You have been deceived by nothing in a form you desired*

In this place, the joy of a transcendent peace leaves the deprivation of a psychological state ... in the dust.

# Suicide: An Attempt to Heal the Split

*Nothing in the world makes sense*
*It is bankrupt, living on borrowed time*
*The time you pay is delay*
*Until you take the time to wake up*

## Introduction

There are times when terror seems to grip your mind ... and escape appears hopeless. When finally, you realize that it is you, you fear. This is when the mind perceives itself as split. Through projection the split was concealed, believing attack could be directed outward or perceived as coming from out there, and thus returned from outside to within. You thought there were enemies outside that you had to fear. But now, the murder is perceived within, intent on punishing you until it can finally kill you. You are at your bottom. All pretense [292] about what you thought about you is laid bare and revealed. You have come to the truth beyond all illusions but one. What are you really? At your bottom, one step beyond the mist of your terror is the truth about what you are ... shining for you to see. Take one more step through the mist of "the valley of the shadow of death"[293] and you will see your way through. You are LOVE.

*There's a path that leads beyond your sorrow*
*Through the mist that path will take you there*
*And when you step through, your fear you will undo*
*As you leave it at your own back door*

---

[292] The folly of your wisdom
[293] Psalm 23: vs 4

## An Ancient Guilt

To depreciate the power of your mind is to miss-create, make a world of bodies, believe this world to be true and then deny that you did it. From this view all you could do is be a frustrated learner in depression and despair.

There is an ancient guilt made out of the lie that you can separate yourself from your Source of Being and succeed. What else could result from this fiction but a fear so deep that you disassociate from it, bury it. To disassociate from this choice is to forget. To forget is to make it unconscious, covering your tracks so you can't see your way back; but it is still alive to the mind that made it real.

This guilt projected on another body is the justification for anger, attack and murder. The projection of guilt on your own body is the justification for anger, attack or self-mutilation and murder. Thus, the basis by which suicide is attempted or occurs.

## The Set-Up

Your attempt to develop self-esteem based on a body/self-idea is futile because it is an attempt to find an identity from the disposition of dis-relation. It is unnecessary to do that because you already "are" in the Mind of Source. But when you try to be what you are not through identify with an ephemeral body, you experience the whims of ever-changing failure, frustration, guilt and fear. You feel failure and frustration because you pursue an impossible goal. You feel guilt because you experience the fiction that you can oppose the Will of Source and succeed. Your persistence in seeking an identity apart from Source demonstrates that you think you are responsible for the making of your own value. This is your authority issue. Who is the maker of your identity? Your fictitious you? Is reality yours to select? Until you grapple with what these two questions mean, you will have to live in the battle ground of your mind.

In your attempts to grasp for an identity through a body born to die, you fearfully and angrily protest any idea of being separate from the body. You solemnly toast to testimonials with tears for those who are dying. You treasure the body by seeking to preserve its memory for eternity with granite markers. All of your cemeteries attest to the fear of a you, you are not.

### The Push

It may seem that your hand is being forced. You find relief at times on your journey. However, release remains elusive. Through a body you seek to be happy and try to avoid pain. It is never-ending. At times you experience a shallow happiness. But it always eludes your grasp. It seems that you are shadowed by depression, anxiety, frustration, stress and fear. The decisiveness for resolve that you seek in the world cannot be found. All too often, there is no solution for your dilemmas that bring you dissatisfaction. So, you place them in a storehouse of the past. At times, your mind goes to that storehouse with no flash-light to illuminate your way through. It becomes easy to get lost in that dark place where you do not see an "exit" sign. The more you try to find resolution in that darkness, the more frustrated you are. The set-up is that you have spent all your resources to find resolve from pain in a place where resolve can't be found.

*Once upon a time there was a wise father who responded to his troubled son with a story.*

*"Son" the father started "I once knew a young man who reminds me of you. This young man gave up everything he had to go to the jungle and capture a rare and beautiful butterfly. To*

317

*catch this butterfly would put this young man at the top of his game compared to everybody else. Through the heat of the jungle, he searched. In spite of mosquitoes and bugs he searched. Through many torrential rainstorms without shelter he searched. Lost for days in uncharted regions he searched. At times he would catch sight of the butterfly from afar. Sometimes he got close enough to catch it. However, it somehow always eluded his grasp.*

*Finally, after much time, energy and frustration, the young man collapsed under the shade of a tree. Exhausted by the chase, the young man sat back against a boulder and cried. In defeat, he decided to give up the chase.*

*Succumbing to despair and declaring himself a failure,[294] the young man felt a soft touch. The butterfly landed on his knee."[295]*

## A Thought that Limits

Your inability to resolve your presenting problems through your self-defeating thinking exacerbates your way of thinking. "I must try harder" you think. How despairing it is to try harder with no resolve and then to think you're a failure because you didn't try hard enough. Is there "no exit?"

A simple thought that limits can also free you. *Your way of thinking* has been to limit you from your heart's desire is to be free. The resolution you seek involves abandoning your way of thinking. "But I can't abandon my way of thinking" you fearfully reason in your darkness. "There are too many things out there to deal with." Ego interjects many compromises meant to distract you from looking

---

[294] Accept your sense of failure as nothing more than a mistake in who you are.
[295] *The Way Home p96-98*

within, to keep you from recognizing your conflict as self-inflicted. The ego's diversions invite a myriad of manifestations to occupy your time and energy, many of which show up as addictions, obsessions, illness, compulsions and a darkness that persists. The ego's business is to bait and switch. You may find placebo relief from some of your dilemmas, but never resolution.

You have been here before and all your decisions have been between meaningless choices. When you finally ask "What am I deciding between?" you are poised for change.

*"Once there was a grandfather who sat his grandson down to teach him about life:*

*"A fight is going on inside of me" grandfather told the boy. "It's a terrible fight between two wolves. One is evil – he is anger, envy, sorrow, regret, greed, arrogance, self-pity, lies, guilt and ego. The other is good – he is joy, peace, generosity, hope, empathy, humility, kindness, truth, compassion and love. This same fight is going on inside you – and inside all other people too."*

*The grandson thought about it for a minute and then asked, "Grandfather, which wolf will win?"*

*The grandfather simply replied, "The one you feed."*[296]

When it becomes obvious that no distractions can save you from you, you are poised to decide between freedom and despair. Decisiveness is your tool for collapsing time. It is your opportunity to move beyond collecting unresolved baggage to die with … only to pick them up again in a different lifetime to deal with.

You do not need any strength of your own to decide. You have already tried this and you are exhausted. Just be

---

[296] A Native American story. *The Way Home p54-58*

willing to want to step beyond your thinking to the place that says *"reality is not for me to select,"* and help will arrive.

*While the master was speaking on the many blessings that are found along The Way, one from among the crowd, tempted by the expectations of life's way, interrupted with a protest.*

*"Master, I have prayed much for these blessings you talk about, but have yet to see any of them materialize! How can you say that God is an ever-present blessing when He has abandoned me?"*

*The master turned to look at the man. She could see that the man was agitated and hungry for an argument. The master calmly leaned towards the man and spoke softly:*

*There once was a man who whispered "God, speak to me," and a meadowlark sang. But the man did not hear.*

*So, the man yelled, "God, speak to me," and thunder rolled across the sky. But the man did not listen.*

*Then the man looked around and said, "God, let me see You," and a star shone brightly. But the man did not notice."*

*And the man shouted, "God show me a miracle!" and a life was born. But the man did not know.*

*So, the man cried out in despair, "Touch me God, and let me know you are here!" Whereupon, God reached down and touched the man. But the man brushed the butterfly away and walked on."*

*The master looked the misguided one in the face to see his eyes soften and spoke softly once more, "You will miss out on your blessing if you have expectations of how it should be packaged."*[297]

Unless you crack the window of your mind open, you will not see the sliver of light that wants to slip through … to illuminate your darkness

---

[297] *The Way Home p185-187*

## Despair

*No matter how destructive the form may appear*
*Every act is intended as resolution*

With your body as your chosen center of being, recognize the experience of the world through the senses of a body to be absolutely futile. You may even take it a thought further by assessing this futility as "dust to dust." Despite all your distractions as escape or a means to empower, you have not found completion outside of yourself. Yet you refuse to walk through the door that allows your inner self to remember its completion with your Spiritual Self.

Again, this is your authority issue. Who is the maker of your identity? Not your fictitious you! Is reality yours to select? No! Until you grapple with what these two questions mean to you, you will have to live within the battle ground of your mind. Only despair awaits those who refuse to align with Spirit's Will. Unwilling to see even the glimmer of a way out in this dark place of the ego mind is where the choice to exit the body seems a viable option.

*You must believe a lie to despair*

The lie you tried so vainly to learn was that you are the experience of a body, and therefore satisfaction and completion comes to you through a body. Because the fulfillment of this lie is impossible, your unconscious guilt leads either to the despair of getting rid of the body ... or to begin to awaken to the journey, the call from your Spiritual Self. There are no other choices but these two. All the other choices the world offers are different forms of the same story line … seek in the world of bodies but do not find. The world was made so you could not find a way out. Suicide, seen as a final act of despair, is a choice that involves tremendous motivation to accomplish resolution.

*To deny self the power of change, is the darkness of despair*

## Suicide as a Choice

*The world is not left by death but by truth*

Your desire to escape the world is the right idea. You just haven't found the right way to go about it. The body, mistakenly identified as the source of your mind's suffering becomes the target of an attack aimed at securing relief. Those unable to choose forward progress through the mind, use the body as a means to facilitate immediate change through the act of suicide.

You facilitate superficial change on a daily basis through all the mental distractions the body seems to offer. To argue "Yea, but those distractions are different than the change suicide calls for," are those who judge the act of suicide as different then all the choices you make on a daily basis between illusions that have nothing to do with waking up … and then the body dies … and you weep.

Fictions can be subtly difficult to see and dispel when it comes to the addiction of your body as "you." What the death of a body means to anyone still comes down to perception. If you are not the body but Eternal Spirit, suicide is just as superficial as any other placebo fix you use to delay your journey. And if one's ground of being comes down to a fiction called a body, death will be perceived as a fearful experience of loss.

*The mast may be one of the sturdiest places on the ship*
*But its grounding still depends on the whims of the sea*

## Suicide as a Speed-Up[298]

If you suspend judgment around the event called suicide, you will see that;

1) The individual made a decision. This decision was a commitment to a change they could not do any other way. You know this is true because suicide is the way they did it.

2) The individual has immediately ended their present body experience negating any further build-up of karma. This is speed-up[299] because they are not stuck in making more present memories to forgive. They were stuck in a cycle of despair, adding karma to their list of thoughts to undo. Now they can start again, anew as it seems,[300] at another time and place.

3) Rather than prolong and add misery to their time, suicide helps the individual start over again. Eventually picking up where they left off in their next incarnation is an opportunity to start sooner, to learn the lessons missed with less karmic build-up to work through. That one may become stuck again through the process of choosing interpretations of life events that are conflictual, can happen. That one begins sooner to choose again is speedup's opportunity.

---

[298] *Symbols of Power in Metaphysics p98-118*

[299] Speed-up or the collapse of time is the result of a particular lesson learned through forgiveness. The illusion of time is shortened any moment you choose to forgive a memory that has held you to times past. Time seems to collapse when there is one less substitution (fiction) between you and your memory of Source. *Symbols of Power in Metaphysics p119-132*

[300] I say "as it seems" because there is no time or place.

4) The event called suicide demands an immediate shift in perception for those left behind. Overcome with misunderstanding, guilt and grief, those left behind are confronted to deal with their fictions about a body/self-idea.

5) Like any other choice that involves the body, *suicide is not an event to spiritualize or demonize*. Your propensity to judge any event does not make it any more special than any other event. Like any other event, through forgiveness all events are opportunities to release you from the chains you made for yourself. [301] You always have the opportunity to start anew.[302]

## Speed-Up

You face life issues as you perceive them. Out of guilt you project an image in the space of your mind through the illusion of time to dance with until you figure out how to end the dance you made. Suicide is a way to temporarily stop the dance; to rest so you can prepare for the next tune . . . without adding more baggage.

A speed-up is a collapse of time, a miracle of the mind that undoes your guilt through a particular lesson learned. Time was made as the time you need to bring the effects or problems you experience in your projection, to its cause. There is only one cause, and that's in the mind that thought it. When all effects are finally brought to their common and only cause, time is needed no more.

Your over willingness to project guilt and deny that you do so is your resistance or *the time you need* to see the obvious. The act of suicide is another way to cut through a resistance, that is massively protected by denial.

---

[301] Plato's Cave, *Symbols of Power in Philosophy* p123-124
[302] *Symbols of Power in Metaphysics* p133-144

## Residual Effects?

Each and every choice has residual effects. Because no thought leaves its source, to judge is to unknowingly condemn yourself to the judgments you make. Either you are a hypocrite like the one you judge or no one is. In other words, you will be doomed to play out your perception of relationships as failed until you figure it out[303] that no one is to be blamed. Either suicide is a real-life event to be taken personally or it is the illusion of death, a passing we all take in our own way and time. The question isn't "Is there life after death. The question is "Is there death."[304]

You take your karma with you to the other side (death). When your guilt catches up with you, you play it again on this side (birth). The last act on this side is to give up the body (dying). From the other side, you are immediately free of all of your fictions; especially the fiction of body identification. The despair that paralyzed spiritual movement on this side of the veil was body centered. Because you do not deal with an ephemeral vehicle on the other side, you do not deal with the trauma of a body center of despair. Thus, suicide is relief, as if a lifting out from a body-centered despair of no exit. Now you can rest to prepare again for the lesson you need to learn. When your guilt catches up you will reincarnate to start again.

For those left behind with their own fiction of a body/self-vulnerability, it will be tempting to interpret events through confusion, judgment, fear and magical thinking. If you judge suicide as a traumatically violent experience, you will assume it to be traumatic for the one

---

[303] No matter how hard you want to evade responsibility, to blame another for a failed relationship, you are the one who chose to dance with them!

[304] *The Way Home p172*

who committed the suicide. It is just the opposite. It is relief. Get past it, it means nothing.

## Will to Empower

*Suicide is not the witness of Self rejection. It is one's attempt to embrace Self through the despair of ego rejection. There is no cost, including the price of a body you are not.*

Friedrich Wilhelm Nietzsche talked about one's "Will to Power," a superman when released of the shackles of traditional ethics and morality, embodied the best qualities of the creative self. In a way;

> *Suicide is one's attempt to empower them-self*
> *It is a form of one's attempt to heal the split mind*

Confusion of identity precedes the suicidal event or else it would not be contemplated.[305] Beyond confusion is a resolution of willfulness that overcomes doubt. Even still, suicide is an act out of confusion because:

1) It is acted on a body identity as if the body is what they are. However, you may end this body life experience but the continuity of what "You really are," remains.[306]
2) One's desire to escape the world is the right idea. They just haven't found the right way to go about it.

> *The world is not left by death, but by truth*

---

[305] We are all involved in confusion of identity or else you would not appear to be here.
[306] *Symbols of Power in Metaphysics p119-143*

Because of the dynamics of karma,[307] how you die is irrelevant. All who die to a body life experience come back to finish what they started, to undo the fiction of dis-relation. Because the effect of your imagined dis-relation is projected as a world untrue to "You," you need to use the world to bring you back to "You." Time becomes your friend as the time you need to undo your karma. And death to birth to death is your means. No matter how the inevitable happens, don't judge it as traumatic.

> *How you die is irrelevant to the truth*
> *How you live is everything!*

## Summary

*You must die as a body until the idea of a body you are not ... dies*[308]

---

[307] *Symbols of Power in Metaphysics p96-118*
[308] *The Way Home p183*

In disappointment, you have looked hard and long for a home. Yet your home, the body, is plagued by disease, disabilities, depression, assault, murder, old age misfortunes, and addictions of all types ... and then you die. And though ethical, moral and religious issues for right living abound, none of them can save you from the death of a body you are not. Therefore;

1) If you are the body you identify with, it matters not how you are to live and die. Only the fiction of a noble humanistic idea would suggest a moralistic reason as to how to live your life ... yet with no basis as to why.[309]

2) If you are Eternal Spirit, the concept of punishment, evil and sin become irrelevant fictions to the fact that Eternal Spirit is unchangeable, otherwise it would not be Eternal.

3) Because reality has never been yours to select, only seemingly in a dream of nothingness, how or when you die is but a matter of the time you take to learn the lessons you need to learn to awaken, and ... any "body" will do.[310]

*Namaste*

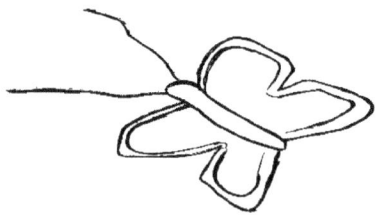

---

[309] *Symbols of Power in Philosophy p50-68*
[310] *Symbols of Power in Metaphysics p133-144*

# IV. Symbols of Power in Psychology

*All writings of truth are not the truth; they are about the truth.*
*We just give them meanings which make them Symbols of Power*

As you find yourself … within the grasp of a body/self-idea, you understand the limits you have accepted for the survival of the body. Mind limited to the association of a process of birth to death is lost in the forest of ever shifting shadows. Now must mind use these shadows, these objects of body orientation as signposts, a means of communication to find your way out beyond them.

Continuous communication is a disposition of knowing. Your mind must use the objects available to its orientation of limitation to remember the communication of knowing. The uses of objects for expression represent a transaction of meaning that is symbolic. Symbolic because they point you in a direction beyond the ever-changing of the ephemeral. A brick to block can be used as a step to heal.

Any symbol you choose has no power of its own. But you can think it has and act accordingly. Your mind cannot give its own power away. However, you can ascribe power to any symbol by the allegiance you pay it. Any symbol you invest in is your attempt to reassign them a power within the limits of the ephemeral for what you can get out of it. For example, money is a symbol that you assign power to for what you think you can get out of it. This is the fiction of magical thinking because what you get out of your symbols that limit is not power, but the slavery of your delay.[311] The body you identify with is your most compelling symbol of delay!

The art of reframing symbols of power is an undoing that re-defines your symbols in a way that helps you step beyond their limited application.[312] Beyond your self-imposed symbols of a body-self-idea is your remembrance of full communication.


## 1985

*Therapy involves the therapist's willingness to participate in the client's readiness. Readiness is the willingness of both to redefine their Symbols of Power.*
*

### Time Line
*Guilt gets its power from living in the past*
*Anxiety gets its power from living for the future*
*Guilt is unforgiveness exposed when projected as blame*
*Blame is protection from guilt, fearing future consequences*
*Future consequences are anxious assumptions based on past guilt*
*None have a reality "now"*
*

*Conflict is a measure that disagreement is not OK*
*If disagreement were OK, there would be no conflict*
*

*Co-dependency is the belief you can find happiness in something or someone outside of yourself. Every addiction attempts to live this out.*

---

[311] Symbols of power as investments would be things like money, cell phones, cars, health, rituals; anything you hold on to for security and happiness.; *The Way Home p149-151*
[312] *Symbols of Power in Metaphysics p26-32*

## 1986

*Impaired judgment does not know the mind is mis-thinking because miss-thinking cannot see impaired judgment. The inability of mind to realize this disposition is its only block.*
*

*The need to explain your behavior is a defense out of self-protection*
*

*The best defense is to tell your opponent they sound defensive*
*An astute opponent will recognize your defensive maneuver*
*

*You can't make me feel anything!*
*My interpretation of your behavior is what makes me feel*
*I just use you to remind me*
*

*Any defense against fear is the feeder of its flame*
*

*Your agenda has made your guilt*
*How can you use the same agenda that condemns you, to heal you?*
*

*Trying to live another's life for them is to put yours on hold*
*

*The sooner you get to feelings you do not like, the sooner you get through them. To fight them off is to put them in your closet. Someday, you will have to wear them.*
*

*Borderline personality types are those who elicit reactions that reinforce their world view.*
*What reaction do they elicit from you?*
*

*Fear is always implied in anger*
*Anger just masks it*

People do not store anger, they store messages of impatience
It only takes one message to light the fuse
*

If my behavior irritates you, you make you my victim!
If your interpretation of my behavior irritates you
You make us both your savior
*

The thoughts you think; do they bring you messages of healing
or messages of conflict?
*

Grandiosity believes in littleness
*

The addict is one who attempts to re-live the moment of
pleasure ... through repetition. Which moment do you try to re-
live?
*

"Yes but ..." is an indication that;
    a)  You don't know
    b)  You are not listening
    c)  You are being defensive
    d)  All of the above
*

When your client measures self-image in terms of good and bad
behavior, it will be at the whims of their own ever-changing
mood ... where nothing is for sure
*

Unmanageability is your interpretation of chaos
Manageability is timing within the occurrence of the natural
*

Because blame is anger's vehicle to nowhere, blame's object is
nothing
*

Every problem is first and foremost a problem of thought

*The only technique to teaching therapeutic play is learning how to play*
*

*Low self-esteem is your judgment against your make-believe self*
*

*What does defiance, provocation, and fear have in common?*
*They're all calls for help*
*

*Your fear distorts your perception*
*A distortion in perception multiplies the possibility of misinterpretation*
*A misinterpretation feeds fear's distortion*
*The cycle of validating the experiences of your distortions completes itself*
*

*The moment of a natural encounter involves patience*
*Beyond patience is the moment*
*

*Be aware of the thoughts you entertain*
*They are the source of your feelings*
*

*Shaming is anger's attempt to control by the defamation of another's character*
*Deny character its reality and shame will have no hold on you*
*

*No one is really afraid of success*
*But you can be afraid that success will change things*
*

*Experience shapes your beliefs while beliefs formulate your experiences*
*

*You teach peace to learn to be at peace with yourself*
*

*Bodies do not communicate, minds do*
*Mind gives motion and sound meaning*

*What meaning have you given behavior?*
*

*Shame involves the sense of being unlovable*
*The unlovable is what you made, not what you are*
*

*Guilt is the reflection of an overactive mind*
*

*Every perpetrator is a victim of their own device*

### 1987

*Criticism always ends where it starts*
*

*It is not any present event that guilt's you*
*It is your reconsideration of the event in question that guilt's you*
*

*To be angry is to expect things to be the way they are not*
*Acceptance is to understand that things are the way they are*
*

*Behind every feeling is a thought you made*
*Only you can interrupt it*
*

*Deny your anger and you will explode*
*Allow for it and you will find a way through*
*

*Your mind is so powerful that if you allow, it will convince you to experience things that are not true*

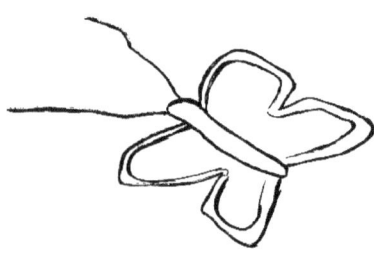

## 1988

*Interpersonal [313] confusion is always a symptom of intrapersonal[314] confusion.*
*

*If you arrange your life according to how another should act, you will be resentful. Yet, you have done this to yourself.*
*

*Before you can resolve an interpersonal issue, you have to look at what you made*
*

*A child is not socialized to feel anger, guilt or fear*
*They bring it with them*
*And if you bring fear with you, the illusion of feeling abandoned is not far behind*
*

*No one can guilt you but yourself*
*

*If you change for another, you will need their support*
*If you change for you, you need no one's support*
*

*To say "I know" and still have guilt is to not know that you do not know*
*

*What some call advocacy, others call enabling*
*There are at least two names for everything*

---

[313] Interpersonal skills are behaviors that help you interact with others effectively, in the workplace, school, or in the larger world.

[314] Intrapersonal ("within the self") skills are the internal abilities and behaviors that help you manage emotions, cope with challenges, and learn new information.

*Those who do not flow are in conflict*
*Those in conflict resist change*
*Those who resist change*
*Invite conflict*
*

*Not understanding life's terms is the basis of all conflict*
*

*The idea of disability involves a body*
*

*To heal is to undo yourself made concept*
*

*Giving rewards and consequences for certain behaviors is not consistent with the world of events. In the world of events, there is no consistency ... and outcomes do not belong to you.*

### 1989

*What is going on outside of you are the projections that started in your mind*
*

*Life is one big adjustment disorder*
*With mixed emotional features*
*

*Trauma belongs to an idea*
*

*Your anger will be of help to you*
*When you see beyond your justifications for it*
*

*If healing is the art of reframing*
*Then your view of the situation is what's upsetting you*
*

*Fear of opening up is not a lack of trust in others*
*You lack trust in yourself*
*

*No one can betray you but yourself*
*And in the end, you can't even do that*

*When I think that resolution of a conflict will make me happy, I think my happiness is at stake*
*

*Blame is a defense to avoid guilt*
*Deny guilt a place and blame will have no reason*
*

*Self-abasement is punishing the body for what the mind fails to understand*
*

*Self-destruction is in the mind of the body that destroys itself*
*

*If you were to say "people are defined by their choices"*
*Then you could say "people are the sum of their choices"*
*Even still, a choice in an instant can undo the sum of all other choices*

### 1990

*Jealously is anger's twin*
*It shares anger's reason*
*

*Self-criticism always misuses hindsight*
*

*Accomplishment has its stress*
*

*Ventilation of anger is fine. But to ventilate again and again and again does nothing for your soul.*
*

*To not want to see the larger picture*
*Is to refuse healing*
*

*The way you see any event is often different for somebody else. What does that tell you about the reliability of your own perception?*

*Denial has its reason*
*You take on only what you can take at any given time*
*

*Two insecure people with multiple needs have the ingredients*
*for an abusive relationship ... or the miracle of a mutual*
*encounter*
*

*To react to things "as if" when they are not, is the magic of self-*
*deceptive thinking*
*

*Hey button pusher, no one pushes your buttons but you! Others*
*seem to facilitate the opportunity for you to push your buttons.*
*And the more buttons you have are the more opportunities you*
*will have to push them.*
*

*According to your belief, is it so for you*
*To not know you do this to yourself is delusion*
*

*The more ready your client is*
*The better your therapeutic approach looks*
*

*Attempting to control your anger without looking at the thought*
*that provoked it, is your justification to not deal with you as the*
*source of your anger*
*

*To feel unjustly treated is to justify your anger*
*

*Blame always protects weakness*
*That's why your blame always victimizes yourself*
*

*Freedom of choice does not involve what you will do*
*It involves seeing things the way you do*
*The way you see things tells you what to do*

*Get yourself straightened out with your parents so they can remind you that what you thought they did to you was not about you*
*

*Ownership always finds misery*
*

*To place value on anything is to take it seriously*
*

*Bitter words of sarcasm is anger misplaced*
*

*Body sickness is an opportunity to heal the mind*
*

*Blame always tries to protect you from a sense of failure*
*

*You're not guilty, just lost*
*

*If you do not take time in your life to cry*
*You will have stress in your life to live*
*

*"Self-Actualization" is a contradiction in terms*
*Unless the "Self" you are actualizing involves everyone*
*

### Witnesses
*Guilt, resentment and secrets witness to how you view your past*
*Guilt witnesses to violation by you*
*Resentment witnesses to violation against you*
*Secrets witness to violation through you*
*All healing involves your release from the past*

### 1991
*Anger, guilt and fear are reminders of your denial*
*

*Irritation is misplaced anger*

*Lasting healing is impossible to explain from a body-self point of view*
\*

*Whenever your tree is shaking, the winds of speed-up are blowing*
\*

*Any problem kept by you remains unresolved*
*Share it so you can be available to receive a gift*
\*

*Explaining is a defense*
\*

*Tension involves fear between bodies*
\*

*Confusion is your step to surrender*
\*

*Figure out what you're really screaming about*
*So you won't have to do it again*
\*

*Here and now encounters are the places where miracles are found*
\*

*Those who complain have not dealt with their grief*
\*

*Readiness is a factor we all share … at the right time*
\*

*Your anger always punishes you first*
\*

*Shame belongs to inadequacy's reflection*
\*

*Lifestyles that cannot include another person will leave you alone*
\*

*Go ahead, weigh all your options … in the end, you will choose the lesson you need*

## 1992

*Guilt and blame go hand and hand*
*Because blame's reason is to hide guilt*
*
*

*That a word can seem to kill is vulnerability*
*
*

*Those who commit suicide are those who have looked hard for a*
*home … and did not find it here*
*
*

*The measurement of personality may result in a summary of*
*something. What that summary is, is not you.*
*
*

*Humor that hides anger is sarcasm*
*
*

*Doubt carries its own tension*
*
*

*If the result of a lesson involves conflict, you have not learned*
*your lesson*
*
*

*When learning is not natural, the effort frustrates motivation*
*
*

*Incompletion in one's world is a reflection of the eye of the*
*beholder. This is the over-achiever's dilemma*
*
*

*Any attempt to make sense out of confusion is an attempt to*
*confuse yourself*
*
*

*The natural student will naturally teach*

## 1993

*Whatever you do out of an attitude of mind, you do to you*
*
*

*Surrender does not need clarification*
*Control does*

*An argument is two people trying to change each other's mind*
*

*Self-empowerment is not about seeing how another set you up.*
*It's about seeing how you set yourself up.*
*

*You are the only one that can choose healing. Therapy merely*
*facilitates opportunities that will increase your motivation.*
*

*Those who need to control are afraid of life*
*

*Special love is hate, as long as you believe God favors you above*
*anyone else*
*

*To change your behavior and not your mind causes tension[315]*
*

*Climb your mountain, whatever it may be*
*See the big picture and be free*
*Step back down, parched by the dust*
*Find your glass of water, relief is never enough*

## 1994
*Money does not heal*
*Desire for healing does*
*

*To despair is to not recognize the inevitable as it truly is*
*

*Speed-up accelerates focus*
*

*Fear always involves a body*
*

*Boredom is an attempt to avoid change*

---

[315] Cognitive dissonance is a mental conflict that occurs when your beliefs don't line up with your actions.

*Anger is the belief that your view is the right view*
*

*Understand how change works so you can work with it*
*

*Arrogance assumes control*
*Humility listens to direction*
*

*Repetition is the practice of doing it over and over again ... until you get it right*
*

*In your search for your kids, don't neglect your child*

### 1995

*Your body never lies*
*Your thoughts do, and they lie about your body*
*

*Whether it's through birth or death*
*Every relationship goes through transformation*
*

*You will always find someone to betray you until you see that you did it to yourself first*
*

*Because your thoughts make your feelings*
*It's not fair to say "feelings lie"*
*

*Trying to avoid conflict, invites it*
*

*Describing behavior is easy*
*Deciding what it means is the hard part*
*

*Get past grieving so you can get on with life*
*

*Because you empowered them*
*Only you can surmise what shame & guilt is for*

*Your body as a vehicle and not an end*
*Will speed you along your way*
*

*Every boundary you make is a limit*
*Every limit you have needs maintenance*
*This involves work … unless you see the whole*
*

*I do not deny the expression of feelings*
*On the contrary, I advocate its ownership*
*

*Arrogance refuses to listen*
*It will try to kill you before the body dies*

### 1996
*In the world of the ever-changing, there is no guarantee*
*So, what are you angry about?*
*

*People talk about needing to work:*
*1) At work*
*2) At home*
*3) On relationships*
*My God! Is everything broken?*
*

*Those who point to others as having boundary issues*
*Are those with mental boundary issues*
*

*Eating disorders are attempts to prove you are a body*
*

*To grab to possess a body that will die*
*Is the making of all your grief*
*

*Is it attention deficit disorder (ADD) or a matter of abstract thinking?*
*

*Every real step involves a degree of acceptance*

*Time heals every wound when you step into the light of your destiny*
*

*The prideful always feel shame*
*

*Attachment has to do with feeling needy*
*

*The "paranoid personality" is sensitive about who or what to trust in their world. There is an element of truth in their paranoia. What can you trust to remain as it is? The paranoid's problem is they take change personally. Do you?*
*

*You must believe in loss to grieve*

### 1997

*Name me a murderer who does not have a need to control!*
*

*Ego is what I believe, not what I am*
*

*Whatever I attach to, I will adjust to*
*This is the seed of grief*
*

*My grief teaches me that I have lost the remembrance of "Self"*

### 1998

*Shame-based implies secrets*
*

*To be abandoned, you must abandon yourself first*
*

*You can't make anybody be where they're not*
*

*The #1 thing that empowers addiction is secrecy*

### 1999

*What I am saying seems intangible because it doesn't meet the standards of social conditioned thinking*
*

*What I see in another is what I wish to see*
*Because it stands for what I want to be the truth*
*

*However much I seem to be impelled by outside happenings*
*I respond to only what I wish to see*
*

*Don't be disappointed that you find yourself with projections to forgive. Be grateful that you recognize them as something you can forgive them.*
*

*Your miracle is simply your ability to perceive differently then what you have decided*

### 2000

*Pity is the break in the storm before the calm of forgiveness sets in*
*

*If you don't get past hate and anger*
*You're doomed to repeat it*

### 2001

*The dirge you see in the world is the one you sing to your heart*
*

*Rage and irritation may appear as different forms*
*But their results are the same*
*They rob you of peace*

### 2002

*Experience is not discrete*
*Memories are*

*To be dependent is to make life decisions based on the life decisions of another*
*

*Fear is the affirmation that you are a body*

## 2004
*Blame is the projection of personal guilt*
*

*Your justification for fear is a preoccupation that attempts to prove it is real*
*

*Suicide is an attack on your projection of "a make-believe self"*
*

*What you take personally you perceive as threat*
*

*Decisions based on the body's eyes is what brings the ego to life*

## 2005
*Self-esteem is a concept devised by ego for its survival*

## 2006
*Your walls do not keep fear out*
*They justify its existence*
*

*The cost of your denial as to what is yours to control*
*Is insanity*

## 2007
*Whenever you assess blame*
*You never get the real story*

## 2008
*We grieve when our love is conditional*
*

*Stress is about taking "nothing" seriously*

347

*You are not angry because you see an angry world*
*You see an angry world because you are angry*

## 2009

*Those who build castles in the air are neurotic*
*Those who live in those castles are psychotic*
*Those who collect the rent are the therapists*

## 2010

*Denial always precedes projection*
*That's why you don't know that what you see out there comes from you*
*

*Anxiety is the witness that you have judged the ever-changing to be something it is not*
*

*You always grieve when you believe a lie*

## 2012

*You don't make fundamental changes through conditioning*
*You become conditioned by making fundamental changes*

## 2015

*When you gossip you haunt your dream*
*

*To know is to be*
*To not know is to perceive endless shades and shadows of possibility*
*

*Mistakes are nothing but memories made*
*

*To think positive about your life fictions leaves you where?*

## 2016

*What you do not understand, you judge as lacking*

*It seems hard to give up your thoughts of safety that make you miserable*
*

*You use your body on how to learn respect*
*Until you know respect through love*

## 2018
*Anger knows no one*
*For if you knew them*
*You would not be angry*

## 2023
*If you are motivated out of guilt to believe the lie that made your guilt, your guilt remains*
*

*You may think people are crazy because all the rules*
*However, we have all the rules because people are crazy*
*

*Isolation can cause obsessive thinking about anything*
*Seek connection*

## 2024
*It's not that people are inconsistent as much as they are conflicted*
*

*When you look outside for meaning you experience anxiety*
*Why? Because meaning cannot be found outside of you*

## 2025
*Accept your sense of failure as nothing more than a mistake in who you think you are*

# Appendix

## The Relationship between Displacement, Disassociation, Compensation & Fiction

Simply stated, to displace is to substitute; to disassociate is to distance yourself from knowing what you substituted (denial); to compensate is to make adjustments that justify/defend against your awareness of your disassociation. All your compensations are about making your fictions workable in denial of what you did. A self apart from Source is your number one fiction. To make this fiction work, you have displaced, disassociated from and compensated for a dream of fear. Sometimes you experience a fleeting happiness. But fear always intrudes on this happiness. All of your compensations are adjustments to keep you from recognizing your mind as split, so you can't heal it.

Your substitution of what you are not, is a violation in thought that breeds guilt. Because it is a thought, your guilt is not real. Guilt imagined, demands punishment for the perceived violation. Suffering and sacrifice is its ends. Because of your willingness to disassociate from this imagined violation, you project and perceive a world untrue to "You."

### Negotiation as a Way of Life

To survive in this world, pseudo-you makes one compensation after another. This is your perceived evolution of the species in all its forms of education, technology, government, psychology, socialization, ethics, etc. Reality seems to be yours to select. But because it is always changing, you don't know what it is. You seem to be evolving, yet, it is always negotiated between other bodies in all its fleeting forms. Society is a collective hunch. That evolution is an illusion; you can't see because you want to believe that to evolve is to change towards the better.[316] The duality of oppositional thinking cannot be escaped because of your need to want to know definitively through the ever-changing. A sabotage at its source. "You" already are, definitive beyond the ever-changing spin of perceptive uncertainty. However, you can't find completion because of your substitutions, disassociations and compensations away from "You." All religions, economics, sociological and educational curriculums, politics, ethics, psychologies and philosophies are fictional attempts to find meaning and understanding in the world of your projection. [317] However, because they are all compensations, you can't find "You" through them.

If you looked closely, you would think that everything *always* being in a state of negotiation would tell you something about your world?

---

[316] Georg Wilhelm Friedrich Hegel (1770-1831), a German philosopher is one of the greatest systematic thinkers in the history of Western philosophy. Hegel claimed that his system of philosophy represented a historical culmination of all previous philosophical thought. A duality of thesis vs its conflictual counterpart of antithesis, resolving to a higher ground of synthesis (conflict resolution). Hegel erroneously saw change as an evolution of progress.

[317] Author Schopenhauer (1788-1860) was a German philosopher, best known for his 1818 work *The World as Will and Representation* (expanded in 1844), which characterizes the phenomenal world as the manifestation of a blind and irrational noumenal will. In other words, Schopenhauer was among the first 19th century philosophers to contend that at its core, the universe is not a rational place. *Symbols of Power in Philosophy p121-139*

*It's white and black like industrial waste*
*Pollution of the highest degree*
*You wonder why I don't hang out much*
*I wonder how you can't see*
George Harrison
The Devil's Radio

## Pseudo-ego's Motto

*The world was made so you could not find a way out*

Symbolically speaking, your "original sin" was the beginning of a time when you sought for something other than everything that you already are. And in that thoughtless instant was your illusion of change. It was a traumatically fearful change because to not recognize your relation with Source is to not know you. To not know you engenders fear, and thus, your detour into fear.[318] This detour is your journey in a world you made to hide from your mistake (guilt). In unawareness does a "you" you are not search for a "You" in a place it can't be found.

Your restlessness comes from a search for completion. Yet through a body it becomes a distracting compensation to endlessly seek comfort and avoid pain.[319] This is the result of part of your mind being in dis-relation with your Ground of Being. Mind knows and rests securely in your identity with Eternal Source. The part of your mind that is split, restlessly seeks peace through the battle ground; the dark shadows of your projections. Nothing in this world of your dark shadows is for sure, and lasting peace you will not find. The guidance you have chosen for direction

---

[318] Genesis 3: 8-10

[319] According to the teachings of Buddha, every living being has the same basic wish; to be happy and to avoid suffering.

is the voice of pseudo-ego. Pseudo-ego's motto is "seek but do not find."

Your search to nowhere are compensations played out as the effects of all the psychological ailments your mind makes up to hide you from an imagined dis-relation with Source. Your body is a compensation; a witness you use to deny the Eternal that you are. Everything in your world of pseudo-ego's guidance is negotiated. In your world of the perception of uncertainty, there is no truth to know.[320] In this light there is no reality for you to select.

*Every conflict is an opportunity*
*Until you see it that way, it will remain as a conflict*

## Summary

What you are not, made a place that isn't, so you would restlessly search for resolution in a "self" you are not, in a place where "Self" can never be found. No wonder you are a frustrated student. You have displaced "The Eternal You Are" for the making of a temporal you are not. That's why you search in vain in a world of ever-shifting shadows to find meaning, purpose and resolution in a place you will never be found. What an insane world it is you live in.

---

[320] *Symbols of Power in Philosophy*

*The world does nothing to you*
*You only thought it did*
*Nor do you do anything to the world*
*Because you were mistaken about what it is*[321]

 *To change your mind about what you thought your world is, is where the miracle is found*

---

[321] A Course in Miracles

Mathias Karayan

*The healed healer stands as a light*
*… Beyond the dream*[322]

*Namaste*

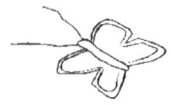

---

[322] *Symbols of Power in Metaphysics p20-32*